Lifestyle Politics and Radical Activism

CONTEMPORARY ANARCHIST STUDIES

A series edited by

Laurence Davis *National University of Ireland, Maynooth*
Uri Gordon *Arava Institute for Environmental Studies, Israel*
Nathan Jun *Midwestern State University, USA*
Alex Prichard *London School of Economics, UK*

Contemporary Anarchist Studies promotes the study of anarchism as a framework for understanding and acting on the most pressing problems of our times. The series publishes cutting edge, socially-engaged scholarship from around the world—bridging theory and practice, academic rigor and the insights of contemporary activism.

The topical scope of the series encompasses anarchist history and theory broadly construed; individual anarchist thinkers; anarchist-informed analysis of current issues and institutions; and anarchist or anarchist-inspired movements and practices. Contributions informed by anti-capitalist, feminist, ecological, indigenous, and non-Western or global South anarchist perspectives are particularly welcome. So, too, are manuscripts that promise to illuminate the relationships between the personal and the political aspects of transformative social change, local and global problems, and anarchism and other movements and ideologies. Above all, we wish to publish books that will help activist scholars and scholar activists think about how to challenge and build real alternatives to existing structures of oppression and injustice.

International Editorial Advisory Board:

Martha Ackelsberg, *Smith College*
John Clark, *Loyola University*
Jesse Cohn, *Purdue University*
Ronald Creagh, *Université Paul Valéry*
Marianne Enckell, *Centre International de Recherches sur l'Anarchisme*
Benjamin Franks, *University of Glasgow*
Judy Greenway, *University of East London*
Ruth Kinna, *Loughborough University*
Todd May, *Clemson University*
Salvo Vaccaro, *Università di Palermo*
Lucien van der Walt, *University of the Witwatersrand*
Charles Weigl, *AK Press*

Lifestyle Politics and Radical Activism

Laura Portwood-Stacer

B L O O M S B U R Y

NEW YORK • LONDON • NEW DELHI • SYDNEY

Bloomsbury Academic

An imprint of Bloomsbury Publishing Plc

1385 Broadway	50 Bedford Square
New York	London
NY 10018	WC1B 3DP
USA	UK

www.bloomsbury.com

Bloomsbury is a registered trade mark of Bloomsbury Publishing Plc

First published 2013

© Laura Portwood-Stacer, 2013

Library of Congress Cataloging-in-Publication Data
Portwood-Stacer, Laura, author.
Lifestyle politics and radical activism / Laura Portwood-Stacer.
pages cm
Includes bibliographical references and index.
ISBN 978-1-4411-8426-9 (pbk.) – ISBN 978-1-4411-8866-3 (hardcover) 1. Radicalism–
United States. 2. Anarchism–United States. 3. Lifestyles–Political aspects–
United States. I. Title.
HN49.R33P67 2013
303.48′4–dc23
2013012214

ISBN: HB: 978-1-4411-8866-3
      PB: 978-1-4411-8426-9
      ePub: 978-1-4411-0512-7
      ePDF: 978-1-4411-5743-0

Typeset by Deanta Global Publishing Services, Chennai, India
Printed and bound in the United States of America

This book is dedicated to my parents,
Norma Portwood-Stacer and Willard Stacer.

CONTENTS

ACKNOWLEDGMENTS

This book represents the collective effort and knowledge of many, many individuals, only some of whom I am able to name here. The editors of the Contemporary Anarchist Studies series, Laurence Davis, Uri Gordon, Nathan Jun, and Alex Prichard have been enthusiastic supporters of this project over the last 2 years, and I'm indebted to them for their efforts in establishing the series in the first place and for their belief that my work could have a home there. I am particularly grateful for Nathan's interest in the subject matter, Alex's comments on my initial proposal, and Uri and Laurence's insightful feedback on the full manuscript. I also thank two anonymous reviewers for their comments on my proposal. Marie-Claire Antoine, Kaitlin Fontana, and Ally Jane Grossan at Bloomsbury have been a pleasure to work with as well, and I appreciate their advocacy of this project.

The manuscript began as a doctoral dissertation at the University of Southern California, and I owe many thanks to all the people who helped me in my career as a graduate student. My research was enhanced by the feedback and support of several faculty at USC, particularly Sandra Ball-Rokeach, Manuel Castells, Carla Kaplan, Josh Kun, Ellen Seiter, and Karen Tongson. Larry Gross has been a guiding force in this project. His knowledge, high standards, and faith in my abilities have pushed me as a scholar in countless, indispensable ways. The close friends I met in graduate school—Inna Arzumanova, Meghan Moran, and Evren Savci—are some of the dearest people to me on the planet, and they have given unlimited and unconditional support over the years. We all live in different cities now, but I can still count on them for virtual partnership in cheese consumption, pop culture processing, and generally trying to be good at life. They've been cheerleaders for this book all along, and I miss them every day.

At New York University, where I worked during the revision from dissertation to book manuscript, Nick Mirzoeff's passion for radical activism has been inspirational. Marita Sturken, who read the entire manuscript toward the end, has been an unbelievably generous department chair and mentor. Many other colleagues and friends have given crucial feedback on various parts of this work since I've been in New York, notably Chris Anderson, Peter Asaro, Christina Dunbar-Hester, Anna Feigenbaum, Lucas

Graves, Dan Greene, Deena Loeffler, Alice Marwick, sava saheli singh, and Lisa Skeen. Laine Nooney read and edited the entire manuscript, and proved to be a valuable reference wrangler.

Several other colleagues and friends deserve mention here as well. Angela McRobbie and Toby Miller both provided feedback on this project in its earliest stages. Robyn Wiegman, Hamilton Carroll, Shaun Cullen, and other participants at the 2010 Futures of American Studies Institute offered insightful suggestions and criticisms. My research depended on the aid, advice, and hospitality of several activists. I would especially like to thank Andrew Burridge, Sara Galindo, Andrew Willis Garcés, Raeanna Gleason, Liz Lopez, Cindy Milstein, James Robinson, Andréa Schmidt, and Nicoal Sheen. Joshua Stephens has been a particularly willing interlocutor. Andy Cornell's writing on anarchist activism has been both inspirational and exceedingly informative. He was also generous enough to read and give feedback on portions of this manuscript, which improved it in significant ways.

Parts of this book have been revised from work published previously. Chapter 5 is a substantial revision of "Constructing Anarchist Sexuality: Queer Identity, Culture, and Politics in the Anarchist Movement," *Sexualities* 13, 4 (2010), 479–93. I thank Jamie Heckert, Gavin Brown, and an anonymous reviewer for their comments on this piece. A version of Chapter 2 was published as "Anti-Consumption as Tactical Resistance: Anarchists, Subculture, and Activist Strategy," *Journal of Consumer Culture* 12, 1 (2012), 87–105. I thank Steven Miles and the anonymous reviewers of that article.

Two individuals who, aside from myself, have spent the most time and effort on this project, deserve extensive thanks. Sarah Banet-Weiser served as my PhD advisor and dissertation chair at USC. Her intellectual profundity and exemplary work ethic are infused indelibly into this book; it would be impossible to articulate precisely how deep her impact goes. I can only hope that the end result makes her proud to have been such an important member of the process. This book would simply not exist without John Cheney-Lippold. He has been an active co-thinker with me almost from the inception of the project, listening and offering advice over innumerable beers, burritos, and afternoons in coffee shops. His camaraderie has been essential to my research and to my life for the past 7 years.

Finally, I must acknowledge the emotional support that has made it possible for me to produce this book. My friends outside of academia, especially Zach Curd, Jesse Fannan, Jemayel Khawaja, Zach Norton, and Ariel Samach all helped keep me sane when I needed distractions from work. Robin Sloan gave me a place to stay while I did fieldwork in San Francisco. My extended family has been ever encouraging and proud of my academic endeavors. The influence of my parents, Norma Portwood-Stacer and Willard Stacer, can really not be measured. Their love and pride, along with the example they have always set through their own hard work and perseverance, made me into a person who could research and write a scholarly book. Lastly, I am deeply grateful to my room/soul mate Brad Waskewich. He cheerfully weathered all the crabbiness and anxiety provoked by this project over our first 5 years together, and he provided me with inexhaustible laughter, pep talks, entertainment, care and feeding, and every other form of support imaginable. I seize the moment of sanctioned earnestness that a book's acknowledgments section presents to say that he means the world to me and I could not have done this without him.

1

Introduction

In March of 2009, I had a long conversation with a young woman named Raychel,[1] a college student and self-identified anarchist. We had met a few weeks previously, at an "anarcha-feminist picnic" in Los Angeles, which she had helped organize. I asked her to meet with me one-on-one for a chat, and we sat down together in a coffee house near her communal home in Long Beach. She rode her bicycle there; she consciously decided not to own a car, a notable choice in Southern California. She sported a short, asymmetrical haircut, had her septum pierced, and wore large plugs in her stretched earlobes. Raychel had spent her adolescence in the Orange County punk scene, and had recently become involved with militant animal rights organizing. We talked for almost 2 hours about her experiences doing activism for anarchist, feminist, vegan, and "genderqueer" causes, and how she tried to integrate her radical politics into her everyday life. Toward the end of our conversation, she commented:

> . . . it gets abstract sometimes, because it's like, where do I attack it, where do I attack patriarchy, where do I attack capitalism? And that's why I think lifestylism is so important, cuz I think that you do attack it by being vegan, or by not buying from Walmart, or not being subjected by the beauty standards. Like, by building those alternative communities and alternative infrastructure, we're not paying attention to them, so we're not demanding anything from them.

Raychel seemed to evince a faith in the power of individual choices to make a difference in political realities. She felt she had a responsibility to resist oppressive forces in her daily life, and she also felt she could empower herself and her peers by refusing to engage with the cultural practices engendered by patriarchy and capitalism.

As an anarchist, Raychel's critique of existing power structures is far-reaching, and separates her from the mainstream in the contemporary United

States. Anarchism is a *radical* political philosophy, meaning that its vision for an ideal society involves a drastic restructuring of the fundamental institutions of power, including but not limited to an overturning of capitalism and the state. Yet, anarchists like Raychel have something important in common with more mainstream citizens—the cherished belief that "one person can make a difference" in the pursuit of a better society. When individuals who desire social or political change are compelled to shape their own personal behaviors and choices toward the ideals they envision, this is known as *lifestyle politics*. While the stakes of each specific episode of activism may be low, the moments of confrontation are multiplied for radical lifestyle activists because every minute decision one makes is implicated in a fight for a new society. The way one dresses, the food one eats, even the people one chooses to have sex with, can become overtly political acts. Radical lifestyle politics reconfigures the everyday life of the individual into an ongoing struggle against domination.

Writing in the 1970s, anarchist ecologist Murray Bookchin (1979: 265) argued:

> . . . the revolutionary movement is profoundly concerned with lifestyle. It must try to live the revolution in all its totality, not only participate in it. It must be deeply concerned with the way the revolutionist lives, his relations with the surrounding environment, and his degree of self-emancipation.

Like the counterculturalists with whom he was in dialogue, Bookchin felt that activists had a responsibility both to live according to their political ideals and to visibly demonstrate the viability of radically different ways of life. With this view, he implicitly subscribed to the feminist adage that "the personal is political" (Evans 1979). Four decades later, this principle has become a truism of contemporary citizenship, and not just for self-identified revolutionaries. It's the premise upon which corporations are able to market "ethical" products to consumers and people regularly include their political beliefs in their personal profiles on online social networks. A cultural study of the practices and discourses of lifestyle-based activism (what Raychel called "lifestylism") can thus illuminate what it means to do politics and to be political today. This book asks, what are the effects of this kind of lifestyle politics? What does it really mean that people are trying to do politics in this way, and what are they accomplishing through their efforts?

I argue that some of the most significant "effects" of lifestyle activism are personal and cultural, and may not be recognizable within narrow understandings of the political. The many personal and cultural needs served by lifestyle politics within contemporary society mean that this form of activism cannot be dismissed as simply ineffective for radical movements. Lifestyle is a major site for the constitution of identity and community among anarchist activists. Shared ways of life bring together diffuse collections of political subjects, and symbolically represent them as a unified movement seeking changes in existing political conditions. The lifestyle practices of contemporary anarchists are also meaningful in so far as they materially enact (or violate) anarchic social relations. Lifestyles may reinforce boundaries between radicals and non-radicals, and among radical activists themselves. The effects of anarchists' ways of life are multifaceted and at times contradictory. A lifestyle practice like veganism may shore up an individual's sense of moral integrity, but it may also be easily co-opted by a capitalist consumer market. A uniquely anarchist style of dress may foster an internal sense of community within the movement, but may also alienate outsiders. A sexual arrangement like polyamory may provide an alternative to state-sponsored monogamous marriage, but it may also prove emotionally daunting for the individuals involved. Even using the term "anarchist" to refer to oneself may prove to be confusing, even while it is simultaneously empowering. These contradictory outcomes suggest that lifestyle activism cannot be fully successful at achieving all the goals that radicals might hold.

While one response to this failure might be to reject lifestyle politics altogether (as some critics have done),[2] a more practical move for activists is to embrace an attitude of trial and error in which outcomes are understood to be context dependent. Any strategic assessment of lifestyle tactics must take into account the range of its potential functions. Assessments must also examine the conditions under which different effects are likely to be realized, and for whom. What is at stake is an understanding of how to effect political change, and how the effects activists sometimes imagine may be more or less achieved, or may be counteracted by effects they haven't quite stopped to think about yet. The question is not, "Is lifestyle an effective site for radical political activism?" Rather, this book offers answers to the questions, "what kinds of political acts are possible within the sphere of lifestyle?" and "how do particular conditions enable lifestyle activism to be effective in those ways?"

A through line in each of the cases presented in this book is the communicative dimension of all political lifestyle practices. Lifestyle activism is premised, both explicitly and implicitly, on the performative and propagandistic effects of its practices. Sociologist Alberto Melucci (1985: 812) suggests that practitioners of cultural resistance are themselves a form of "new media," who, through their activities, "enlighten what every system doesn't say of itself, the amount of silence, violence, irrationality, which is always hidden in dominant codes." Melucci goes on to say that, "through what they do, or rather through how they do it, movements announce to society that something 'else' is possible." This book examines how, and under what conditions, radical activists are able to make their lifestyles into communicative performances that effectively make the kind of "announcement" that Melucci suggests.

A life that is completely free from hierarchical power relations is impossible to achieve within contemporary material and ideological conditions—no individual can achieve anarchist purity. Despite this, the individuals discussed in this book still *try* to make their everyday lives congruent with their utopian political ideals. Here, I describe their attempts, in order to understand what they *do* accomplish, and how this might guide other ongoing struggles to make a better world. This book also reveals the intense labor of trying to "live one's politics," especially when those politics are oppositional to the status quo. Although I take a critical approach to radical activists' use of lifestyle politics, this critique should be understood as a way of "caring for and even renewing the object in question" (Brown 2005: x). I approach this project from a position of sympathy and solidarity with radical activists. While I do not personally self-identify as an anarchist, I take anarchism seriously as a political philosophy, and feel it has much to offer in the way of alternatives to hierarchical distributions of power.[3]

Definitions: Lifestyle, lifestyle politics, lifestyle activism, and lifestylism

Lifestyle is a set of routine choices an individual makes about practices as various as dress, diet, housing, leisure activities, and more (Weber 1978).[4] These lifestyle choices signify who people are and who they want to be (Featherstone 1987). For instance, participants in "ethical consumption" communicate through their choices that they are environmentally conscious or sensitive to social justice issues.[5] Lifestyle also extends beyond consumption activities to the language one uses, the choices one makes about marriage and family, the career path one pursues, and so on. These are all elements of what sociologist Anthony Giddens (1991: 5) has called the "reflexive project of the self" which arises when individuals attempt to create coherent narratives of their lives while choosing from what lifestyle scholar Sam Binkley (2007a: 116) describes as the "overwhelming range of options" made available to them in consumer societies.

Lifestyle choices that depart from the mainstream are particularly noticeable and they seem to indicate an active effort to differentiate from the status quo. Such alternative lifestyles often bespeak alternative ways of thinking about society, sometimes extending to radical visions for how society should change. Individuals who hold radical political beliefs may see their cumulative daily choices as a reflection of their political integrity and authenticity (Haenfler et al. 2012: 9). A "lifestyle anarchist," for example, is someone who intentionally lives one's life according to specifically anarchist principles, attempting to incorporate their political philosophy into the minute activities of everyday life (Purkis and Bowen 2004: 8). When culture is seen as a site of domination, the direct alteration of cultural forms—including lifestyle habits—makes sense as a means of liberation from dominant ideologies (Marcuse 2001; Whittier 1995). I use the term *lifestyle politics* to refer to the whole cultural formation around individuals' use of everyday choices as a legitimate site of political expression. The discourse of lifestyle politics reaches beyond radical movements; indeed, it is a feature of mainstream contemporary politics in the United States as well.

Politically inflected lifestyle practices contest divisions between what counts as "the personal" and "the political." Since personal acts hold political meaning for people, it becomes necessary to rethink what it means to engage in political activism. This book looks at the times in people's lives that occur *between* discretely identifiable moments of political involvement and action, since many people who identify as radical activists "integrate movement values into a holistic way of life" (Haenfler et al. 2012: 7). It's also important to recognize that what counts as activism is a discursive construction. I argue that whether a practice can be considered activism does not depend on the measurable *effects* of the action, but rather on the *meaning* people attribute to it. The concept of political communication, too, must be enlarged to account for the symbolic messages that individuals are sending on an everyday basis, outside of "official" political institutions. This book intervenes in previous discussions of political activism and political communication by offering sustained attention to lifestyle as a site where social actors implicitly, and sometimes explicitly, understand these processes to be taking place.

Many sociological accounts of the role of lifestyle in social movements position activists' turn toward lifestyle as a personalistic retreat from previous forms of political action which were aimed directly at the state (see Beuchler 1995; Kauffman 1990). But many contemporary activist movements (such as the queer and global justice movements) *both* place heavy investments in personal issues *and* retain a radical critique of capitalism and the state (Feixa et al. 2009). The conditions of the neoliberal consumer culture that have matured over the past two decades cultivate a climate in which lifestyle activism is a common-sense part of the path toward radical change. There is a need for theory and empirical research that accounts for radicals' deployment of lifestyle for activist purposes, which I will call *lifestyle activism*.

It is the case that while political citizenship in general is often enacted within the private sphere of consumption (Cohen 2003), radical political positions *in particular* are strongly enmeshed within private lifestyle practices. Histories of US activist movements show that radicals have a long tradition of making connections between their political ideologies and their habits of everyday life.[6] A repressive political environment—one in which active disruption of capitalist processes is strictly policed, for example—pushes radical movements toward private efforts at expressing their dissent, even while engendering that dissent *through* its repression. Geographer David

Harvey (2007) argues that the neoliberal state sees itself as the guarantor of the smooth functioning of consumer markets, given its ideological commitments to private property rights and free markets. This ideology spawns policies under which radical dissent is often quickly squashed in the name of protecting free trade; activists face less threat of repression when they pursue resistance in private, cultural realms.[7]

Harvey and other critics of neoliberalism (e.g. Rose 1999) point out that the same ideology also calls upon individuals to see themselves as "entrepreneurs," to pursue their own projects of self-enterprise, often in lieu of state welfare provision. The emergence of what cultural scholars Sarah Banet-Weiser and Roopali Mukherjee (2012) term "commodity activism" speaks to the overall cultural environment in which individualized tactics—such as the consumption of commodities—are widely accepted as logical solutions to collective problems. Lifestyle activism has been recognized as an instantiation of this "responsibilization" of individuals to take ownership not only of their own personal well-being, but also of the well-being of society at large (Littler 2009). The emergence of activist projects that seem to have much in common with individualized pursuits of consumer satisfaction is one manifestation of neoliberalism's effect on culture. Yet, as I will show, the strategic deployment of lifestyle tactics pursued by radical activists is not the same as the astrategic preoccupation with the self encouraged by neoliberal ideology.

As I demonstrate in this book, rather than participating in *either* lifestyle activism *or* radical dissent, many anarchists do both, and do not see attention to their lifestyles as separate from their concerns with altering state power and mounting strategic protest. On the contrary, lifestyle practices are heavily politicized among anarchists, and are taken up by them alongside other forms of activism. Anarchists bridge a divide between cultural movements which are oriented toward personal change and political movements which are oriented toward social change. This book therefore fills what sociologists of lifestyle movements Ross Haenfler, Brett Johnson, and Ellis Jones (2012: 2) have called "a scholarly blind spot concealing the intersections of private action and movement participation." By examining how lifestyle politics works within a radical political formation like anarchism, we can understand the contradictions introduced by modes of activism that both grow out of the conditions of neoliberal consumer culture and attempt to resist these very conditions. Scholars of political activism need to attend to the specific processes and outcomes of lifestyle tactics, in order to understand how these tactics are both empowered and limited by the contexts in which they have emerged.

Isolated tactics of resistance may coalesce into a radical activist *strategy* when they are discursively articulated to a recognizable way of life with which many individuals can identify.[8] Subcultural formations enable such recognition—people who feel affinity with a subculture can see themselves and their activities as part of a larger collective of individuals who are living in similar ways and working toward shared goals. The anarchists who are the subject of this book are part of a subcultural formation. They have their own patterns of consumption, sociality, and identity that unite them with each other and set them apart from the mainstream. They are also part of a radical political movement. They collectively wish to resist and someday replace the political system in which they find themselves. I argue that anarchists—and others in today's society who hold a commitment to oppositional lifestyle politics—can only be understood through both lenses at once, as both subculture and movement.

The utility of the concept of subculture has been much debated in recent years (see, e.g. Bennett and Kahn-Harris 2004; Haenfler et al. 2012: 7). I find it useful for thinking about anarchists because they are often unified by conventions of style and taste that symbolize and enact their opposition to the dominant culture and its attendant ideologies, which is the definition of subculture elaborated by Hall and others in a landmark collection, *Resistance through Rituals* (2005), and by Hebdige in *Subculture: The Meaning of Style* (1981). The use of the terms "subculture" and "movement" can also be contentious within activist social formations. For example, one of the first people I interviewed for this project took issue with my referring to anarchists as a "subculture," due to his perception that the term has been used by outsiders to misrepresent anarchists in some way. Presumably, he was apprehensive about anarchism being dismissed as a youthful trend or phase, rather than a serious force of resistance. Another interviewee later decried the fact that anarchism can sometimes seem like a "scene," used purely for socializing and stylistic performance rather than organized resistance. I use the terms "subculture" and "scene" throughout this book, in reference to the sociological literature that defines these terms (see Gelder [2007] for an overview of how each of these terms is defined and used in this literature). I also use the terms "milieu", "community", and "movement" to refer to anarchists' social formations. All of these terms have utility for highlighting various aspects of anarchists' social formations, and so I use each of them in this book when appropriate to capture the aspect I wish to emphasize. (During my fieldwork, I only used the latter terms, so as to avoid creating a false impression among participants that I took a negative or condescending view of their political views and activities).

An understanding of how activism happens must take into account, first, that cultural work is necessary to produce political resistance and, second, that resistant practices perform cultural work as well. Shared norms and discourses of identity enable individuals to coordinate their behavior into collective practices that resist dominant ideologies and structures. At the same time, these collective practices of resistance performatively reproduce the same norms and identities that enabled them. Lifestyle activists make clear that culture and politics are co-constitutive; to resist one is to resist the other. Yet, there is a tension here, because cultural resistance—the characteristic activity of subcultures—is often seen as a retreat from more direct, "effective" forms of political confrontation. Also, despite the strength that comes from collective recognition and cultural unity, anarchists' subculturalism threatens to undermine their status as a political movement that can reach beyond a constricted cultural milieu. Anarchists who are perceived to be too preoccupied with individual, cultural resistance are derided by other anarchists, often branded with the pejorative label "lifestylist." In such situations, the figure of the "lifestyle anarchist" takes on negative connotations and such an individual may be suspected of believing that lifestyle change is the *only* necessary means to social change. So, while the subculture and movement dimensions of contemporary anarchism draw strength from each other, they also pose seemingly irreconcilable conflict.

Some cultural theorists have argued that under neoliberalism, lifestyle projects have become experienced purely as the products of individual choice and pleasure, rather than "tests of character or expression of devotion to long-term goals requiring the control of impulse and postponement of gratification" (Binkley 2007a: 8). However, the lifestyles of the anarchists in this book tell a slightly different story. As we will see, many radicals do take ethical commitments and visions of social change as motivators for their lifestyle practices, and often defer personal gratification in the interest of their utopian political ideals. That said, the sense of responsibility and empowerment they feel, as individuals, to effect social change through their own lifestyles, is in part the product of neoliberal ideological conditions. For this reason, there is widespread concern, among both radical activists and cultural scholars, that a focus on lifestyle constitutes an evasion of the project of radical social transformation.

An irony inheres in the fact that those radicals who are able to freely make "choices" about how to live their lives might, in fact, be seen as the greatest beneficiaries of the policies and ideologies to which they are so strongly opposed. Critics argue that lifestyle tactics are only available to the very privileged who have the freedom and means to make agentic choices for themselves among many options (e.g. Braunstein and Doyle 2002; Littler 2009; Schutz 2009a, 2009b). Yet, cultural and stylistic resistance has never been the exclusive purview of those with social and economic privilege. Studies of working class youth in mid twentieth-century Britain (e.g. Hall and Jefferson 2005; Hebdige 1981) and politicized ethnic movements in the United States (e.g. Cosgrove 1984; Kelley 1996; Mercer 1987; Ogbar 2004; Van Deburg 1992) convincingly show how style has been an important tool of resistance for those who are disempowered by official social and political institutions (Duncombe 2002). However, it *is* the case that highly visible forms of consumption-based activism *have* either favored the affluent, or, more often, been co-opted by corporate interests who have used the imagery of resistance and rebellion for their own campaigns *targeting* the affluent consumer. The history of the commodification of Black Power iconography, for instance, provides a key case of symbols that once signified a militant threat to US capitalism and white supremacy being incorporated into the advertising of products that fit seamlessly into these oppressive systems (Mercer 1987). The cycle of politically informed subcultural innovation and subsequent commercial co-optation has intensified as the US economy has increasingly transitioned to conditions of flexible production and niche branding. In this context, critics argue that desires for cultural alternatives are catered to and contained within the capitalist market itself (see Frank and Weiland 1997; Heath and Potter 2004; Klein 1999).

The idea that lifestyle activism might favor those coming from privileged positions is a troubling one for radical activists. There is a conflict here between privileged individuals needing to act on the terrain in which they find themselves, and their desire to avoid playing into the dynamics engendered by that terrain, thereby reinforcing those dynamics. This conflict haunts each of the practices that will be documented in the pages of this book.

I use the term *lifestyle politics* to refer to the whole cultural formation around individuals' use of everyday choices as a legitimate site of political expression. The discourse of lifestyle politics is common sense in contemporary US society. The belief that "one person can make a difference" with the choices that one makes is pervasive not only among radicals such as anarchists, but also among all who are interpellated by the ideology of neoliberalism. When individuals' lifestyle practices are mobilized toward the goal of "making a difference" in the direction of a strategic political project, we can say that lifestyle choices are functioning as *lifestyle tactics*, which are collectively and repeatedly wielded for resistant ends.

Another aspect of the conflict that arises from lifestyle politics is the status hierarchies that often form within movements around individuals' lifestyle practices. This aspect of lifestyle politics might usefully be thought of as what I call *politicking over lifestyle*. Because lifestyles take on such ethical significance among radical activists, lifestyle practices often become targets of self-righteous moralizing and other forms of social policing. In this sense, the larger discourse of lifestyle politics includes the relations of power that arise between individuals based on their own performances of lifestyle as well as the ways in which individuals discipline themselves and their peers in line with accepted lifestyle norms. This is related to the idea of "political correctness" which developed in social movements of the 1970s and 1980s as a discursive mechanism through which activists regulated each other's "personal conduct in everyday life" (Kauffman 1990: 78). Within the regime of political correctness, those who are perceived as failing to prefigure the political goals of their movement within their own lives may be assumed to be weak in their beliefs and commitment, labeled hypocrites, or otherwise socially ostracized (Epstein 1991; Veysey 1973). Within radical movements, such individuals may even be suspected of being infiltrators and informants, working on behalf of law enforcement to surveil and undermine activist communities (Jeppesen 2003: 70).

Politicking over lifestyle can fracture bonds of solidarity among activists who make different lifestyle choices. Movements may also end up failing to recruit individuals who, for various reasons beyond their control, are unprepared to fully commit to a particular lifestyle. While many participants in and scholars of social movement culture celebrate the potential for cultural practices to bring cohesion to political movements (e.g. Gordon 2008; Purkis and Bowen 2004), cultural preferences can just as readily lead to division and exclusion. Important critiques of countercultural persuasions within activist scenes have questioned whether people of color, especially, are implicitly excluded from movements whose adherents fail to account for what sociologist Patricia Hill Collins (1986) terms the "interlocking nature of oppressions."[9] The very idea that lifestyle is completely open to individual choice is an ideologically biased one, which does not take into account the way symbolic boundaries work to reproduce pre-existing sociological stratifications (Binkley 2007b; Bourdieu 1984; Chaney 1996). Among anarchists, these dynamics become even more complicated: one is at risk of being judged for not having the "correct" activist lifestyle, yet one is negatively labeled a lifestylist if one is seen as being *too* focused on lifestyle. So-called lifestylists are also criticized for being disproportionately drawn from socially privileged identity categories, namely male, white, straight, and middle class. In fact, the topic of lifestyle anarchism has proven so controversial among anarchists that it was expressly *banned* as a topic of discussion on one internet forum.[10]

Looking at the lifestyles of people who identify with a philosophy like anarchism highlights the political and cultural implications of what I call "identities we choose," drawing on anthropologist Kath Weston's (1997) concept of "families we choose." Weston's idea captures the destabilization but continued importance of a construct—family—that has traditionally been understood as "naturally" given but is more accurately understood as both sociologically and ideologically *achieved*. Similarly, there is nothing "given" about anarchist identity; it is something that must be established and maintained through behavior and performance. Yet, radical political identity is a tricky thing to perform since, as a mental construct, it is not immediately evident on one's physical body, and because radicalism is by definition outside the recognizable narratives available in mainstream society. This is where lifestyle emerges as a site of political subject formation and an expression of political identity. As writer and activist L. A. Kauffman (1990: 78) puts it, lifestyle choices project "a sense of 'being' political at a time when the options for doing politics may seem limited." While performativity theorists (e.g. Butler 1990; Sedgwick 1990) have argued that, in fact, *all* types of identity may be constituted through performance, the case of anarchist political identity is a useful one since it can expose the obviously performative dimensions of subject and movement formation. As a political identity, anarchism has no intrinsic link to a pre-constituted social position such as race, gender, sexuality, class, nationality, or religion. Yet, the commitment and identification that activists bring to anarchism make clear that such pre-constituted positions are not necessary for mobilizing political activism.

"De-essentialized" identities—those which are not assumed to be naturally given (Mohanty 2003)—highlight the importance of meaning and interpretation in the construction of political identity. It is not just the commonality of experience that is important—it is a commonality of *interpretation* of experience through a critical, political lens that forms the basis of political identification (Scott 1992). The dynamics of anarchist movements also show that the absence of more conventional identity narratives does not preclude some of the problems of identity politics that have dogged other movements, such as debates over who can claim authentic membership (as discussed above). And, despite the potential for openness and diversity among those who join anarchist movements, people do not simply leave behind their other social identities when they take up radical activism. By showing how issues like essentialism and authenticity play out even within a movement based on a de-essentialized identity, I offer a perspective on how these concepts operate within social movements at large. The conflicts over which lifestyle practices anarchists should adopt and the extent to which lifestyle should figure in activist strategy at all, highlight how important it is to consider issues of power and privilege when studying the formation of political identities and movements. This book examines and explains these dynamics, as they play out within contemporary US anarchism. In examining how one set of radical activists attempts to navigate the conflicts introduced by lifestyle politics, this book offers insight into the challenges faced by many contemporary formations which exist at the intersection of subculture and social movement.

The culture of contemporary US anarchism

I undertook the research for this book as a "strategic ethnography," which looks at one particular aspect of anarchist culture[11]—in this case, lifestyle politics. There is much more to contemporary anarchism than the lifestyle choices its adherents make, so this book should be seen as *one* story about anarchists, rather than a definitive, exhaustive account of an entire movement. In the interest of looking at the use of lifestyle within anarchist movements, I employed a combination of methods, which included interviews with individuals who either self-identified as anarchists or claimed an affinity with anarchist politics, participant observation at formal and informal anarchist events, and discourse analysis of anarchist print culture. In recognition of the diversity of contemporary anarchists, I gathered data from a variety of sites, interviewing individuals and attending events in dispersed geographic locations around the United States. While I did gather evidence of what some anarchists' everyday practices are like, I was most interested in understanding the *meaning* everyday practices hold for dissident individuals and the ways cultural and subcultural discourses around the politics of lifestyle impact those individuals' subjective experience of everyday life. The book provides some descriptive accounts of what some anarchists *do*, but its focus is more on the ways that anarchists think and talk about what they do.

My fieldwork involved attending several anarchist events between 2007 and 2010. These included book fairs, conferences, organizing meetings, and social events such as potlucks and parties. Often, these were public events; otherwise, I attended on the invitation of an interviewee or other contact. Whenever feasible, I made my role as a researcher known. Most of the events I attended took place in Los Angeles, where I lived, but I also traveled to other locations (such as Vermont and Northern California) for conferences and book fairs. Attending anarchist events proved to be useful for observing some specific trends in behavior across time and place, and for corroborating some of the accounts of reality found in anarchist texts and given by my interviewees. I did, however, limit the types of events I attended to those I felt were appropriate for a researcher to attend. The notion of "security culture" influenced the types of events I attended and the individuals I approached for interviews. Security culture refers to the norms of privacy and information control developed by anarchists in response to regular infiltration of their groups and surveillance by law enforcement personnel.[12] Though many subcultures may be hard to observe carefully because they are resistant to "gawkers" (Thornton 1996: 87), the stakes are often much higher for anarchist activists, because they are a frequent target of state surveillance and repression. For this reason, I restricted my observation to public and otherwise innocuous activities, so that I would never be in a position to expose sensitive or potentially threatening information about what I was observing. I also avoided asking for interviews with individuals whom I knew had been frequently targeted by the police. In fact, I tended only to approach people for interviews if I had met them personally or had an acquaintance in common who could vouch for my not being a cop. Though it is possible that the data I gathered were skewed by these self-imposed restrictions on my fieldwork, I do think that I was able to observe a great deal that was relevant to my research focus on lifestyle.

Currently, there are thousands of anarchists in the United States, but as a stigmatized identity with no clear "criteria for membership," it is impossible to collect accurate data as to their numbers and demographic make-up (Stein 1997: 6); this, in turn, makes it impossible to construct a "representative sample" of anarchists. I conducted a total of 39 interviews.

The format of the interviews varied. With interviewees located in Los Angeles, where I lived, I conducted the interviews in person, recording them so that I could transcribe them later. The rest of the interviews were conducted electronically, either via email or instant messenger. In all cases, I attempted to make the interviews as open and conversational as possible. When the interviews were conducted via email, I preferred to send a question or two at a time and then follow up on the responses before moving on to new topics. Usually, this meant exchanging several messages over the course of a few days. I began each interview with a question about where the person first learned about anarchism, because I felt it was a question that could be definitively answered, rather than requiring too much introspection or subjective analysis from the interviewee. At times, I purposely asked questions that were not strictly relevant to my research, because I thought they would put the interviewees at ease, or allow them to perform their anarchist identities in a way that felt comfortable for them. For example, one of my first interviewees expressed surprise that I hadn't asked him more about his organized activism, as he thought of that as crucial to his political identity as an anarchist. In subsequent interviews, I generally asked what kind of activism and organizing work the interviewees were involved with, even if I didn't expect to find this information to be within the scope of my definition of lifestyle politics. As interviewees became more comfortable with the conversation, I asked more personal questions. I nearly always reserved questions about potentially sensitive issues—sexuality, ethnicity, personal appearance—for the end of the interview, or did not ask them at all, if I got the impression that the interviewee would find them offensive. Although I aimed to make the interview format feel somewhat conversational, I said relatively little, in order to let the interviewees follow their own trains of thought and not feel that I was judging them or foreclosing certain topics or opinions.

Contemporary anarchists are often geographically mobile and electronically connected across national and cultural borders. Many of my interviewees, for instance, had participated in anarchist movements in locations outside North America, including Central and South America, Europe, and Australia, though they were all living in the United States or Canada when I met them. Yet, the particularities of US culture, and the specific history of political resistance in the United States, have a definite effect on the way lifestyle functions within contemporary anarchism here, and perhaps accounts for the perception (expressed to me on multiple occasions) that American anarchists are more preoccupied with lifestyle issues than their counterparts elsewhere. Even within the United States, there is no monolithic way to characterize all anarchists or anarchist organizations. There are commonalities of culture and collective identification across the US context however, and this book focuses on those, in the interest of providing an analysis that is somewhat generalizable to contemporary

American radical movements. I hope too that activists and scholars in other parts of the world find this research useful, though it may be less reflective of their own observations and experiences.

The core philosophy of anarchism is that human well-being is best ensured by a decentralized, non-hierarchical, radically democratic society. Anarchists seek revolutionary change to existing society in the pursuit of a more just world. Although anarchy is often misperceived as being synonymous with chaos or violence, it denotes only an absence of hierarchy. Anarchists are not against organization or structure; rather, they object to organizations or structures that are based on unequal relations of power or are maintained coercively. Because of their critique of hierarchy, anarchists often work in solidarity with feminists, anti-racists, socialists, environmentalists, and any number of other radical and progressive movements that share this critique. Capitalism and the state are chief among anarchists' targets of critique, since these structures are seen as centralizing authority in people and institutions that are unaccountable to the people who are subject to their power. Anarchists are also critical of other systems of oppression, such as patriarchy and colonialism. Thus, they are interested in mounting challenges to authoritarianism in many cultural spheres, not just in the capitalist market or in state governments. To put the anarchist project more positively, anarchists try to cultivate social forms that will foster egalitarian relationships of voluntary association and freedom of creative expression for all. While anarchism is clearly a utopian philosophy, it is also a philosophy for the here and now. As anarchist activist and scholar Uri Gordon (2008: 41) explains, anarchy is "a lived reality that pops up everywhere in new guises, adapts to different cultural climates, and should be extended and developed experimentally for its own sake, whether or not we believe it can become, in some sense, the prevailing mode of society."

Gordon also points out that contemporary anarchism is a "political culture," which entails "a family of shared orientations to doing and talking about politics and to living everyday life" (2008: 4). In this, anarchism is typical of contemporary social movements in which a very blurry line separates everyday life and political orientation, if any such line exists at all. Anarchists present a rather extreme case, since, as anarchist writer Cindy Milstein (2010: 41) suggests, "Embracing anarchism is a process of reevaulating every assumption, everything one thinks about and does, and indeed who one is, and then basically turning one's life upside-down." The radical subversiveness of anarchist political philosophy translates to the striking contrast between the ways of life pursued by anarchists and those in the mainstream, hence the idea that one's life is turned "upside-down" in the process of shifting from mainstream ideology to the ideals of anarchism. Although, as I argued above, the discourse of lifestyle politics is not unique to anarchists, they do provide a vivid illustration of the way this discourse manifests in material practices.

Today's anarchist lifestyles must be understood as partially continuous with the efforts of earlier radical and utopian movements that attempted to put principles of anti-authoritarianism into practice at the most minute levels of everyday life, dating back at least to the nineteenth century in the United States.[13] Many of these movements explicitly identified with anarchist principles; others were implicitly aligned with anarchist philosophy. The hippie counterculture of the late 1960s, for example, had significant anarchist elements and became one of the most culturally resonant alternative lifestyle movements in modern history. Many of these groups experimented with the lifestyle practices still adopted by anarchists today and discussed in this book, such as communal living, veganism, alternative styles of dress, and sexual non-conformity. The most direct influence on the cultural texture of contemporary anarchism is probably the punk subculture that emerged in the late 1970s and rose in popularity through the 1980s. Certain bands and publications (namely Crass, the Dead Kennedys, *MaximumRockNRoll*, and *Profane Existence*) helped to link punk music, lifestyles, and attitudes to a whole set of political philosophies closely aligned with anarchism, often explicitly (O'Hara 1999; Thompson 2004).

It is clear that few if any of the specific lifestyle practices that will be discussed in this book can be fairly described as truly unique to the contemporary moment. Yet, the practice of lifestyle politics today does occur amid historically specific conditions. These conditions include the nearly complete interpenetration of the capitalist market into processes of everyday life, the broad incorporation of alternative cultural movements into commodity culture, the transfer of social and environmental welfare projects away from the state and into the private sector, intense class and race stratification masked by rhetorics of meritocracy and equal access, and the simultaneous liberal advancement of some women and sexual minorities alongside the draconian disenfranchisement of others. Contemporary anarchist lifestyle tactics certainly bear the traces of earlier countercultural movements but they are also shaped by and respond to the forces of their own time.

As noted briefly above, contemporary anarchism is far from a monolithic movement, philosophy, or social formation. Anarchist historian Andrew Cornell (2011a: 41) concisely explains, "It is more accurate to talk about an array of continuously evolving, sometimes overlapping, sometimes conflicting *anarchisms* or anarchist tendencies." The diversity of contemporary anarchism is germane to a critical analysis of anarchist lifestyle politics, since different subformations may deploy lifestyle in different ways. The divergent goals of various types of anarchists may also be differently compatible with an activist strategy that draws on lifestyle tactics. In this book, I draw on various strands of contemporary anarchism in the United States in order to paint a general picture of the way lifestyle functions in the anarchist scene, broadly conceived. I study practices of culture and collective identity that can be found across contexts, rather than focusing on specific organizations or institutions.[14]

I would argue that culture and collective identification are, in fact, the primary basis upon which an anarchist "movement" coheres at all.[15] Investment in anarchism is a basis upon which individuals form community and think of themselves as part of a distinct group (Gordon 2008). People identify as anarchists, recognize that there are others who also identify that way, and experience actual and imagined bonds with those people because of this shared identification. In keeping with social movement scholars Verta Taylor and Nancy Wittier's (1995: 173) sociological definition of collective identities, the identity anarchist is something that is recognizable across specific communities and settings, and is "widely available for adoption." As individuals become involved with the political and cultural activities of anarchism, they may develop a "movement identity," which further solidifies anarchists' collective identification and solidarity with each other (Polletta and Jasper 2001: 291).

Yet, complicating this picture of anarchism as a coherent collective identity is the skepticism of identity and identity politics that many activists bring with them to contemporary anarchism. Anarchist anthropologist David Graeber (2002: 62) points out that "there are some who take anarchist principles of anti-sectarianism and open-endedness so seriously that they are sometimes reluctant to call themselves 'anarchists' for that very reason." Furthermore, anarchist organizers doggedly resist centralized institutionalization and incorporation into mainstream political structures. Anthropologist Jeffrey Juris (2009: 213), drawing on the work of Manuel Castells (1996), describes the structure of the anarchist movement as driven by the "cultural logic of networking," meaning that it is made up of autonomous entities (individuals and local groups) that are horizontally connected through information circuits and may voluntarily come together through physical or discursive means to organize around particular issues and events. This decentralized structure, which has its roots in the autonomous networks of anarchists involved in the Spanish Civil War of the 1930s, is meant to keep power from becoming concentrated in the hands of a movement elite and to keep recognizable leaders from emerging who might attempt to speak for anarchists as a whole (Sheehan 2003). As I will show, the commitment to a lack of formal structure can unintentionally foster informal hierarchies of power, in which individuals' tastes and lifestyle practices are used as status markers.[16]

The lifestyle practices and discourses I will be discussing in this book are crucial to contemporary anarchism as a movement, because they are key sites for the maintenance of anarchist culture and identity. Suffice it to say here that contemporary anarchism can be both a kind of "politics of identity," to the extent that some people invest in their identities *as* anarchists, and a "politics of articulation," in that the identity and the community that form around anarchism are seen as always in process, contestable, and negotiable.[17] The movement culture[18] of contemporary anarchism attempts to reflect anarchists' philosophical commitments to decentralization, egalitarianism, cultural freedom, and positive social transformation. Anarchists form what social historian Sharif Gemie (1994: 357) calls "counter-communities," in which anarchist political theories are developed and practiced in the interest of modeling a more general social formation and inspiring confidence in the achievability of anarchist iwjadeals. Like other radical movements, anarchists aim for a political culture out of which actions and affinity groups might arise as needed, rather than as directed by a centralized institution (Epstein 1991: 118).

Local affinity groups and collectives undertake ongoing projects and provide a general sense of community through both formal meetings and spontaneous, informal gatherings. Collectives may form around fixed sites such as group houses, community centers, cafés, or "infoshops" (an anarchist infoshop is something like a radical bookstore or library and is also usually used as an event space for the local anarchist community).[19] These institutions may endure for months or even years, or they may be designed to be more temporary. Collectives may also convene to facilitate more sporadic events, including protests, book fairs, festivals, conferences, speaking events, reading groups, music performances, film screenings, and art showings. Consumption often plays a central role in these events (a point of contestation among anarchists that I will discuss in Chapter 2).

Events such as protests and book fairs bring anarchists out of their local situations, fostering a sense of a larger activist community that transcends geographical space (Juris 2004: 244; see also Juris 2008b). While the events themselves may be sporadic, the lifestyle practices observable at these events (e.g. styles of dress and consumption) are understood to be ongoing aspects of daily life for the individuals involved. For anarchists, events like these are what ethnographer Clifford Geertz (1993) would call "paradigmatic," in that they are key occasions for performing the ethos of anarchist movement culture. The spectacle of dozens or hundreds of people engaged in typical anarchist lifestyle practices normalizes those practices and reinforces their status as constitutive of anarchist identity and activism. The actual bodies of attendees at events also create a visual spectacle. The sight of hundreds of similarly styled strangers in one place contributes to the sense of a unified anarchist culture that extends across geographic space as these individuals disperse after the event.

Events and meetings serve as sites for the cultivation of a distinctive "habitus" among participants in anarchist activism. Sociologist Pierre Bourdieu's (1984) notion of the habitus refers to a regular set of dispositions among members of a social group that directs those individuals' everyday choices into patterned, empirically observable lifestyle trends. These common tastes among social group members become what Bourdieu calls "a unitary set of distinctive preferences" (1984: 173). For example, the Bay Area Anarchist Book Fair annually features a Bike Valet where attendees can park their bicycles. The hundreds of bicycles parked outside during the fair sends the message to participants that it is normal and even preferable to use a bicycle as a means of transportation. Similarly, the food provided at such events is usually entirely vegan (or at least there will always be readily available vegan options), establishing the normalcy of a vegan diet in one's daily life.

More isolated convergences also give anarchists the chance to try out lifestyle practices they may not yet have experienced or figured out how to implement in their daily lives. Anarchist geographer Gavin Brown (2007) describes how at mass protests, to which activists may travel long distances, temporary communal housing is usually set up near the convergence site for the duration of the protest. Here, individuals experience what it is like to work collectively to meet everyone's basic food and shelter needs in financially and environmentally sustainable ways (Feigenbaum, Frenzel, and McCurdy, forthcoming). These spaces also often actively encourage consensus decision making and other forms of interpersonal interaction that are important to anarchists. For those who have never had the opportunity to incorporate such practices into their everyday lifestyles, these experiences are crucial for demonstrating the viability of these practices.

Organizing spaces, conferences, and festivals are not only sites of performance and practice, but also home to explicit discussions and debate about lifestyle and its relevance to anarchist principles. Formal presentations on specific lifestyle practices teach the uninitiated how to partake in these activities and provide ideological justification for why one should incorporate them into one's everyday life. For example, I attended a workshop on DIY ("do-it-yourself") gynecology, in which the facilitator explained anarcha-feminist principles and provided space for the women (and men) in attendance to learn methods of monitoring their own health and treating common ailments with at-home remedies. The personal implementation of such a lifestyle practice might be quite intimidating for some women, due to mainstream norms and taboos around health and sexuality. Formal presentations like the one I attended help make such practices feel familiar and practicable, thus making them accessible to newcomers to the subculture. The presentations are also explicitly focused on deconstructing the ideologies behind the norms and taboos of women's health care and sexuality, giving attendees reasons to feel attracted to anarchist philosophies and practices.

The culture of contemporary anarchism extends beyond physical interactions into a rich print culture as well, in the form of books, newsletters, and photocopied booklets—known as "zines"— which are ubiquitous at anarchist gatherings and infoshops.[20] Anarchists also communicate with each other via websites, blogs, and posts on social media networks. As with other subcultures, there is a sense that one can go anywhere in the country, and some parts of the world, and find other anarchists, especially if one is willing to do a little exploring on the internet or put out some feelers among one's social networks (Gordon 2008; Juris 2004). For those anarchists who have the means and inclination to travel, and even for those who never come into physical contact with the far-flung members of their imagined community, these electronically networked connections are key to the understanding of anarchism as a movement with real political potential (Rupp and Taylor 1987). As Cornell (2011a) shows, anarchist movements have always been heavily sustained by their print cultures, particularly in times and places where public airing of anarchist philosophy has been unwelcome and where activists have been separated from each other by geographic distance. Because of this, I supplemented my interview and observational research by immersing myself in the textual world of the broad anarchist movement, consuming written material published by and about anarchists.

In these texts lies an expression of the shared values of the movement subculture, in which anarchists document their own culture for an anarchist audience, representing themselves to themselves (Duncombe 2008). Texts often impart explicit information about specific lifestyle practices, including in some cases detailed instructions for how individuals might implement them.[21] These representations both shore up the self-identity of the authors and provide models for others to imitate. The circulation of these texts also solidifies the sense of a cohesive subculture, a fact about which the authors and distributors of these texts are self-reflexive. For example, one book produced by the anarchist collective CrimethInc. (2005a: 16) suggests that even texts such as graffiti or wheatpasted posters serve an important cultural function in that they "help others who share this [political] sentiment to feel that they are not entirely alone and insane, and [they] might inspire them to turn their silent rancor into expressive projects of their own."

Commitments to certain fundamental principles of anarchist praxis run across all incarnations of contemporary anarchist culture. Praxis refers to the way in which political, philosophical ideals are strategically put into activist practice to bring about material change (Amster et al. 2009: 181). *Direct action* and *propaganda by deed* are two aspects of anarchist praxis that bear directly on the contemporary use of lifestyle as a site of activism. Anarchist strategists differ in the extent to which they believe lifestyle politics are mandated by these principles of praxis (I will say much more about these debates in Chapter 6). As a precursor, my discussion here will explain why *some* anarchists find lifestyle tactics to be consistent with their activist principles.

Direct action expresses the anarchist ideal that power should not solely reside in a centralized institution, such as the state, which must be appealed to in order to effect change. According to the principle of direct action, if one desires a change in one's conditions, one should empower oneself to do whatever is necessary to actively bring about that change (de Cleyre

2004a). If one is successful, then one has accomplished change without working within and legitimizing hierarchical institutions. But even if one is unsuccessful, one has at least not reinforced the legitimacy of the institution by appealing to it for the results one desires. While direct action sometimes refers to acts of destruction undertaken in order to bring down an existing institution or event, it also refers to the coordination of efforts to establish new, anarchist organizations and activities. A strike in which workers attempt to seize and collectivize the means of production is a classic example of direct action (Goldman 1969). But direct action can also refer to, for example, a group of anarchists who come together to provide baskets of food to needy people in a park each week, as a group called Revolutionary Autonomous Communities does in Los Angeles's MacArthur Park each Sunday (Imani 2011). These people act because they see the operations of the liberal state and the free market neglecting to ensure that everyone in their community has enough to eat.

Lifestyle practices can be understood as direct action because they attempt to materially change one's everyday experience without appealing to a central entity. When an individual attempts to put anarchist principles into action in one's everyday life, one acts on the assumption that one has the capacity to determine the shape of one's personal experience. One may be more or less successful at actually putting anarchist principles into effect. For example, one may try to live without participating in capitalist exchange relations, but one will probably have to engage with capitalism at some point in order to survive, given its dominance and pervasiveness in contemporary societies. Nevertheless, any attempt to reduce one's complicity through one's own purchasing habits could be a form of direct action, however limited the outcome may be.

Gordon (2008: 38) suggests that the alternative lifestyles of anarchists might function as a kind of "propaganda by deed," by setting an example for others to follow in attempting to free their own lives of oppressive forces. Originally developed by European anarchists of the late nineteenth century, propaganda by deed was a concept referring to spectacular acts of insurrectionary violence, undertaken with the intent to rouse the masses to action (Sheehan 2003). These acts, including attempted assassinations of world leaders and businessmen, were supposed to expose as irrational the ideological dichotomy between "legitimate" uses of force (exercised by state rulers and capitalists) and "illegitimate" uses of force (exercised by the insurrectionists). The idea was that where people were systematically oppressed by hierarchical institutions, they had a responsibility to rise up against their oppressors.

That the concept of propaganda by deed might be applied to lifestyle practices owes to a historical shift in the meaning of the concept. Cornell (2011a) shows how intense repression of anarchists by the state in the early twentieth century stamped out activists' aims of inciting revolution through class warfare. Social theory also developed such that state and class oppression were no longer the only targets of anarchist critique. Cornell suggests that the recognition that mass insurrection was both unlikely to happen and inadequate to address all the forms of oppression they opposed pushed anarchists toward projects of "practical anarchism," such as building utopian communities in which life could be lived more anarchistically without facing violent repression by the state.

Practical projects, such as utopian communities, were thought to be useful because they would, first, serve as experimental incubators for anarchist lifestyles, and second, prove that such ways of life were possible and desirable (for a litany of specific examples of such projects and the strategic philosophies behind them, see Cornell [2011a]). Anarchists see the achievement of alternative, anti-oppression lifestyles not just as an end itself, but as a means toward expanding the public appeal of revolutionary projects. The term "prefigurative politics" (Breines 1982) is often used in reference to organizing structures and processes taken up by activist movements (e.g. the use of consensus decision making within anarchist organizations), but it may also be applied to patterns of everyday life among members of those movements as well. The capacity for activists' personal practices to communicate about the viability and appeal of anarchism is what makes lifestyle a potential tool of propaganda and prefiguration.

Tactics of direct action and prefigurative politics are especially salient for anarchist activists within the contemporary conditions of receding state responsibility and new sites of civic participation. Within neoliberalism, power is understood to operate outside the narrow structures of the state. Thus, radical change must also be effected outside the state as well. Anthropologist Marianne Maeckelbergh (2011: 2) points out that "the veritable obsession with process found within the alterglobalization movement is indicative of a crucial shift in the way movement actors understand how social change can be enacted."[22] By process, Maeckelbergh is referring to the processes of democratic participation and agenda setting within activist organizations. As she explains, many radical organizations since the 1990s have made fundamental commitments to enacting principles of democracy, diversity, and horizontalism within movement structures. Enacting these principles is so important she says, because movements are attempting to "build a new world in the shell of the old."[23] These movements desire a radical alternative to neoliberal modes of citizenship and thus attempt to realize this alternative for themselves in their own organizations, which for them *are* the public sphere apart from the state and the market. I argue that lifestyle has also become a "veritable obsession" for contemporary radical activists, in part for precisely the same reasons that process has become central in radical organizations. We might thus see the lifestyles of radical activists as responses to and proposed remedies for the failure of neoliberal societies to actually ensure the everyday health and happiness of their members.

As stated earlier, my research was strategic in that I attempted to focus on one particular aspect of anarchist culture. Another strategic move I made was to seek out interviewees, events, and texts that would destabilize some of the enduring stereotypes that have characterized previous portrayals of anarchists and their subcultures. From the nineteenth century to the present, mainstream media representations have oversimplified, vilified, and sensationalized anarchists and their aims, usually painting anarchists as pathologically violent and irrational.[24] In contemporary times, portrayals that are more sympathetic to the political philosophy of anarchism—usually only appearing in niche or underground media outlets—frequently criticize the contemporary anarchist movement for its homogeneity. To be more specific, anarchism is critiqued for its apparently disproportionate appeal to white, straight, middle-class men. This book gives particular attention to the perspectives of the many women, queer people, people of color, and working-class people who embrace anarchist politics. In doing so, I attempt to amplify these voices and to show that contemporary anarchism is actually *not* homogeneous at all. My analysis shows that lifestyle politics may reproduce white, male, heterosexual, middle-class privilege, leading to increased *visibility* and *status* for individuals who bring these kinds of privileges with them to activist scenes. The point here is that anarchism is a more heterogeneous movement than it has frequently been *represented* or recognized as, and lifestyle politics may be to blame for these representational distortions in some instances. By accounting for some of the specific processes by which mainstream dynamics of privilege are replicated within activist movements, I hope this book might prove illuminating for those looking to interrupt such processes.

Each of the individual chapters of this book has a dual purpose: (1) to provide rich description of practices and discourses of lifestyle politics which are central to contemporary US anarchism in particular, and (2) to make a theoretical argument that can be applied to lifestyle politics as a broader phenomenon. All the chapters consider the motivations and consequences of a wide range of lifestyle practices undertaken by anarchists as part of their radical activism. Together, they build an argument that lifestyle-based activist tactics are complex cultural phenomena which must be considered from many angles in order to arrive at a full understanding of the way they function in activist movements and in the lives of individual activists. Furthermore, analyses of activist tactics must consider how power relationships shape the ways several tactical practices get enacted and taken up, as well as how power relationships may be reproduced or unsettled through those processes. Such assessments of power are important, not only for analytical clarity, but also because they can inform future activist strategy.

In Chapter 2, I describe anarchists' practices of "anti-consumption" in which they avoid participating in mainstream consumer culture, or at least discursively position themselves as having done so. This chapter argues that lifestyle tactics, such as anti-consumption, "do" more than simply fulfill material, strategic goals, such as subverting capitalism. Thus, they need to be analyzed, critiqued, and evaluated for *all* their potential effects. I make this argument by showing how individuals may be motivated by many factors, not just straightforward activist outcomes. Specifically, I identify five distinct types of motivation for anti-consumption practices: personal, moral, activist, identificatory, and social motivations. My analysis focuses especially on the social motivations and effects of anarchist consumption patterns. I then illustrate how this typology can be usefully applied to specific practices and the effects thereof, in order to arrive at a strategic assessment of any given lifestyle-based tactic.

The third chapter describes several self-presentation practices of anarchists. I argue that the meaning of subcultural stylistic practices is context dependent, and travels in a circuit among producers and consumers (wearers and observers) of stylistic practices. The meanings assigned to anarchists' self-presentation in various contexts, and the practical implications of these meanings (such as social prejudice, in-group boundary policing, and even mainstream co-optation through commodification), are important to consider in assessing self-presentation as an activist tactic. I present perspectives from individuals who adopt typical practices of anarchist self-presentation, and from those who choose not to. I also apply theories of representation, performance, and power to the production and consumption of embodied, stylistic "texts."

Chapter 4 describes how individuals relate to the identity category "anarchist," what attractions it holds, and what problems it presents as a category of identity. I argue that subcultural commitments to "authenticity" are both productive—in that they engender self-discipline and community accountability among activists—and destructive—in that they often lead to internecine drama and boundary policing within movements. These phenomena relate to lifestyle in that lifestyle practices are often the means by which an individual's sincere commitment to the principles and goals of anarchist movements is gauged by one's peers/comrades. This gauging of sincerity proves problematic when the individual lifestyle habits of anarchist subcultures are recontextualized within the dominant culture under which all individuals must live. Differential levels of privilege within the dominant culture may translate to differential abilities to undertake the practices which serve as measures of subcultural authenticity. Some anarchists attempt to cope with this problem through a kind of ironic stance toward authentic anarchist identity, which tries to balance the benefits of cohesive group identity with an awareness of its limitations.

In Chapter 5, I show that lifestyle practices may be symbolic *and* material, and that both dimensions can be considered when assessing the strategic fitness of a given tactical practice in a given personal and historical context.

I make this argument by comparing three sexual lifestyle practices adopted by anarchists as part of their anarchist orientations—polyamory, queer self-identification, and consent-seeking—and considering the expressive and instrumental motivations for each. This chapter also argues that while sexual identities may be performatively constituted through everyday, embodied practice, the symbolic act of sexual identification is also seen as a kind of activist practice in itself.

The sixth chapter addresses self-reflexive attitudes toward lifestyle politics within anarchist movement culture. I discuss how the terms "lifestyle anarchist" and "lifestylism" are sometimes used as epithets within movement discourse to separate supposedly worthwhile forms of activism from illegitimate, superficial forms of activism. The discourse around lifestylism highlights the many issues at stake when individual, everyday practices become significant—even prioritized—for a political movement. This chapter surveys those issues as they are manifest within contemporary anarchism. The book's conclusion remarks upon the significance of lifestyle politics within the broader contemporary culture, specifically its relation to neoliberal political subjectivity.

2

The anti-consumption lifestyle: The cultural work of activist practices

It's March 2009, and I'm in a car with four anarchists in Oakland, California. I've hitched a ride with them back to Los Angeles from the annual Bay Area Anarchist Book Fair, where we've all spent the weekend. Two of the people in the car are people I've interviewed for my research, Tina and Raychel. I've known them for several weeks, and have spent time with them at events and meetings of the anarcha-feminist group they're involved with. We had all traveled to the book fair to distribute literature and network with other activists. When I get in the car and thank them for giving me a ride, they say it's no problem, that it's just "mutual aid"—the anarchist principle of cooperation and generosity.[1] Before leaving Oakland, we stop for lunch at a vegan, organic restaurant (everyone in the group is a practicing vegan but me). It turns out to be quite expensive, so we drive around for at least 20 minutes looking for another restaurant that serves vegan food (we end up settling on a vegetarian Thai restaurant). Our last stop before hitting the road is a gas station to fill up. The driver and owner of the car insists we find a Chevron station—he's recently read an article about the 20 "worst" corporations and Chevron was one of the only oil companies not on it (the criteria for "worst" are unclear to me but I presume some sort of ethical standard was given in the article). I'm able to locate a Chevron station using my cell phone, and we make our way there. While he fills up the tank, Raychel goes into the station's bathroom to brush her teeth.

As Raychel is walking back to the car, a man asks her for change, saying he is hungry and wants to buy some food. In keeping with the spirit of mutual aid, she goes back into the station and buys him a burrito using her credit card, since she didn't have any cash on her to give to him. Raychel relates this to the rest of us in the car as we are setting off on the highway. She expresses regret that she purchased non-vegan food for the man (the burrito contained cheese), since she herself is a militant vegan who is very active and outspoken in the animal rights movement. Though Raychel is apologetic, Tina still points out that Raychel was supporting a system of cruelty by paying for the dairy product. This hurts Raychel's feelings—she is obviously bothered by Tina's comment and spends the next several minutes trying to justify her act.

While this road trip was one of the more informal experiences I had as part of my fieldwork, it ended up being paradigmatic because of the observations I was able to make about how these anarchists approach everyday practices of consumption. It was a paradigmatic episode because it encapsulated so many aspects of how anarchist activists approach their everyday decisions about consumption. The individuals in this group readily shared their resources with both acquaintances and strangers, citing anarchist principles. They sought out particular kinds of commodities for themselves, going out of their way when other options would have been more convenient. They also held themselves and each other accountable for purchases that involved compromises to their ethical values. And this was all in the space of about an hour. Their practices seem to be clear illustrations of what Sam Binkley calls, drawing on the work of Michel Foucault, "self-problematization": "a holding up of some aspect of one's daily conduct as the object of serious ethical scrutiny and concern, at the center of which is a discourse with others on the appropriate shape of such behavior for the purposes of an ethical goal of one sort or another" (Binkley 2007a: 131). These individuals' discursive activity *around* their acts of consumption is particularly consistent with Binkley's Foucaultian picture of ethical practice.

I use the term "anti-consumption" to refer to the kinds of consumer activism that some anarchists, like the ones on my road trip, engage in. The range of specific practices encompassed by anti-consumption will become clear as this chapter progresses. Anti-consumption is part of the fabric of everyday life for the anarchist activists I discuss here. Anarchist anti-consumers do not universally abstain from consumption; indeed, such a feat would be impossible. Rather, they consume differently, in ways that *signify* an opposition to the kinds of lifestyles encouraged by the bourgeois consumer culture. To say that anarchists consume differently is not to say that they never participate in the same kinds of consumption activities that "regular" people do, just that, on the whole, they cultivate a different consumer habitus (Bourdieu 1984) or "way of being in the world" (Clarke et al. 2005: 54). And when they do consume in similar *material* ways to mainstream consumers, they often *discursively* frame their consumption activities as contra to the overall system of consumer capitalism. This is what makes their anti-consumption lifestyles understandable *as* activism.

In this chapter, I emphasize the ways in which anti-consumption carries cultural and political significance for participants in activist movements, despite the fact that a purely non-consumptive lifestyle is an impossible achievement for anyone. My hope is that this emphasis on the discursive work of anti-consumption will provide a counterpoint to dismissals that see anti-consumption as simply ineffective or hypocritical in its attempts to overturn capitalism. Like all resistant practices, anti-consumption "does" much more than directly subvert its object of opposition. In other words, the objective of anti-consumption cannot simply be reduced to opposing consumption. People may espouse an anti-consumption position for a variety of reasons, only some of which have to do with fighting the system of consumer capitalism. I will discuss these various reasons in depth in the second half of this chapter. In doing so, I hope to reinforce the idea that any analysis or evaluation of anti-consumption as a political practice must work from an enlarged understanding of resistance and its potential "effects."

Practices of anti-consumption

Several of the individuals I interviewed explained that once they began to identify as anarchists, they started refusing to consume things that many middle-class Americans consider to be basic features of everyday life. Anarchists, in fact, have a centuries-old tradition of assuming "voluntary poverty," which is the chosen state of having just enough to meet one's basic needs (Woodcock 1979: 32). Josef described himself as "an anarchist Los Angeles pirate" because he chose to forego "luxuries" like having a car and a stable home. For anarchists like Josef, needs are distinguished from luxuries through a critical lens that understands most consumer desires to be the product of false consciousness, induced by corporations, in the interest of promoting rampant material acquisition. The logic of voluntary poverty is that once individuals become aware that their needs are falsely imposed by marketers, they can willfully decide to do without many consumer products they may have previously considered necessary.

Personal hygiene is a notable area in which many anarchists do without products that mainstream consumers buy as a matter of course. Grant said that since becoming involved with anarchism, he no longer felt it necessary to take a shower every day. For him, this was about "being comfortable with the way your body naturally exists and not succumbing to pressure from the dominant society." Mass-marketed soaps, shampoos, and deodorants are all seen as unnecessary chemicals foisted upon consumers by greedy capitalists. The authors of a popular anarchist book *Days of War, Nights of Love* (CrimethInc. 2000: 121) assert that "western" [sic] standards of cleanliness are rooted in class hierarchies, wherein "those who possessed the wealth and power required to have the leisure to remain indoors, inactive, scorned the peasants and travelers whose lifestyles involved getting their hands and bodies dirty." They go on to argue that "these days, cleanliness is defined more by corporations selling 'sanitation products' ... When we accept their definition of 'cleanliness' we are accepting their economic domination of our lives" (122–3). The way to subvert these hierarchies, they argue, is to reject hygiene standards in one's daily routine.

Veganism is another common form of anti-consumption among anarchists. Vegans refuse to consume meat and dairy, along with fur, leather, wool, and cosmetics tested on animals. The decision not to consume any animal-derived products may be constructed as a practice of political solidarity with non-human creatures, against an industry that systematically exploits human power over animals. Many of my interviewees were vegetarians before they learned about or identified with anarchism, but "went vegan" when they became able to connect an anarchist opposition to hierarchy with their previous distaste for animal slaughter. Sally explained how veganism is, for her, also an explicit protest against ideological manipulation by capitalist interests:

> I had become vegetarian for a couple months at a time in high school and that was very much based on sort of the emotional not wanting to eat animals sense, but then I don't think it really stuck until it became a lot more political and about consumption and about . . . the kinds of consumption that capitalism encourages you to have . . . especially the marketing to think you need to eat so much meat and need to drink so much milk, that really started bothering me and seeing it as just creating a need that just isn't there . . . .

Another interviewee named Branch similarly explained that anarchist vegans see their diets "as avoiding 'the system' in terms of the meat industry or the dairy industry, practices of, you know, modern-day sort of farming and agriculture and things like that." For Branch too, specialized dietary practices had followed his politicization and integration into a local anarchist community. Importantly, anarchist veganism is about resisting the systemic power relationship between humans and the animals they consume; that is, it may not have much to do with an actual distaste for the human consumption of animal products per se. As Josef, who is also vegan, explained, "Yeah, believe me if I had my own cow, I would make my own cheese! And I'd love it and I'd make it a dharma cow and it'd have jewelry, but you know, that's not feasible for me, I live in the city. I don't want to contribute to animal slavery." Anarchists like Josef are against the *industrialization* of animal production, which turns capitalism's exploitative relations against animals on a mass scale.

Anarchists are especially wary of consumer "needs" that involve environmental degradation or the waste of natural resources. Of course, this criteria covers almost all consumption, but a few practices in particular are notable. Flushing the toilet, for example, is a rather mundane and automatic activity for most people, but it is problematic for many anarchists. (Many people may not even consider toilet flushing an act of "consumption," but of course it consumes fresh water). In response to my questions about everyday things he does "because of his politics," Josef laughingly volunteered, "I pee outside because of my politics, not because I'm a freak." He went on to explain:

> I'm not gonna waste like a gallon and a half of water that we're stealing from the Colorado River just cuz I took a pee, you know like, 'if it's yellow let it mellow,' you know, don't flush it. But I mean, you gotta keep some sort of hygiene, but urine is pretty clean. I mean, water a bush, you know?

An anti-consumerism zine I picked up at an anarchist book fair also includes a section on water consumption, in which it admonishes readers, "Don't flush when you pee! It won't hurt you, pee just sits in the toilet, not bothering anyone; it doesn't warrant the 10 gallons per flush just to get rid of it" (koala!, n.d.: 10). The inside of the front cover of the zine is a sheet of warning labels reading: "DON'T FLUSH! If it's yellow let it mellow! (or go outside . . . fun for you, good for plants!)." Handwritten instructions on the page also urge readers to photocopy these labels onto sticker paper and post them in bathrooms.

Another consumer item that many people consider a need, but which anarchists do not, is an automobile. Even in a city like Los Angeles, a sprawling metropolis which is known for its car culture, most of the anarchists I met did not own an automobile. This was true for interviewees located in other cities as well. Even if they did have access to a car, they usually chose to commute to work, school, and other activities by bicycle. As evidence of the close relationship between bike culture and anarchist identity, several interviewees said they got into cycling as a serious mode of transportation around the same time they became politicized, even if they had ridden bicycles recreationally earlier in their lives. As Tina recalled, "I started riding a bike probably three, three and a half years ago, I think the whole radicalization happened around that time, so bike riding comes with it you know." Branch described the link between anarchism and cycling in this way:

> An important thing with anarchism is, anything can be done if you set your mind to it, and you don't have to sort of conform to typical ways of living, or the system. And I think a large part of that is driving, and I think a large way to overcome that is through cycling, and I think it's a much more effective way [than driving] to build community and it's a much more effective way to act environmentally, ethically.

Although he didn't believe that cycling exhausts "what anarchism is," Branch did say that "if you're truly trying to understand and practice anarchism I think they just go hand in hand." For many anarchists, riding bicycles is a form of consumption-based resistance against the automobile-centric transportation industry and its influence on mainstream social norms around personal physical mobility.

There are, however, some circumstances in which commuting by bicycle may be impractical. To give one example, anarchists often form Food Not Bombs (FNB) organizations, which prepare large quantities of food and distribute it to homeless people and attendees at political events.[2] Transporting the food from the preparation site to the distribution site (e.g. from a kitchen to a public park) can pose a problem when all the activists travel by bicycle. The creative solution employed by the Downtown Los Angeles FNB group was to hook trailers up to their bicycles to get the food from the cook site (a communal household in the Silverlake neighborhood) to Skid Row (a site where homeless people congregate, located a few miles away). Activist groups and communal households may also take on shared ownership of an automobile, reserved for occasions where bicycle transit is prohibitively impractical.

This points to another means by which anarchists reduce their commercial consumption, which is sharing commodities among many people, taking advantage of economies of scale to avoid expending a lot of money on necessities. A related example is the common anarchist practice of co-habiting together in large numbers—anywhere from half a dozen to more than 20 people—a practice known as cooperative housing or collective living. By living together in groups, anarchists spend less on rent, groceries, utility bills, and other household expenditures than they would if they lived alone or in small numbers, as is the norm for mainstream middle-class Americans. An interviewee called Revbaker explained his involvement in cooperative housing (or "co-ops") this way:

> I first learned of collective living after visiting a few student coops [sic] in Boulder. I was definitely impressed and heavily influenced by the whole idea. It seemed like a natural and even necessary embodiment, or manifestation, of radical politics. Something like, 'If you believe that humans can live in different ways from mainstream society, and in fact can live in ways that are counter to prevailing societal institutions (nuclear family, competition, over-consumption, coercion, etc.) then prove it.' And so we did, or are at least, we are trying.

Anarchist cooperative houses are direct descendents of hippie communes and earlier experiments with "intentional living." Like their forerunners in earlier countercultural movements, anarchist communes are meant to denaturalize the idea that people are meant to live in small, private family units and to care most for those closely related to them by blood. Intentional living situations are also attempts to reinvent members' own class status and in the process protest the idea of class status altogether (Rossinow 1998: 249). As might be expected based on anarchists' attitudes toward personal hygiene, standards of cleanliness in these group houses are generally relaxed. Group houses often open themselves up to visiting travelers, and many host music shows or organize meetings in the house's communal space. Local activist groups such as Food Not Bombs also often utilize group houses for meetings and food preparation.

One of the most cherished principles of anarchist lifestyles is "DIY," which stands for "do-it-yourself." The idea behind DIY is that when possible one should put one's own, unalienated labor toward producing the things one needs, rather than putting money toward practices and industries that exploit workers and natural resources. Knowing how to repair things for oneself also keeps one from having either to pay others to do it or to spend money on new things to replace the old. An interviewee named Orlando explained to me that he saw bicycle commuting as an example of DIY, in that it involves using one's own physical energy to transport oneself rather than gasoline purchased from a corrupt oil corporation. Anarcho-cyclists (a term used by some anarchist bike enthusiasts) may also become versed in DIY bicycle repair, with the aid of specifically anarchist books, zines, and instruction from comrades. Politicized bicycle cultures often build institutions that foster DIY practices and operate under anarchist organizing principles. For example, the Bicycle Kitchen in Los Angeles is a non-hierarchically organized, volunteer-run workshop that exists to promote cycling as an alternative to driving, and to provide the means for cyclists to build, maintain, and repair their own bicycles using salvaged parts, rather than further contributing to capitalist patterns of waste and alienated labor.

The DIY principle can be, and is, applied to almost everything anarchists consume. For example, growing one's own food (or even hunting it, as one non-vegetarian interviewee from rural Vermont did) is a common DIY practice, as is making and mending one's own clothing. At the TOW Warehouse, a collective space in downtown Los Angeles, organizers put on regular workshops where participants share their knowledge and skills to make things that they would otherwise have to buy from corporations, such as LED bike lights or home-brewed beer. As a collective member named Tom explained to me, TOW stands for Theater of Work, which symbolizes that the space is a place to work and be productive, but for one's own benefit and not through selling one's labor to others who have the means to exploit it. The reference to theatricality could be thought, furthermore, to symbolize a commitment to performing alternatives in a visible way, so as to communicate a political message. Josef explained the activities at TOW in less abstract terms: "that's another thing we do because we're anarchists! We brew our own beer now, cuz, fuck supporting the liquor stores, and you know what, fuck liquor stores."

There are even some consumer services that most people would not think of as feasible to do for oneself, but to which many anarchists apply the DIY principle. Take, for example, the practice of DIY gynecology, which focuses on self-examination and diagnosis and herbal treatments for things like menstrual cramps, yeast infections, sexually transmitted diseases, and unwanted pregnancies. I attended a workshop on DIY gynecology at a festival co-organized by Gabby, an interviewee. In this workshop, the facilitator showed participants how to use a speculum on themselves and what to look for while doing examinations. She also encouraged frank discussion and questions from the audience, and offered medical advice on topics such as infections, masturbation, and sexual intercourse. Workshops like this are extremely common—it was my experience that several of the anarchist book fairs and conferences I attended featured a session in this vein. Zines on DIY gynecology are also ubiquitous—in addition to the one I purchased at the workshop, called *Hot Pants* (Gauthier and Vinebaum 1999), I've seen similar ones at every book fair that I've attended.

The political principle behind DIY gynecology is explained by the *Hot Pants* zine in its assertion that the practice is an attempt "to help break away from the medical establishment's tentacular grip on our bodies and our approaches to health and healing" (Gauthier and Vinebaum 1999: 1). An interviewee named Minty said that she would rather rely on herself and her anarcha-feminist friends to take care of her physical and mental health, because their practices are "holistic and healthy and women-centered" and she won't have to deal with a doctor "that will call me crazy anyway and give me fucked up medicine." Raychel, another interviewee, makes her own menstrual pads because they are more comfortable and less environmentally destructive than store-bought pads. DIY approaches to menstrual products are also a way to avoid supporting "the 'sanitary hygiene' industry" which feeds into the patriarchal taboo on menstruation by treating it as something that needs to be hidden and sanitized in the first place (Gauthier and Vinebaum 1999). Like other DIY practices, DIY gynecology is about empowering oneself rather than handing power over to someone—be it a doctor, a pharmaceutical company, or a tampon brand—who profits by exploiting others' needs.

In some cases, refusal of consumption or doing-it-oneself are not feasible options. In these instances, anarchists utilize what I call extra-commercial means of obtaining goods, which allows them to consume without providing financial support to capitalist corporations. One common means of doing so is to share and trade with friends. For Minty, consuming in an anarchist way is about finding alternatives to capitalist exchange within her own circle of acquaintances. She explained this using a few examples:

> It's knowing the resources that are already in the network of people that you trust and using them whether it be DIY gynecology or clothing. Like,

a lot of my friends knit, so when I'm in New York, [it's] buying their scarves and their hats and mittens, or doing like a barter versus going to like Urban Outfitters you know? So knowing what resources are in your group of friends and utilizing that versus anywhere else.

Minty thus sees her social network as an alternative to capitalist retail establishments. In this vein, Gabby also finds friends who can provide services she needs, and, in turn, she shares her own skills. She mentioned, for instance, that she was taking violin lessons from a friend and cooking meals for him in exchange.

Some anarchists have more permanently institutionalized the practice of sharing, establishing "free stores" where people can convene to donate their unwanted belongings to each other. The idea of relying on the resources of your community is also at work in events like Really Really Free Markets (RRFMs), which anarchists have organized in several cities across the United States. At RRFMs, people bring things to give away that are still usable but just not useful to them anymore. The markets are often held in public parks, and look like a cross between a yard sale and a swap meet, only there is no monetary exchange or even barter involved. At the one I attended in Los Angeles, folks spread blankets out in a corner of a municipal park, and put out old clothes, books, and other consumable items for "shoppers" to take at will. There was also a station set up for people to bring their bicycles and get free bike repair lessons. The local Food Not Bombs group provided free snacks and water. The guiding principle at RRFMs is that things are given away as "gifts" and anyone can freely take what they want without having to give anything themselves. The point is not to make money off one's old possessions—just to find them a new home as an alternative to throwing them away. And the provision of services like bike repair instruction is meant to spread knowledge for its own sake. Besides providing for people's material needs and wants, RRFMs are meant to function as demonstrations of the viability of an alternative to the neoliberal capitalist free market in which state policies and economic practices favor big business and exploit individuals in the name of corporate profits. The name of the event itself is a verbal play on the view that the "free market" does not actually ("really really") promote freedom for most people, especially those who must sell their labor in order to earn the living wage that is required to enable them to consume in fulfillment of their needs.

Outside of structured consumption encounters like free stores or RRFMs, anarchists may also scavenge for discarded goods which are not necessarily intended to be shared or reused, but which still hold value. A common term for such scavenging is "dumpster diving" (sometimes abbreviated to "dumpstering") owing to the fact that commercial institutions often discard perfectly usable goods in trash bins, which the plucky scavenger can climb (dive) into and root through. Dumpster diving has become something of a refined skill among anarchists, with zines and articles written on the subject of how to most effectively and efficiently obtain the best refuse. Depending on the availability of well-stocked dumpsters in one's area, one may be able to obtain most commodities, including food, for free. Food retailers in particular often discard mass quantities of edible products for purely cosmetic reasons—the produce is marred, the boxes are crushed, or the expiration date has recently passed. In addition to being a practical strategy for finding food, clothes, appliances, and furniture, dumpstering is positioned by anarchists as an act of protest against the wastefulness of the commercial retail system, in which things that are superficially damaged or just out of fashion are thrown away, though their use value is intact.

Another means by which anarchists may attempt to obtain consumable goods without monetary expenditure is shoplifting. Obviously, this method poses a certain amount of risk to the practitioner, as it is a criminal activity. Ideologically, anarchists can justify theft as an act of legitimate property redistribution within a system that they believe to be "criminal" in a more metaphorical, moral sense. In other words, because the system of capitalist exchange enables corporations to "steal" labor and natural resources, there is nothing morally objectionable in anarchists reappropriating the products those corporations sell for profit. This logic accounts for Gabby explaining to me that she doesn't shoplift at "mom and pop" establishments, only big chain stores. Furthermore, subcultural theorist Stephen Duncombe (2008: 88) explains that as a transgression of the law, theft is a symbolic "refusal to become part of the cycle of 'responsible' work and consumption."

Practices which involve the appropriation of consumer items at no monetary cost are encompassed under the umbrella designation of *freeganism*. The term "freegan" is a portmanteau of the words free and vegan, and it refers to a diet in which animal-based (non-vegan) food products may be consumed, but only if they can be obtained for free, so as not to contribute to the market demand for animal products. Joel, for example, regularly consumes dairy products if they will otherwise be discarded. I actually witnessed Joel deftly take a piece of lemon meringue pie off a vacated table at a restaurant when he saw that the diner had left it untouched and was told by the server that it would be thrown away. Because he was not paying for the pie, he did not see himself as financially supporting the producers or distributors of the eggs and dairy that had gone into making it, thus he did not see himself as contributing to the economic demand for animal products. Freegans register their critique of consumer capitalism and its attendant hierarchies not by abstaining from consumption, but by abstaining from *paying for* their consumption. They also see themselves as extracting material value from the system without putting value back in, thus weakening the system in a small way. The freegan lifestyle may extend beyond dietary practices to encompass a holistic orientation toward not making a financial contribution to the offenders in the capitalist system.

Perhaps the mode of anarchist anti-consumption least identifiable as such is the patronage of anarchist businesses. Anarchist businesses—seemingly self-contradictory entities in the eyes of some—explicitly identify themselves as anarchist and run themselves according to anarchist organizing principles. The practice of purchasing commodities from an anarchist business is obviously an act of consumption. Yet, we can analyze it as anti-consumption, since such purchases are made with a conscious intention *not* to purchase from a more conventional capitalist institution. Generally, anarchist businesses do not exist to turn a profit through the sale of commodities (they may even have non-profit status with the US Internal Revenue Service). Rather, their mission is to provide consumers with products that are not always readily available in the mainstream market, such as fair-trade coffee, vegan food, and radical literature. Furthermore, they usually try to put value back into the local radical community by sponsoring activist efforts. Some anarchist businesses are transient, only setting up shop at events like book fairs and festivals. Others have a permanent physical space—often a storefront or residence—which they also make available for organizing meetings and traveling presenters. These spaces are sometimes called "infoshops" because they generally keep a stock of political books and zines for local community members to borrow or purchase. They may also provide public computers and internet access or host public events. Joel Olson (2009: 40) describes the anarchist infoshop as "a space where people can learn about radical ideas, where radicals can meet other radicals, and where political work (such as meetings, public forums, fundraisers, etc.) can get done." Some paradigmatic examples of institutions like this are the Wooden Shoe in Philadelphia and Red Emma's in Baltimore.

Another anarchist business enterprise, AK Press, is a publishing outfit that prints and distributes books and other media on topics of interest to radicals. AK's self-stated goal is "supplying radical words and images to as many people as possible" (AK Press, n.d.). The press runs a website and print catalog, and is a ubiquitous presence at anarchist book fairs; every book fair I've attended has had a large AK Press table with hundreds of books as well as shirts and other items for sale. Based in the San Francisco Bay area, AK also runs a warehouse in Oakland that hosts organizing and social events, particularly near the time of the annual Bay Area Anarchist Book Fair held in nearby San Francisco. Like the Wooden Shoe and Red Emma's, AK is run by a collective of its workers, who democratically decide which titles to carry as well as how to divide the labor of the press. The collective management structure is, in all these cases, an attempt to resist replicating the worst practices of capitalist businesses, even while participating in the commodity marketplace.

AK's mission illustrates a point made by cultural studies scholar Jeremy Gilbert (2008: 108) in his book *Anticapitalism and Culture*, which is that commodification is not equivalent to capitalism. It is theoretically possible to embrace the communicative potential of commodification without advocating an exploitative system based on the principle of the maximization of capital. Businesses like AK Press are aware that they are inevitable participants in the capitalist system:

> like it or not, capitalism is the only game in town at the moment. The paper that books are printed on, the building we work in, the packages we send and receive, the computers we use—all are the result of the exploited labor of the working class. Until we take power away from private economic tyrannies like corporations and investment groups, until we're in control of our creative energies, almost every good or service we use or provide is administered by capitalism. (AK Press, n.d.)

However, the collective that runs AK also points out that the press "doesn't exist to enrich its members at the expense of consumers." Instead, they use commodification as a means of providing what they call "tools for intellectual self-defense." As proudly self-proclaimed "propagandists," AK is a business that channels commercial exchange toward the spread of revolutionary ideas. All of these businesses arguably use consumption relations as an infrastructure upon which can be overlaid other processes that are important to anarchism as an activist political movement; processes such as the circulation of discourse, the performance of identity, and the sustenance of community. Anarchist businesses use discourse to position their enterprises as oppositional to capitalism and contributory to the anarchist project of revolution. In this way, the practice of working or shopping at an anarchist business is of a piece with the other anti-consumption practices described above.

Although lifestyle and consumer politics are often thought of as individualistic in nature, many of the examples described above point to the importance of community for political anti-consumption. Communal housing obviously cannot be undertaken by one person; nor can RRFMs or free stores. Other anarchist anti-consumption practices are greatly facilitated by a network of informed and skilled people who can share their knowledge and experience with new adopters. Caring for one's gynecological health with DIY examinations and remedies is a daunting prospect without the help of people who are qualified to hold workshops and author pamphlets in which they pass along their expertise. In some cases, DIY lifestyle practices are only cost-effective if the tools for making and repairing things oneself can be shared across many individuals. Cycling, for instance, can require prohibitive amounts of financial and knowledge capital if attempted by an isolated individual. In extolling the virtues of having an anarchist community around him, interviewee Branch commented that, "when you have a local bicycle workshop it becomes much cheaper and easier to maintain a bicycle and learn how to keep things running." In this capacity, the Bicycle Kitchen in Los Angeles (and collectives like it in many other cities) is indispensable for those who practice their anarchist politics through cycling.

Where the anarchist lifestyle calls for the consumption of alternative products, a relatively large number of people with similar needs and preferences is needed to sustain demand for any given commodity. For example, for fair-trade coffee to be a viable consumer option for any one person depends on there being enough people who demand it to generate enough revenue to sustain the workers involved in fair-trade production. Furthermore, in the absence of systemic support, many individuals may find individual resistance a practical impossibility. Alyssa was an interviewee who had moved to a small Canadian town after having lived in Northern California for many years. She explained that many of the anti-consumption practices she had engaged in while living in Santa Cruz (a California college town known for its progressive community), such as dumpstering and participating in a bicycle collective, were simply not feasible in her new location. So, while she still stuck to a vegan diet and commuted by bicycle, "so many of those things were available to me in the culture of Santa Cruz, and really aren't here (the dumpsters are locked, there are no collective spaces like the Bike Church or Free Radio, etc)." Each of these examples reminds us that lifestyle and consumption practices are social productions, and must be analyzed as such.

Typology of anti-consumption motivations

It would be easy to see anti-consumption as a purely negative phenomenon, a practice constituted only by what is *not* done. The writer of the *Why Freeganism* zine remarks, "I couldn't really justify buying anything, I couldn't get behind any aspect of the corporate death consumer machine so I decided to boycott everything" (koala!, n.d.: 4). One might be tempted to see the image of "boycotting everything" in an attempt to escape "the corporate death consumer machine" as a bleak one. But as I have shown above, anti-consumption lifestyles are actually rich with practices and meanings of their own. Also, the consequences of anti-consumption cannot be reduced simply to the market impact of not buying—there is a range of motivations to be found among anarchist anti-consumers, including personal gratification, moral rectitude, activist intervention, identificatory performance, and social communication.

I use the term "motivations" cautiously, since individual anti-consumers are not always highly conscious of and striving toward the outcomes I enumerate below. Rather, anti-consumption practices are social objects, in the sense that they represent the collective work of innumerable individual subjects and thus take on a cultural meaning that exceeds the consciousness or experience of any specific actor. While I have framed my analysis in terms of motivations, I could have framed it in terms of consequences or effects. The decision to frame my analysis in terms of motivations rather than consequences or effects was, in part, a matter of convenience and method. It is easier to observe and document the stated intentions behind practices than it is to reliably assess whether anti-consumption practices actually achieve their intended effects. Hypothetically, the analytic typology I elaborate *could* be used to evaluate outcomes in addition to intentions, an idea which I will also discuss further below. The typology I offer makes analytical distinctions between several different kinds of goals that might motivate anti-consumption behavior. These goals may overlap in the real world, and they are often not clearly demarcated in the minds of practitioners—that is, multiple motivations may converge in the same behavior.[3] I will discuss the real-world overlaps further below, but for now I will present the typology in terms of pure categories, in the interest of analytical clarity.

Personal motivations for anti-consumption practices have to do with finding immediate personal benefit in these alternative consumption experiences—what Binkley (2008: 601) refers to as "individualistic anti-consumerism." In short, personal motivations for consumption or non-consumption seek the betterment of one's own situation. Many anarchists believe that capitalist entities will try to exploit and alienate them through consumerism, and so they try to thwart these effects on themselves by abstaining from commercial consumption as much as possible. Anti-capitalists argue that capitalism retains its power by "integrating" consumers into the system of wage labor, keeping them docile and foreclosing the development of a "revolutionary consciousness" (Marcuse 1972: 14). By rejecting commercial consumption, anarchists reduce their own incentive to earn money, thus releasing themselves as much as possible from the intrinsically exploitative conditions of wage labor. Expressions like this one (from the zine I referenced above)—"You don't have to compromise yourself and your humanity to the evil demon of wage-slavery!" (koala!, n.d.: 2)—are not uncommon in contemporary anarchist discourse. The zine goes on to say, "Working sucks and if a little scavenging can keep you from needing a job than [sic] go jump in a dumpster!" (3). Consumption habits such as dumpstering are thus offered as a solution to the problem of the alienation that comes of "working long hours at a dehumanizing job" (2).

Along similar lines, Emily explained one of her reasons for getting around by bicycle and public transit, instead of owning her own car, "I also don't like to work that much . . . and if you don't have a car, you don't have to work as much, because you don't have to pay for a car. Cars cost a lot of money—I think people don't realize how much they cost because I don't think people sit back and look at it." Here, Emily demonstrated that she had thought critically about exactly what was involved in participating in a consumption practice most people take for granted. For her, like many anarchists, owning a car is not an automatic fact of life, it is an intentional activity which involves real trade-offs in terms of time and money, which could be spent otherwise. While most of the anarchists I spoke with did hold some kind of job in order to maintain a baseline income, they were still able to work less than they would have had they been trying to earn enough money to consume at mainstream levels.

Anarchists also understand their conscious rejection of consumerism as a means of resistance against being personally ideologically manipulated. In other words, they attempt not to succumb to the "false needs" imposed by dominant consumerist ideology, and as a result, they see themselves as being able to lead more enjoyable, liberated lives. Josef alluded to the personal benefits that come from actively rejecting the standards of mainstream culture: "I'm not gonna subscribe to all that shit because it's just gonna make me depressed anyway, cuz I don't look like Cindy Crawford and I wouldn't want to be Brad Pitt anyways!" Joel expressed his feeling that "it makes you a more interesting person" when you "diverge a little bit from the mainstream." He brought this up in the context of talking about how being a vegan has forced him to try different kinds of cuisine than he might have, had his diet been more conventional.

Branch said that he made a habit of seeking news and entertainment from independent media producers, like Indymedia, an electronic network in which independent individuals and organizations can directly upload news stories for public consumption. To him, alternative media outlets were a "much more informative and reliable form of information, of what's going on, as opposed to a commercial network, television news and things like that, where they are influenced by media companies, by government." In Branch's view, his practice of not consuming mainstream media allowed him to liberate himself (at least somewhat) from dependence on sources of information he saw as untrustworthy.

Moral anti-consumption describes practices that are motivated by judgments about right and wrong. Here, acting morally is about being able to live with oneself, about holding oneself personally accountable for living consistently with one's values, and with feeling personally responsible for the concrete impacts one's consumption has on others. The "others" in these cases may include animals, the environment, and/or exploited laborers. Moral anti-consumption is "a case of integrity" (Newholm 2005: 114). Anti-consumption practices are construed as moral in that, by reducing one's demand for goods produced under objectionable conditions, one reduces one's complicity with the system or entities that perpetuate those conditions. To give a basic example, several interviewees said they made a point of wearing used clothing so as to avoid personally contributing money to companies that employ sweatshop labor. Furthermore, by establishing a regular lifestyle habit of not consuming new clothes, anti-consumers attempt to remove themselves from a global economic circuit in which clothing manufacturers tend to locate their production in places with lax labor regulations, the result being exploitative conditions across the clothing industry. By not participating in the consumption of new clothes, anti-consumers can feel they have acted with integrity in the face of widespread corporate immorality.

Veganism too is frequently understood as a moral practice. Joel explained that he believes human dominance over animals is unjustifiable in moral terms. For Joel, to eat meat or wear leather shoes would be to personally benefit from the industrialization of that dominance, and thus those acts of consumption on his part would be illegitimate exercises of human power. In Joel's words, coming to that belief made it "so easy for me to be vegan." The way he put it, veganism was for him less about an emotional connection to animal suffering and more about an ethical objection to the ways in which humans attempt to use ideology (about human superiority) to legitimize an illegitimate exercise of power. Although another interviewee, Josef, said he respected other people's decision not to be vegan, he went on to point out an ethical consistency between anarchism and certain forms of consumption: "just do whatever the fuck you want, but don't be, like, promoting what you're trying to fight against. Like, if you're, if you're an anarchist but you're like, gonna go eat at McDonalds, you gotta check yourself right there, you know?" For Josef, acting morally means subjecting oneself to "checks" to ensure that one is not violating one's own political commitments.

Activist motivations for anti-consumption go beyond adopting a practice because it is morally right in itself. Activist anti-consumption is done in order to put pressure on a system or larger entity to *alter a pattern* of immoral practice. Whether a practice has activist motivations or not depends on whether the practitioners are attempting to use their actions to effect a change in current conditions. For anarchists, activist consumption often involves attempts to leverage personal finances toward subverting or correcting the objectionable aspects of the entire capitalist system. Craig O'Hara's *The Philosophy of Punk* (1999: 131) expresses this view: "One of the best ways to *refuse and resist a destructive capitalist system* is to vote economically, spending dough where you feel it has the least harmful effect" (emphasis mine).[4] Anti-consumption which occurs under the aegis of a strike or boycott falls into this category.[5] The reasoning behind activist anti-consumption is that if enough individuals withdraw their resources from the system of corporate capitalism, that system will eventually "have a real battle on its hands," in the words of one commenter on an anarchist email list I followed.

As an example of activist consumption, many interviewees said that they try to buy from local or independent businesses (including the specific ones mentioned above). Matthew, a professor living in a small college town in Texas, offered his book-buying practices as an instance of this habit:

I prefer to buy books secondhand. When I lived in Chicago and Philadelphia, I bought as many books as possible this way. If I couldn't get them from a shop I'd buy them online. Now that I live in a town that doesn't have a single independently-owned bookstore, I get nearly all my books online. For newer books, I'll usually try to abuse my academic privileges and ask for review copies first. Anything to beat the media conglomerates, though obviously the smaller presses are fine!

Matthew's habit of avoiding corporate chain stores in order to "beat the media conglomerates" could be understood as a kind of boycott or consumer strike. His coinciding habit of patronizing second-hand and independent bookshops could be understood as a "buycott," which takes up "an oppositional or 'anti' product that is promoted as the alternative to a brand that is being avoided for reasons of wider social purpose" (Littler 2009: 35). Matthew's patronage of alternative booksellers is not part of any specific consumer activist campaign. Yet, the fact that it is, for him, connected to his political identification with anarchism means that he can envision his consumer practices as collective, since many other anarchists are engaged in similar practices. The fact that such actions are discursively promoted as part of the culture of anarchist movements means that they are not really isolated personal acts, but rather "individualized collective action" (Micheletti 2003: xi). Because anarchist individuals are aware that there are very many of them adopting similar lifestyles, they can see themselves as contributing to a project that makes a measurable impact.

Activist anti-consumption may also entail a communicative motivation, as a kind of propaganda by the deed or prefigurative politics (as discussed in the introductory chapter). The communicative logic of prefigurative politics rests on implicit assumptions about the capacity of small-scale actions to work as theatrical spectacles which publicly represent political ideologies and convince others of their correctness. In this way, lifestyle practices are seen as rhetorical acts with the capacity to persuade and inspire others. Recall Revbaker's comment above, about collective housing being a means of "proving" the legitimacy of anarchist alternatives to consumerist society. Emily also expressed that she felt it was important for anarchists to show that their way of life "actually work[s]," that "it's a viable model" for a more just society.

Identificatory motivations for anti-consumption can be detected from the fact that many of the practices I discussed above (e.g. veganism and bicycling) are adopted alongside the assumption of an anarchist identity. This supports the idea that politicized subjects call on anti-consumption practices for their performative value. In other words, these practices are important in part because they are rituals that establish the practitioner as a certain kind of (politicized) person (Goffman 1959). The performative dimensions of consumption (and by implication, anti-consumption) are discussed by sociologist Anthony Giddens (1991) in his exploration of "life politics." As Giddens explains, "A lifestyle can be defined as a more or less integrated set of practices which an individual embraces, not only because such practices satisfy utilitarian needs, but because they give material form to a particular narrative of self-identity" (81). In the case of anarchist anti-consumers, practices of refusal, DIY, and the like, are material expressions of what it means to be an anarchist. Constructing such an identity narrative is both an individual and a collective process. That is, performances of self are both intrasubjective and intersubjective: the performance is done for oneself and also for others. Material performances of anti-consumption, in this capacity, become a Foucaultian "technology of the self" (Foucault 1988b), a dramatization of political commitment that constitutes the performer as a particular kind of subject.

Emily described her transition into vegetarianism, as a teenager, in such terms:

> I was also really into imagining myself in certain ways and I wanted to imagine myself as the kind of person I wanted to be—you know, when I grew up—and I kind of figured that the kind of person I wanted to be would be a vegetarian, you know? I guess I just sort of figured it went along with the lifestyle.

Josef expressed a similar sentiment, a bit more succinctly: "I'm vegan because I think that's what real anarchists should be." Josef's offhand invocation of authenticity is telling. The rhetorical figure of the "real" anarchist is a powerful one that features largely in the internal discourse of anarchist movements. It is unsurprising then that those who wish to be identified as anarchists would be motivated to orient their behaviors toward those habits which are most commonly accepted by their peers, and themselves, as authentically anarchist. This discourse of authenticity also causes individuals to feel pride and shame associated with their consumption habits, depending on the degree to which they recognize those habits as being consistent with an acceptable narrative of activist identity (Giddens 1991). Sally observed that norms of food consumption could bring about "this weird kind of pressure and guilt and I don't know, this moral righteousness from some people." Others I interviewed expressed feelings of guilt as well over things such as using beauty products, owning an iPod, and using a car, because of the sense that "actual" (Orlando's word) anarchists do not do those things.

Social motivations for anti-consumption come into play when performances like those just described are used as a means of achieving solidarity among participants in anarchist movements. Beyond establishing one's own identity, one may also use cultural practices to unite one with others who share similar political goals, and to differentiate one from those who don't (Taylor and Whittier 1992: 111). Where consumption practices are performed publicly, particularly where they take place in "alternative" spaces, as they often do for anarchists, they may be quite meaningful in the establishing of a community of anarchist consumers. Individual habits may reinforce one's affinity to an imagined community of fellow anti-consumers, in much the same way that consumers of the same product or brand cultivate a sense of community (Muñiz and O'Guinn 2001). The difference is that while mainstream consumption communities unite around meanings they share with marketers and the dominant culture, anarchist anti-consumers unite around their symbolic rejection of mainstream consumption. Anti-consumption may even spur more social cohesion than shared consumption practices do, due to its association with radical resistance to mainstream ideologies and mores (Kozinets and Handelman 2004).

By cultivating particular lifestyle practices as a community, anarchists are engaged in what I call *conspicuous anti-consumption*. Thorstein Veblen's (1994) concept of conspicuous consumption sought to explain how wealthy Americans established their identities as elites through their visibly sumptuous consumption habits and leisure activities. Although Veblen was concerned with the role of goods in the communication of economic status, the notion of conspicuous consumption can also be applied to the practices of contemporary consumers, who are more likely to define themselves in terms of cultural identity rather than economic class. This means that, while income levels still structure the consumption options available to particular individuals, the variety of commodities available at all price points allow for people to establish any manner of cultural identities based on the goods they appropriate and the style in which they appropriate them.[6]

Commodities are important vectors for the communication of identity in public life. While goods may fulfill material needs for individuals, they also carry social meanings, as objects of "collective appropriation, within relations of solidarity with and distinction from others" (Canclini 2001: 46; see also Douglas and Isherwood 1979). Matthew's explanation of his decision to throw away his television set resonates with these ideas. Matthew told me that he hated television and had thrown his set away around the time of his becoming politicized in the 1990s. He later explained that he and his fellow activists were influenced by cultural critics Max Horkheimer and Theodor Adorno, as well as Guy Debord and Raoul Vaneigem, and objected to television on the basis that it is a tool of capitalist control. He went on to note that no one he knew was really afraid that their television would brainwash them, but for them, "the rejection of TV . . . was more symbolic than anything else." The fact that others were engaged in similar performances of disgust with the culture industry and its products was crucial for Matthew; he reflected, "I'd like to chalk it up to deep-seated conviction but in 1999 it was just the hip thing to do, at least in the anti-globalization movement. In all honesty I was just going with the flow!"

Often, people are rewarded for "going with the flow" through the conferral of *cultural capital*, a concept developed by Bourdieu (1984) to refer to the status that accrues to individuals who possess certain tastes and habits which are valued in a particular social context. Sarah Thornton's

(1996) repurposing of this concept as "subcultural capital" is usefully applied to those instances in which individuals accrue social status in the anarchist milieu based on the extent to which their tastes deviate from the mainstream and conform to anarchist norms (the notion of "anarchist norms" may seem like a contradiction in terms—this contradiction will be explored in depth in subsequent chapters, particularly Chapter 4).

What distinguishes the normative tastes of political movements from those of other subcultures is their basis in explicit political critique. All subcultures are engaged in struggles for power, and might thus be thought of as political, but anarchists are somewhat unique in that they quite self-consciously define their subcultural identity by a collective vision for social change. This is clear from the way that most of the practices discussed here are positioned by their practitioners as expressions of political philosophy. For instance, Josef told me, "I wouldn't want to cipher or hang out with somebody who is like, like really obsessed with the Beyoncé dance routines so they can impress people at a club, like that to me is kinda lame." At first this seems to be a simple taste distinction, but he quickly positioned his tastes in terms of his political project, elaborating with, "what I'm trying to say is I wouldn't want to like surround myself with, you know, people who watch football games and drink Budweiser and go to strip joints or whatever, who contribute to the violence, you know." Importantly, Josef claimed that he doesn't want to hang out with people who do these things not just because he happens not to like the activities, but because he sees the activities as, in themselves, "contributing to the violence" of the capitalist, hierarchical society to which he positions himself in opposition.

"Aesthetic revisioning" is a concept that captures the impact that politicization can have on individual tastes (Soper 2008). The idea is that, as individuals come to radical political consciousness, their tastes change accordingly. "Persons or objects or behaviours or practices that were formerly erotically seductive or aesthetically compelling yield their enchantment to others that previously held little of those attractions" (Soper 2008: 580). So, for example, Matthew's taste for television was "revisioned" due to his politicization and simultaneous immersion in a subcultural community in which a rejection of mainstream media was the norm. The multiple aspects of Matthew's decision to throw away his television show the complex intersection of motivations behind anti-consumption practices—the personal hatred he felt toward television was inextricably bound up with his activist critique of the culture industry and his tendency to "go with the flow" of the social movement with which he identified.

The anarchist businesses described above also concretely illustrate how consumption can become a collective activity, with the physical venues of consumption serving as hubs around which social networks can be forged. Places like these, along with places like group houses and bicycle workshops, provide the physical materials necessary for maintaining aspects of anarchist lifestyle, while also bringing people together and enabling them to learn from each other about various lifestyle practices and how to implement them. Branch said that, for him, one of the most important aspects of shared housing was that it had given him opportunities to meet people who taught him about things like bicycle repair and vegan cooking. The fact that his group house was seen as an accessible space for community projects and political organizing meant that there was a "flow of people and information constantly coming through the house." Joel had a similar experience with collective housing. In one of his houses in particular, he remembered "always hav[ing] these people coming in, [who had] really interesting politics, really interesting experiences, staying there, coming to parties." For Joel's anarchist community, the social space of the house facilitated interactions and relationships upon which a political network could be built and sustained.

While the social aspects of these spaces of consumption may not be conscious motivating factors at first—an individual may wander into an infoshop simply looking for a book—consumption-related practices are often a point of entry into the larger world of radical political movements. Jerome, an interviewee from Philadelphia, didn't know much about anarchism until he started shopping for books at The Wooden Shoe. He told me about how one of his friends had taken him there when he was a teenager, and he "absolutely loved it." He explained that it made him feel like there was a place where people understood his political views and could help him make sense of them: "I felt like I was home after thinking I was nuts for a long time." When he had the opportunity to become a volunteer there, Jerome found himself, "quickly thrown into a world that was really eye-opening to me. Interacting with customer[s] and staff was something that put me into an entirely different way of thinking." He told me that his experience at "the Shoe" (as he called it) brought him into contact with anarchists for the first time (apart from seeing them at punk shows) and made him aware that an anarchist community existed. After a few months, he started identifying as an anarchist himself, and he still did over a decade later and was still a committed volunteer at the Shoe.

Jerome was already aligned with leftist politics when he got involved with anarchism through the Shoe. In other instances, consumption may start out as an apolitical activity, generating feelings of identification with a community, feelings which are later utilized as a foundation for political organizing. The consumption of punk music, for instance, is a common factor in many anarchists' introduction to radical political ideologies and organizing efforts. Many interviewees explicitly named punk artists and zines as the source of their first exposure to anarchist ideas. Several more referred to their participation in punk scenes as bringing them into contact with individuals whose political beliefs they found compelling. Listening to records, circulating zines, and attending punk shows are all consumption activities which may start out as a product of aesthetic preferences and end up producing political subjectivity and social networks, as consumers communicate and identify with each other, both remotely and in person, both in "imagined" (Anderson 1991) and in material senses.

Applying the typology

As other studies before this one have shown, any specific instance of anti-consumption is likely to be motivated by multiple goals, with varying degrees of consciousness on the part of the actor. One goal may even "over-determine" others (Soper 2007: 212); for example, if one's identity is defined by the extent to which one acts in a moral manner, the moral and identificatory motivations will be practically inseparable (Barnett et al. 2005). Practices of anti-consumption may also have multiple outcomes, independent of the motivations of the practitioners. It is important to sketch out the multiple dimensions of political lifestyle practices, both to see how they may work to constitute each other, and to identify potential points of contradiction. The multiple, and potentially contradictory, outcomes of anarchists' consumption practices may bear on judgments about the appropriateness of lifestyle politics within movement strategy.[7]

Leo was one interviewee who had at one time been enthusiastic about typically anarchist lifestyle practices like veganism and bicycling, but he had since abandoned them. Unlike many of my other interviewees, Leo did not look particularly like an anarchist: he wore a clean, loose-fitting button-down shirt, had no visible tattoos or piercings, and arrived to our interview driving a car. He was 32 years old, working in a hospital, and attending community college. He described himself as the child of a Salvadorean communist, and was raising a young daughter of his own. When I asked Leo why he had given up many of the typical anarchist consumption practices, he said that one reason was that, "I guess I thought that maybe the position of struggle might be somewhere else. That that wasn't even a struggle?" He also pointed out that a lot of the lifestyle practices adopted by self-identified radicals, like gardening and bicycling, might seem appealingly "revolutionary" but that ultimately those choices don't radically subvert the state or the capitalist economy. In part, this realization came about for him due to the ease with which corporate brands were able to integrate his lifestyle choices into their profit models. By way of example, Leo voiced his distaste for Whole Foods consumers and his frustration at seeing, "my desires and my moral position, ethical position, be so co-opted into a whole other kind of consumer class." Although he had at one time felt good about his ethical consumption practices, he stopped feeling so good when he realized that he shared many of them with people whose politics and social position he didn't share.

Frustration like Leo's is ostensibly fueled by the fear that commercial co-optation necessarily implies a draining of dissenting ideological content, and thus causes the defusion of oppositional potential. That is, when a taste is catered to, even if that taste was originally based in ethical commitments, it may only retain a superficial connection to oppositional values. Some fear that anarchist political critique is actively defused when it is expressed through individual consumer practices. Of particular concern is the potential for the reincorporation of anti-capitalists back into the capitalist marketplace as consumers through *commercial* appeals to political dissatisfaction. The incorporation of oppositional symbols and their consumers into the marketplace means that they will probably become implicated in capitalist exploitation at some point in the supply chain. To be sure, commodification is a material process and, within conditions of mass production, it usually entails exploitation of people and the environment. Rosemary Hennessey argues that when commodities become meaningful for identity or politics, this accretion of meaning only furthers what Karl Marx refers to as the fetishism of the commodity (Hennessey 1994–95; Marx 1978). According to arguments like Hennessey's, capitalism is deplorably strengthened by this renewed demand for commodities. Some take the position that if a practice or style is co-optable by the market or compatible with state policy, then it *must* not be radical (and maybe never was), and by extension should not be supported by authentic anarchists. For some anarchists, the risk of co-optation is enough to render lifestyle politics untenable as part of anarchist strategy. Others are less resigned; as one participant in an online debate over lifestyle anarchism remarked, "it's been said that capitalism can co-opt lifestyles etc . . . so what, we just stick with the shit they offer us in the first place? I'd rather run the risk of being eventually co-opted than starting at the place the capitalists want me to start."

The typology offered above can help to illuminate what was at stake for Leo when his lifestyle practices were co-opted by the Whole Foods consumer class. The *personal* and *moral* outcomes of Leo's consumption habits were ostensibly unchanged, yet the *identificatory* and *social* ramifications were shifted as a result of the mainstreaming of his habits. Leo also saw the *activist* potential of his practices as being defused through their co-optation by the Whole Foods corporation, since his motivation had initially been to subvert capitalism itself. Indeed, this example demonstrates that certain personal and moral orientations may be quite compatible with capitalism, provided corporations are willing to adapt to "alternative" preferences (and they usually are). Individual practices of veganism, for instance, are not *intrinsically* incompatible with capitalism, as has been shown by the burgeoning niche market for vegan food and other consumables. Yet, just because vegan consumers have been targeted by capitalist corporations doesn't mean that the moral justifications for veganism held by those consumers are eviscerated. Gardening and biking may not be intrinsically anti-capitalist if capitalist enterprises can find a way to exploit the demand for them, but certainly there are other benefits to these practices. The analytical separation I advocate is important here, because it allows for a critical assessment of lifestyle politics even in light of corporate co-optation.

It is true that commercialism can diffuse anarchist styles and practices beyond a bounded subcultural milieu. Although conventional wisdom among anti-capitalists has it that once a political subculture is integrated into the commercial market, it necessarily loses its subversive power, we might also see something positive in popular culture's capacity to facilitate a certain kind of democratic accessibility to dissenting political discourses. Because there are both political and apolitical attractions to cycling, veganism, and other lifestyle practices, it may be that people who get drawn into consumption communities around these practices become exposed to people who do have political reasons for participating in them. For instance, a collective institution like a café which makes itself welcoming to its local community regardless of political orientation may find that people who don't know anything about worker self-management (a key component of anarchist businesses) become interested in the political philosophies behind this organizing principle once they see it in action. Commercial exchange thus enables the diffusion of anarchist ideals to a broader audience than those who might be predisposed to seek out radical political discourse. For many people like the individuals I interviewed, an interest and involvement in anarchism ends up extending beyond just listening to punk music or reading CrimethInc. books or wearing circle-A patches, though these subcultural consumption habits serve as an initial introduction to anarchist ideas. Even if more deeply engaged people like these interviewees are the minority among consumers of "anarchist" merchandise, it's not the case that commercial exposure necessarily *precludes* political activism in other forms. Even in the case of corporate co-optation, the picture is not unequivocally bleak. As Jeremy Gilbert (2008) argues, even while capitalism may try to exploit the creative products of bohemian subcultures, even anti-capitalist ones, it cannot fully control those products or the way they are used by consumers.

The analysis of anarchist book fairs offers another example of how being attentive to the multiple effects of consumption as a cultural practice can be helpful. Whenever an anarchist book fair is held, people both within and outside of the anarchist community are quick to point out that vendors selling literature to crowds of anarchists is not exactly an overturning of capitalism. For instance, in a *Los Angeles Times* article about the 2010 Los Angeles Anarchist Book Fair, an attendee at the event was quoted as saying, ruefully, "We don't fight here. We hold book fairs" (Linthicum 2010). The journalist who authored the article attributed this attendee with the belief that the "event itself proved the need for revolution." The underlying assumption here is that book fairs and other activities that revolve around consumption are taking away time and effort that could be devoted to "fighting." This is a kind of all-or-nothing logic that doesn't really allow for the reality that lifestyle politics is not the only form of politics in which people are engaged. When that same *Los Angeles Times* article circulated on Los Angeles Anarchist email listserv, one person responded, "lol [lauging out loud] at 'People don't fight here. They hold book fairs.' some truth to that, we fight though, just not at book fairs I guess." This response reveals that while it may be true that some people participate in book fairs to the exclusion of other political activities, one does not *necessarily* exclude the other. Book fairs coexist with other forms of activism that look more like "fighting." The people who organize anarchist book fairs rarely intend them to substitute for other forms of political engagement. Book fairs also serve functions other than direct activism. They are fun and personally enjoyable to activists, they provide a space where activists' identities as anarchists can be openly performed and validated, and they are an opportunity for social togetherness and network building. Furthermore, if we consider the communicative potential of an event like a book fair, we could see it as having activist dimensions. Book fairs are large, public events that require collective effort and organization. By demonstrating that anarchists are capable of such things, book fairs may persuade skeptics that anarchy is not synonymous with chaos and violence and instead offers many more wholesome values, such as mutual aid and community.

To offer another concrete example, the organizers of an anarchist event held in downtown Los Angeles in 2009 were targets of criticism on the basis that their event was too oriented toward lifestyle and consumption activities. The event, called an "Anarchist Café" by its organizers, was declared "a bust" by one anonymous critic who posted a review to a blog called *The LA Anarchist Weekly*. In the review, the café attendee criticized the fact that the event was too focused on "subcultural" aspects of anarchism like vegan nutrition; the attendee also found it objectionable that there was an admission charge in addition to vendors selling books and shirts. The reviewer's damning conclusion: "The Downtown LA Anarchist Cafe = anarchist (as in vegan, trendy, hipster) identity for SALE. Epic Fail." Yet, the organizers were aware of the multiplicity of motivations potentially involved in such an event. They responded to the criticism by saying that that particular event "was not about bring on a Revolution or lets over throw [sic]." On a local listserv, another commenter argued that the purpose of every event does not need to be to stage revolution, saying, "These types of events should be enjoyed as social decompressors, spaces which are provided for, hopefully, activist and anarchist networking. But they are in no way a substitute or alternative for actual community organizing & movement building which we are ALL responsible for." Comments like these show that practices of lifestyle politics are meant to serve multiple functions beyond their activist effects, and not all of these functions are necessarily aimed at revolutionary social change. Anti-consumption practices are fruitfully understood as a set of rituals through which anarchists accomplish many things, not least of which is the reproduction of themselves as a resistant subculture.

An understanding that practices may fulfill different goals to different degrees allows for flexibility and adaptability rather than wholesale condemnation or celebration of a given tactic. Anti-consumption clearly "does" things other than effect sweeping social change—it performs identity, it builds culture, and so on. Along the way, it may shore up new forms of distinction—social divisions based on taste (Bourdieu 1984)—that prevent anarchists from reaching people outside their subculture and even pit them against each other in struggles over authenticity. The fact that individual practices are accorded such political significance within activist discourses encourages people to be all the more invested in distinguishing themselves from those who make different choices. The rhetorical construction and defense of these distinctions may take a moralistic tone, claiming superiority for certain lifestyles and shutting down productive discussion about the tactical benefits of specific consumption practices (see Littler 2009). This is just one reason why it's useful to maintain an analytical separation between multiple motivations and potential outcomes of politicized lifestyle practices. If one is interested in evaluating lifestyle practices as political *tactics*, one needs to know what they are trying to accomplish and whether they are actually accomplishing these things. While one motivation may be legitimately served by an individual's consumption activity, other goals may be less effectively realized. It is up to the actors in any particular situation to debate and decide (as the organizers and attendees of the Anarchist Café did) whether a given tactic is appropriate in that context.

Becoming highly conscious of the many potential motivations and effects of anti-consumption can also help activists not to fetishize anti-consumption as a tactic, not to conflate its satisfaction of personal fulfillment with its fulfillment of the promise of social change, for example. In fact, it is strategically useful to be able to recognize when anti-consumption fulfills one goal and works *against* another. To go back to the anecdote with which this chapter began, had Raychel not purchased the burrito with cheese in it, she may have fulfilled the identificatory goal of performing pure veganism, but she would have sacrificed the moral imperative she felt to feed the man who was hungry. The ultimate implication of an analysis that identifies multiple and potentially contradictory motivations or outcomes for lifestyle practices is that it's self-defeating for activists to be "puristic" or "black and white" (as Joel put it) about any specific practice. As Grant pointed out, "When you attempt to create a hierarchy of personal purchase choices it will ultimately fall to pieces when put under any type of scrutiny." What this chapter suggests is not that all consumption practices are equal or that scrutiny should be avoided, but rather that a careful, contextual scrutiny might be adopted, in which the conditions of the situation are taken into account and the immediate goals are decided upon and clearly communicated so that tactics can be assessed accordingly. This principle can be applied to any practice of lifestyle politics, in order to determine whether it should be pulled out of the activist toolkit in any specific circumstance.

3

"I'm not joining your world": Performing political dissent through spectacular self-presentation

It's February 2009, and I'm sitting in a coffee shop in Los Angeles. Across the table sits Minty, a woman I was introduced to by a mutual friend of ours. I've seen her before—she's a regular presence at anarchist events in the Los Angeles area—but this is our first real conversation. Minty is in her late twenties; her appearance is conventionally feminine, with long strawberry blonde hair. She smiles a lot, and strikes me as a warm, friendly person. I've noticed her tattoos before—she has large, colorful ones on her back and upper arms. It's not unusual to see anarchists sporting tattoos, since it's actually something of a norm in the subculture,[1] but I noticed Minty's in particular because they are somewhat similar in style to my own tattoos. Minty's forearms are unmarked, which makes sense since she holds a professional job at a non-profit organization. People in such careers often strategically place their body modifications, such as tattoos and piercings, so that they can be hidden under clothing while at work. During our conversation, it comes up that Minty has an appointment the following weekend to get her forearms fully covered in tattoos. I ask if she is concerned about getting tattoos in such a visible place, given her need to appear professional at her job. She's not concerned. On the contrary, she says her new tattoos will be, "a way to really make it visible, and, like, there's nothing I can do [to cover them up], I don't wear long sleeves ever. So it's a really great way to communicate, 'I'm not joining your world.'"

Minty is using the style of her self-presentation to produce for herself what subculture scholar John Clarke (2005: 54) calls "a coherent and distinctive

way of 'being-in-the-world.'" In the case of many anarchist activists like
Minty, their "way of being in the world" is actually a refusal to silently join
the mainstream. This stylistic production is "spectacular" in the sense that it
is meant to be looked at, to be seen by others; the styled anarchist body is a
spectacle (Hebdige 1981). In fact, all bodies are "spectacular" in this sense—
the ways that humans present themselves are always culturally shaped and
are thus communicative of social meaning. What makes anarchist style an
illustrative case is that it is often spectacular in both this technical sense and
in a more colloquial sense: by styling themselves in non-mainstream ways,
some anarchists make a spectacle of themselves. They seem to invite the
looks of others by consciously adorning themselves in ways that stand out
from the crowd of more politically moderate subjects. The non-normative
appearance of some anarchists sets them apart and demands interpretation,
both by outsiders and by members of their own stylistic community. A
common thread among all the forms of self-presentation associated with
anarchist subcultures is that they are all designed to enact what cultural
studies scholar Dick Hebdige (1981: 102) calls the "communication of a
significant difference" between anarchists and mainstream culture. This
is, as Hebdige explains, the "'point' behind the style of all spectacular
subcultures" (Ibid.).

Personal style is a form of representation that presents to the world
information about the individuals themselves, particularly where they situate
themselves socially. By situating oneself within an anarchist subculture, the
individual represents many layers of meaning, including a set of political
ideologies and ethical commitments associated with anarchism. For Minty,
it wasn't the content of her tattoos that would carry the most significant
meaning. The important meaning for her would come from the fact that she
marked herself in a way that was atypical of the mainstream, and possibly
even taboo in certain settings. The mere fact of her having permanently
modified her body in this way was, as she put it, "a 'fuck you' to society."
Upon further reflection, she mused, "How does this really say anything
about me? It really doesn't, but I guess it does, because not everybody does
it." My analysis in this chapter will echo Minty's question, asking *how*
anarchist modes of self-presentation actually say anything about anarchists
themselves. The question of "how" forces us to look at the *process* of
symbolic communication inherent in anarchists' presentation of self. Minty
also reminds us that the content of stylistic practice would be meaningless
apart from the contexts in which these performances circulate, contexts
in which the performances stand out as non-normative. This chapter is
concerned with the subset of anarchist lifestyle practices related to self-
presentation by activists, such as dress, adornment, and body modification.
I will examine how activists perform and produce themselves as members
in a subcultural community through practices of personal style; I will also
discuss why some anarchists choose *not* to conform to the subcultural

norms of dress adopted by many activists. Furthermore, I will consider the strategic potential for practices of self-presentation to function as effective propaganda for radical movements. This potential is limited by the ease with which symbols of such movements are decoupled from the ethical and ideological content with which activists endow them. This implies that while subcultural lifestyle practices may serve a variety of social and identificatory functions, their communicative, activist capacity is highly constrained by the hegemonic context of mainstream media and culture.

Anarchists' modes of self-presentation are signs which can be read and decoded. These signs are situated within communicative circuits—texts have consumers as well as producers, they live on in the world past the moment in which they are assembled and made public. Stylistic performances are the same way, and thus it's not enough to figure out what the producer—in this case the stylist or the "wearer"—meant when they first put the look together and went out into the world wearing it. Cultural objects, texts, and practices acquire and shift meanings at their moments of production, consumption, and recirculation, and thus one must attend to each of these moments, and the power relations involved at each, in order to understand the full significance of a given cultural phenomenon.[2] A strategic assessment of stylistic self-presentation as an activist tactic requires attention to the way practices such as dress, adornment, and body modification circulate meaning at the subcultural level and beyond. In this regard, my discussion aims to open up a set of questions that might be asked of any given activist performance, situating it within a circuit of cultural production and consumption.

The "generic anarchist suit"

Matthew explained that when he began to identify as an anarchist, he habitually wore "the 'generic Midwestern anarchist suit,'" which he described as consisting of, "a black hooded sweatshirt, black pants, black combat boots, a black shirt of some kind (usually a tee), a black bandana tied around the neck, and a black hat with a home-made haircut." Although Matthew was living in Illinois and Indiana at the time of his first identification with anarchism, the "generic anarchist suit" he described transcends geographic region. Black is indeed a prominently worn color at anarchist events across the country, with many individuals dressing solely in black items. Dressing in black has historically held associations with alternative subcultures of many kinds (Garber 1992: 22), but there are several reasons for the preference for black clothing by anarchists in particular.

The first reason is symbolic: the plain black flag has been a symbol of the anarchist movement in Europe since the nineteenth century (Wehling 1995), hence adorning oneself in black is a way of wrapping oneself in the flag of anarchism, so to speak (Sawer 2007). The second reason is a combination of symbolism and material practicality that is tied to protest techniques employed by some anarchists. Anarchists at protest events sometimes form a Black Bloc, in which a large group of individuals collectively attempts to inflict damage on corporate or government property, sabotage a political event, or physically confront law enforcement personnel. Because Black Bloc activities are generally illegal, the participants attempt to dress similarly so as to frustrate the identification of individuals by media and police. This is also the reason why bandanas and face masks are a common element of anarchist style—they can be pulled up to cover the face in case anonymity is desired.[3] Anarchists don't tend to be engaged in violent, illegal altercations on an everyday basis, and many will never participate in these actions. Yet, the symbolic cachet of the Black Bloc look transcends the time, place, and bodies of actual Black Bloc protests. Dressing on an everyday basis as if one is ready for such an event is a way of indicating a kind of militant preparedness to fight—if only metaphorically or ideologically—when the need arises. The symbolism is all the more powerful when one's subcultural peers are all dressed similarly on a daily basis, with the conscious or unconscious message being something like, "together, we'll be ready for the revolution when it comes."

Another reason why anarchists prefer black clothing has to do with anarchist attitudes toward consumption. Black clothes do not show stains easily, meaning they do not have to be replaced as often as light-colored garments. This allows the wearer to reduce their overall consumption of clothing in the long term. Black garments also require less frequent washing in order to look "presentable" (though clearly presentable is a relative term when we're talking about subcultures), which is convenient if one is transient or wishes to conserve the money and water involved in doing laundry. I should point out here that having one's clothing look or actually be clean is hardly a top concern for many anarchists. In fact, there may be a kind of cache associated with wearing obviously dirty clothes, insofar as it is a material expression of one's refusal of consumption as well as "bourgeois" standards of cleanliness. For example, Matthew expressed his feeling that, among his anarchist peers, "all the clothes had to be very faded and dirty and gross."

Anarchists' consumption habits when it comes to hygiene practices and products have further impacts on the content of their self-presentation. In an essay on what he calls "radical men's fashion," anarchist blogger Adam Tinnell asserts, "Deodorant is for losers and compulsive washing a thing of the past. Always wear your hygiene as a part of your look, if it calls for dirt, then bring it on . . ." (Tinnell 2008). Greasy, matted hair, sometimes in the form of dreadlocks, may also be an indicator of infrequent bathing. What's more, anarchist spaces often smell strongly of body odor—further evidence of the occupants' rejection of soaps, deodorants, and chemical perfumes. Anti-consumption practices influence other aspects of anarchist style as well. Clothing may be tattered or patched many times over, rather than replaced right away. The fact that clothes are sometimes thrifted or dumpstered may also account for their poor condition. The prevalence of veganism means that leather is not generally worn, while certain fashion brands that provide alternatives to leather products are commonplace. In some locales the intersection of anarchism and the bicycling culture results in certain stylistic quirks, such as short or rolled-up pants (so they won't get caught in the bicycle chain), and the staple accessories of the messenger bag and water bottle. Though these obviously serve practical functions, they also end up being stylistic markers of one's involvement in anarchist subcultures.

Probably the most straightforward practice of anarchist stylization is the adorning of one's body with traditional symbols of the anarchist movement on clothing, patches, pins, stickers, and even tattoos. The circle-A insignia (featuring a capital letter "A" inscribed within a circle, with the points of the letter often transgressing the bounds of the circle itself) is probably the most recognizable anarchist symbol, but many others are used. The colors black and red in combination carry anarchist connotations, owing to the color scheme of a flag used by anarcho-syndicalists in early twentieth-century Europe (the flag is bisected diagonally, with each half colored red and black, respectively). A modified version of this flag in the shape of a star may be worn as a button or used as a t-shirt or patch emblem. The images of famous historical anarchists, such as Emma Goldman or Sacco and Vanzetti, are often emblazoned across shirts and tote bags. One interviewee, Ahmad, commented that he tries to make his "politics more visible" through subtle symbols, such as an International Workers of the World (a labor union associated with anarchist politics) patch that he wears on his backpack. During my fieldwork, I commonly observed individuals wearing hooded sweatshirts bearing the names and insignias of other anarchist organizations, such as the anarchist publishing collective AK Press, whose logos reference historical anarchist imagery, such as the red and black flag. There's often an element of DIY ("do-it-yourself") involved too, as individuals creatively embellish their own garments with ink, buttons, and patches that depict anarchist symbols. The DIY ethos pervades other aspects of anarchist style; recall, for example, Matthew's mention of having a "home haircut" as part of his so-called "anarchist suit." DIY tattooing and piercing is even practiced; I met two women at a book fair who had done their forearm tattoos themselves using sewing machine needles and ink pens. Simply by marking themselves with recognizable anarchist symbols, individuals express their dissidence from the cultural and political mainstream. These symbols become "stigmata" which "warn the 'straight' world in advance of a sinister presence" (Hebdige 1981: 3).

Anarchism is inevitably defined in relation to dominant political ideologies; specifically, it is defined by both insiders and outsiders as *oppositional* to dominant liberal, capitalist ideology. Hence, the performance of *stylistic* difference from the mainstream is homologous with the underlying *ideological* differences espoused by anarchists, though it may not literally depict the content of those differences. Take Miles' appearance for example: Miles is a professor in his late thirties. When I met him at an anarchist conference, he was dressed entirely in black. His head was shaved bald, and he had a long goatee, which he groomed into two braids secured with colored rubber bands. Although there was nothing explicitly anarchist about his style (there were no circle-As in sight), his dramatic appearance marked him as standing outside the mainstream. When I later asked him in an email interview if his style of self-presentation was an expression of his politics, he was hesitant to draw a direct connection:

> If I were to boil down the relationship, it would be one of form not content. That is, it is not that my undying commitment to wearing black (with a smattering of white from time to time) is something I think is anarchist, nor is my ridiculous hair, etc. They are simply an aesthetic, one that I find engaging/attractive.

Yet, he went on to admit that it was not a coincidence that his personal attraction to this aesthetic ends up aligning him with others who would politically identify in similar ways. Although he didn't necessarily see his style as a direct representation of anarchism, he did see it as political because it flies in the face of what mainstream society expects him to look like, particularly as a professor at a prestigious college. This is a striking illustration of Hebdige's (1981: 89) point that subcultural style "challeng[es] at a symbolic level the 'inevitability,' the 'naturalness' of class and gender stereotypes."

A desire for personal autonomy from mainstream norms is a major reason offered by anarchists to explain their lifestyle practices. As Miles explained, "I feel like I am making aesthetic and/or consumption-based choices strictly following my own desires/interests," which are not necessarily, "those requested/expected/demanded by the mainstreams." Thus, Miles made an implicit distinction between his own choices and those of others whose tastes are determined by something other than their own autonomous will. His implication is that, while most people may be happy to go along with consumer trends and mainstream norms, he does not allow these things to dictate his decisions. Like other anarchists, Miles values the power of the individual to resist dominant, disciplining forces; as he said, "thus, in that sense, I am enacting at least some tangential element of my politics."

Style as self-construction through self-representation

The use of style as a means of performing identity is self-evident in modern societies. In cultures where sartorial options can be freely chosen from among many alternatives, the way an individual styles oneself is a communicative act about who that person is. Among all the forms of everyday practice discussed in this book, personal style is perhaps the one most easily linked to the representation of political identity, since, as Veblen (1994: 103)—who coined the term "conspicuous consumption" in the late nineteenth century— observed, "our apparel is always in evidence and affords an indication of our pecuniary standing to all observers at first glance." Although we are less directly concerned with economic class ("pecuniary standing") here, the communicative dimensions of conspicuous consumption still hold. In fact, acts of communication *about* identity, in the form of embodied performance, are constitutive *of* identity, according to some theorists of performativity (Butler 1990, 2005; Cavarero 2000). This goes beyond the idea of conspicuous consumption to say that dress does not only reflect a pre-existing subject position, it also constructs subjectivity in the moment of dress and display. By producing a narrative of the self through style and other visible performances, an individual makes oneself into the type of person whose identity can be narrativized that way. So, in the moments when an anarchist individual dresses "like an anarchist," one makes and remakes oneself into an anarchist. Each time one taps into a shared notion of "what an anarchist looks like," one implicitly tells oneself and those who witness her, "I am an anarchist." One's performance also works to shore up that common understanding of what an anarchist looks like; it's an endless, recursive loop.[4]

Instructive parallels can be drawn between radical political identities and minority sexualities. Performance has been such an important concern for scholars of queer identity precisely because hegemonic understandings of sexuality see sexual identity as emanating from *within* the individual rather than being constituted through visible practice. Political beliefs are similar, in that they are internally held; both sexual and political identities are "invisible" until made otherwise.[5] In a society where hegemonic identities are assumed *de facto*, visible performances of difference are a prerequisite for establishing, socially, that marginal identities even exist. In order for an oppositional identity to have any valence as a social category—to be a basis for community formation and political mobilization—it must be made visible, it must be performed. Symbolic representations of identity are the means by which individuals can recognize a shared identification between themselves and others. Embodied self-presentation is clearly an important site for the symbolic representation of identity. Thus, one can see style as an arena in which anarchists bring themselves—and their social movement—into being. Seen in this way, one can understand stylistic performances as part of what Bourdieu (1987: 8) calls the "complex historical work of construction" that goes into making a social class. As Bourdieu explains, "It is through this endless work of representation (in every sense of the term) that social agents try to impose their vision of the world or the vision of their own position in that world, and to define their social identity" (10–11).

Anarchists' distinctive modes of self-presentation operate on two levels of representation. First, they may physically enact particular lifestyle habits, which may be taken as evidence of ethical commitments based on political beliefs. So, for example, being dirty is physical evidence that, among other things, one does not hold a job that requires a certain level of cleanliness, one does not wish to expend one's personal financial resources on hygiene products, and/or one is ideologically opposed to a marketing system that creates false needs where cleanliness and hygiene are concerned. At this level, anarchist style takes a set of beliefs and makes them visible by translating them into material practices, the traces of which may be observed on the body. At the second level of representation, anarchist modes of self-presentation tap into shared discourses of social identity in which observers associate symbols with particular identity categories. Here, it doesn't matter so much whether the style corresponds in any material way to an ethical practice, just that it is widely understood as standing for "anarchism."

Along these lines, Adam Tinnell (2009), the anarchist fashion blogger quoted above, argues that, "While these [anarchist] fashion choices are often portrayed as based on necessity, more often than not, they are nothing more than a desire to fit in and feel part of a subculture." Tinnell attests to the idea that visible performances are as much about their communicative value as their material content. Anarchist activist Uri Gordon (2008: 19) concurs:

> Cultural expression can serve as a shorthand designation of affiliation and connection with others. It thus plays an important role in the articulation of personal or collective identities in the anarchist movement. External appearances like styles of clothes or hair are important cultural signifiers, visible before any political conversation begins.

To put it another way, after describing the look adopted by many anarchists he knew, interviewee Orlando remarked, "if you want to meet more people who think like you—looking like that is a way to do it." The implication of this is that once individuals learn to read and write the signs of anarchist identity on the body, they can locate each other in mainstream settings and potentially grow their activist networks. None of this is to say that style is a substitute for actual political beliefs and commitment. Rather, an anarchist's style functions as a signifier for one's political identity. Thus, anarchists cultivate a sense of solidarity through their collective adoption of recognized signifiers of anarchist identity.[6]

The intrinsic problem with using stylistic representations to signify actually held political beliefs is that the chain of signification between beliefs and styles is easily disrupted. That is, there is no mechanism to ensure that all people who adopt similar practices of self-presentation actually share the same political commitments. It is precisely this fact that puts Black Blocs at risk of being easily infiltrated by *agents provocateurs* during protest actions.[7] Since just about anyone can adopt the symbolic markers of a subculture, the markers may eventually lose their semiotic linkage to that subculture and its political ideologies, as the "poseurs" become indistinguishable from the "authentic" members. Indeed, if a subcultural style is adopted by too many people, or even goes mainstream, it is rendered void of any symbolic value as an expression of oppositional ideology. The cultural diffusion of radical lifestyles, by proliferating the arenas of visibility and consumption, enables the disarticulation of symbolic gestures from their oppositional meanings. This, in turn, creates a potential bifurcation of anarchist identity—there are those who identify with anarchist politics and those who identify with the aesthetics of anarchist subcultures, and there is little *necessary* correspondence between the two. The utility of an individual's distinctively anarchist mode of self-presentation for communicating identity and group membership is thereby greatly reduced.

On the one hand, the constitution of political identity through stylistic performance can be democratizing, in that it makes anarchist identity available as a social position for anyone willing to take the time to understand and perform the recognized modes of self-presentation. Hypothetically, this opens up the group to anyone who wants to identify with it, which allows for a diversity of membership. Yet, on the other hand, it also introduces a new social boundary, in that personal style becomes a terrain for judgments to be made about who should be accepted and who should be excluded from the group. An interviewee named Samantha described some of the anarchists she knew as having a "punk rock aesthetic." She went on to say that, among these people, "It tends to be more of a scene where you are either in or out." Considering the social dynamics of inclusion and exclusion around aesthetic practices helps us to see that subcultural tastes are more than mere preferences that happen to unite certain individuals. The tastes one is able to express publicly—what Bourdieu calls "manifested tastes"—get converted into a form of capital—"cultural capital"—that is used to establish and secure one's position in society (Bourdieu 1984: 56). And as Bourdieu has convincingly shown, individual tastes are always conditioned by social structures, which are often inflected by relations of power, hierarchy, and domination. The tastes one has the opportunity and inclination to cultivate are shaped by one's economic position, access to education, and so on. This is how taste works to "classify" individuals: one's social position can be read off the tastes one has cultivated (6). Furthermore, one can be functionally excluded from a social class if one fails to share the tastes associated with it. But there is a kind of mystification at work here: because the cultivation of taste is usually a slow process that happens over years of immersion in a particular social sphere (or "habitus"), aesthetic preferences are often experienced as natural desires. By extension, the differential levels of social power that accrue to those with different tastes are perceived as a natural hierarchy rather than a constructed one. What are the implications of these propositions for anarchist subcultures?

Style as distinction and boundary

Just as anarchism is defined by its extreme critique of the dominant political system, so anarchist tastes are defined by and valued for their extreme divergence from dominant cultural norms. As other scholars have shown, power dynamics over taste are often found within subcultures. David Chaney (2001: 82) explains that lifestyles "are ways in which members of a group can display their privileges, or, more actively, use their mastery of symbolic capital to control access to desirable status." As noted in Chapter 2, Sarah Thornton's (1996) concept of subcultural capital refers to the way in which people are rewarded for specific tastes within a specific subcultural milieu. As with regular cultural capital, these rewards come in the form of social acceptance, respect, and admiration from one's peers (Bourdieu 1984). And, should particular tastes not be in evidence, the result can be non-recognition, chastisement, or even ostracism from the group. Even political subcultures that are philosophically opposed to hierarchy—such as anarchism—are not immune to such dynamics. Whereas Bourdieu's cultural capital is mostly the product of education and upbringing and has currency within a dominant or mainstream social milieu, Thornton's subcultural capital is developed through immersion in subcultural lifestyle and is valuable as distinction only within the relevant subcultural milieu, for it is only within the subculture that particular tastes are coded as valuable.

Comfort with dirtiness, for instance, is unlikely to bring status to an individual in mainstream society, whereas among one's anarchist peers it can serve as valuable proof of one's ideological commitment. Often, the tastes coded as most valuable within anarchist subcultures are in direct contradiction to mainstream norms. Joel was an interviewee who described the importance, among some of his anarchist acquaintances, of not looking like someone who "fit in" with mainstream culture. For example, the wearing of a button-down shirt, with its white-collar professional connotations, was a no-no among his anarchist peers. He also joked that he couldn't be a member of an anarchist organization in his city because he didn't own a black hooded sweatshirt. Since garments like black hooded sweatshirts were understood to be de rigueur among the anarchists in his community, Joel's identity as an authentic adherent to the shared anarchist politics underlying the organization was questionable. Although Joel was being facetious when he said that he was barred from membership in the organization on the basis of his not owning a particular clothing item, he was gesturing toward a real feeling of alienation experienced by individuals who do not conform to subcultural norms.

Because anarchism entails a set of values or ethics, the subcultural tastes associated with anarchism take on ethical significance. Even where a direct relationship cannot be drawn (is there truly any direct ethical difference between wearing a ratty hooded sweatshirt and wearing a clean button-down shirt?), adherence to stylistic conventions stands in, symbolically, for adherence to ethical standards (Chaney 2001: 82). Within anarchist subcultures, this assumed relationship between ethics and style provides ideological justification for the reproduction of hierarchies based on taste. In other words, individuals may feel justified in judging others based on their appearances, because appearance is thought to signify internally held values, which may be legitimately judged on the basis of their ethical validity. While it is understandable how such judgments are justifiable to the people who make them, the history of radical social movements offers many cautionary tales about the power of such taste hierarchies to breed conflict, which may threaten cohesion within the movement and ultimately drive some individuals out of it.[8] Furthermore, taste judgments work to marginalize the uninitiated who may not have had the benefit of moving in anarchist circles—that is, have not cultivated an anarchist subcultural habitus. For those who are not determined enough to stick it out and make it beyond the learning curve, their desire to stay with the movement may be short lived. Revbaker, an interviewee who had been involved with anarchism in Denver for several years, described his initial feelings that the scene there was "closed off" and "cliquey." It's not hard to imagine that many people who are interested in working on anarchist political projects get scared off by such feelings early on and simply go away. Thus, judgments around taste work, almost invisibly, to maintain the insularity and homogeneity of the subculture. There is a strategically significant trade-off here, between defending a movement against the diffusion of style for the purposes of maintaining subcultural unity on the one hand and broadening a movement's appeal and increasing the diversity of its participants on the other.

As I have noted, the stylistic boundaries around anarchist subcultures are not random. They often map onto other social boundaries such as gender and race, hence the oft-stated perception that the anarchist movement is largely populated by white males. While it's important to challenge the assumption that most anarchists are white and male, it is quite clear that most anarchists *who are recognizable as such* through their stylistic self-presentation *are* male and white. This is an important point that I want to emphasize. It is not necessarily the case that women and people of color are less likely to identify as anarchists or to hold anarchist principles. What is evident is that, for various reasons, many having to do with the structural relations of power in society at large, women and people of color are less likely to style themselves in a way that is immediately recognizable as being associated with anarchist subcultures. Indeed, several interviewees explicitly connected the "anarchist look" to young, white men. For example, Winona commented that she had been to an anarchist book fair in Montreal, attended by what she described as "a lot of white men wearing black. It was pretty limited and not the world I personally feel connected to—macho, activist-oriented, all young." Although she said she respected the political ideas discussed at the book fair, she obviously felt alienated by the stylistic presentation of some of the participants.

Angela McRobbie (1991: 24) asserts that the style that defines a subculture is often the style of its male members. My own observations of the LA anarchist scene in particular support McRobbie's assertion. At many of the events I attended in Los Angeles, the men tended to dress similarly and in typical anarchist fashion—in clothing that was mostly black, tattered, and dirty—whereas the women tended to dress and style themselves in more mainstream ways—including brightly colored and clean-cut garments in their wardrobes. This was not a universal rule, but it was enough of a trend to be readily noticeable. One reason for this is that women may feel more internalized pressure than men to live up to mainstream beauty standards, and thus might be reluctant to reject conventional hygiene practices or to adopt what one interviewee described as anarchists' "aggressive" style of dress and body adornment. In many respects, anarchist style contradicts hegemonic disciplinary practices of femininity (Bartky 1990) much more strongly than it bucks dominant standards of masculinity. For some women, this is a point of attraction to anarchist subcultural style. Yet for others, the style may conflict too sharply with their other social identities. The performance of masculinity encoded in anarchist style may be particularly trepidatious for women of color, who can face extra censure for gender transgression beyond what is experienced by their white counterparts (Moore 2006: 130).

Other structural factors can further complicate an individual's desire and capacity to adopt subcultural modes of self-presentation. Ahmad was an Afghan immigrant living in San Jose, whom I interviewed via email. He observed that some of the activists in his area "wore their anarchism on their sleeves—sometimes literally" in the form of "buttons, shirts, visible tattoos and . . . other symbols from a particular subculture." While he said he admired the political work they were doing, he felt alienated from them because of their style. Part of the reason for this was that he relied on a retail job at an electronics store for his income, so his appearance had to be somewhat mainstream if he wanted to keep his job. He added, "my family also did not have a green card and our immigration status was up in the air. Especially after 9/11. So as a first generation immigrant I had some general fears about how people, the man, would perceive me."

Like Ahmad, other people of color I interviewed had concerns about the scrutiny their appearance as anarchists might draw from authority figures. Alma was also an immigrant; she had come to the United States with her family from Mexico. She expressed to me that she had been afraid that her long dreadlocks would arouse suspicion of her radical activities among the officials who interviewed her during her process of obtaining US citizenship. Gabby, a Filipina-American woman, mentioned that she attempted to look "less crusty" when engaged in shoplifting, so as not to draw more attention than she would already receive as a person of color. Each of these interviewees' experiences speaks to the surveillance faced by people of color in white supremacist societies. It is understandable that, as individuals who are already very vulnerable to scrutiny and repression, they would be hesitant to draw even more negative attention to themselves through stylistic association with a radical political movement. When one's body is always already a spectacle in the dominant culture, as it is for women and people of color, the prospect of inviting further looks may lack a certain appeal. One consequence of this is that the reluctance of women and people of color to adopt recognizable stylistic practices may translate into their marginalization—and certainly their relatively low visibility—within anarchist subcultural scenes. The means by which individuals win recognition, authenticity, and subcultural capital may be precisely those means which are more available to subjects who are already privileged in mainstream society.

Although it is extremely unlikely that any anarchists *intend* for their scenes to be unwelcoming for women and people of color, it is clearly the case that anarchist scenes *are* often unwelcoming, and the maintaining of stylistic boundaries is a contributing factor. Some feel strongly that this must change. A few interviewees distanced themselves from anarchist style for this reason. Pritha, for instance, was careful to tell me that she avoids wearing black. Helena too, remarked, "I like not conforming to people's expectations of what an anarchist looks like." Adam Tinnell's (2009) blog, which I have quoted above, is similarly devoted to contesting norms of anarchist style, particularly where they work to discipline expressions of gender identity within anarchist scenes. He argues:

> With such a diverse politic as anarchism, being interpreted and enacted in thousands of different cultures around the world, not to mention the contributions of anarcha-feminism and queer anarchism, it's totally unacceptable to let one or two subcultures dominate the look and the feel of this movement.

Tinnell believes that anarchists should make a conscious effort to cultivate a variety of anarchist looks that challenge some of the forms of privilege that have heretofore been reproduced within anarchists' stylistic norms.

An interest in evading norms—even subcultural ones—is one that speaks to many anarchists, for philosophical and tactical reasons. Matthew, the interviewee who described the "Midwestern anarchist suit" he used to wear, explained to me his reasons for eventually giving up on that look. In an email exchange with me, he said that over time he had grown "increasingly disillusioned" with Black Bloc tactics, and didn't like the symbolic associations between his wardrobe and that subset of anarchist activists. He said:

> I've had enough with senseless violence, with masked anarchists all dressed up in identical uniforms like fascists! I started feeling this way in 2005

or '6 when I started putting color back in my wardrobe. It seemed like a trivial thing but it's not. All these self-proclaimed individualists wearing uniforms . . . should we be surprised that when they get together they act like a fascist horde? It bothered me, all that uniformity. I mean, I understand the symbolic cache . . . I understand what the look is trying to promote, but it hardly seems worthwhile on balance. It just carries too much negative weight. So I decided anarchism 'is something you do and not something you wear' after all.

Many anarchists struggle with the problem of how to live in opposition to dominant cultural patterns without alienating and foreclosing solidarity with people who may not understand or approve of anarchist lifestyles. Particularly because of the associations with violent protest activities, many prefer not to risk alienating outsiders with an appearance that would evoke those associations. As scholar of global anarchist movements, Jeffrey Juris (2008b: 87) observes, "the same factors that generate affective solidarity among militants may also complicate efforts to recruit more broadly." Even where associations with violence are not intentionally invoked, the mere "communication of a significant difference" involved in "looking like an anarchist" may be enough to divide individuals from those with whom they might otherwise wish to establish common ground. The sense of cohesive group identity produced through stylistic performance may thus hamper the movement's potential impact beyond its existing subcultural milieu.

Some anarchists are therefore ambivalent about using their presentations of self to construct or highlight differences between themselves and non-anarchists. Several interviewees expressed their commitment to doing political work with people who do not identify as anarchists. In their view, the adoption of a subcultural style of self-presentation could be counterproductive in that it could alienate people to whom they were interested in reaching out and partnering. Rilla was an interviewee in her late twenties who had spent many years doing what she described as "community-oriented or labor-oriented anarchist work." She had been involved in founding a community center in Los Angeles and running radical programs for local youth. Rilla had never cultivated a particularly distinctively anarchist appearance; she found this to be useful when recruiting youth to get involved in her programs. As she put it,

the kind of stuff I did didn't really mark itself as subcultural. Because a lot of the work we were doing had to integrate with the community. Actually it would be almost to our disadvantage to look in a particularly marked way. If I'm gonna go out and do work in high schools, I want the teachers to, like, want me to come into their classroom, or the parents of these kids to trust me with their kids. So it's not that I changed the way I look, but it actually is to my advantage if I look somewhat unremarkable.

Rilla's brother Mark, also an anarchist and also involved in community and labor activism, expressed a similar view. Mark was another interviewee who didn't immediately look like an anarchist. I saw him on several occasions, and his clothes were always unassuming, just t-shirts and jeans; he had buzzed blonde hair that he sometimes covered with a baseball cap. Although he confessed to owning "a whole collection" of political t-shirts, and a red and black star button he wore on his hat, he was clear on the point that, for him, "it's important to look like a fuckin' regular guy." He felt that, "You don't have to look a certain way or listen to a certain kind of music to be an anarchist, it just means you fuckin' believe in a world without boxes or borders, you know, without fucking, uh, exploitation or oppression . . . ." He hoped to demonstrate through his actions and appearance that anarchism is "not something so hocus pocus." Mark's view was that by looking like a "regular guy" and simply "living by [his] principles," he could more readily win political allies. For example, he expressed an interest in forging alliances with and possibly politicizing his fellow bike messengers, who were not necessarily aware of or interested in radical activism.

In considering the perspective of activists like Rilla and Mark, one can again draw parallels to queer politics and performance tactics. Sexual geographers David Bell and Gill Valentine (1995) draw on the work of John Dollimore (1991), introducing the idea of the "passing pervert": the queer individual who does not actively signify queerness on one's body and thereby is allowed passage into straight spaces. The political power of such an individual is that, by bringing one's queer sexuality into straight space, one actually "carries the potential for disruption more meaningful – more *dangerous*" to the status quo (Bell and Valentine 1995: 153). Anarchist activists who "pass" as more mainstream political subjects can similarly insinuate themselves into settings where people may not be predisposed to look favorably on radicalism. They then have the capacity to quietly politicize their students, co-workers, neighbors, or whomever, without bearing the stigma that the label "anarchist" carries in mainstream society. Given that visibility can be "a trap," which "summons surveillance and the law," it may be a matter of strategy to be unmarked (Phelan 1993: 6; Foucault 1995). Some anarchists *can* present themselves in unmarked ways, if they wish, and those who do may find themselves less scrutinized by officers of social control (Clarke et al. 2005). Evading such scrutiny by both police officials and less official enforcers of hegemony, such as social peers, may empower activists to undertake different forms of resistance.

One can see a conflict here between two diverging activist strategies: one, to symbolically communicate difference from the mainstream and thus cultivate an alternative space of identity and community formation; the other, to draw potential philosophical sympathizers to anarchism without immediately communicating the radicalness of one's position. Historian of American radical movements Lawrence Veysey (1973: 449) notes that this is an enduring dilemma among political dissidents: "radicals have always been torn between the desire to express themselves in an openly unconventional fashion and the opposing desire . . . to melt inconspicuously into the crowd." As anarchist activists, practitioners of both techniques are interested in provoking critiques of dominant ideology among the people with whom they interact. The difference perhaps lies in these individuals' implicit understanding of the capacity of self-presentation to accomplish this goal. In the following sections, I give more sustained attention to the idea that self-presentation can serve a tactical purpose beyond the mere communication of subcultural identity.

Style as tactical critique and propaganda

As I have just shown, there are merits to looking like a "regular" person and perfectly understandable reasons why a person would not want to mark themself in disruptive ways. And yet, there are those, like Minty, who see the symbolic "fuck you to society" as a worthwhile political act. Is it possible to see Minty's refusal to conform to mainstream styles of self-presentation as having material consequences beyond a symbolic disruption? That is, can one understand the stylistic "communication of a significant difference" as constituting, in itself, a material threat to dominant power? At a strictly individual level, deviance from mainstream stylistic standards is a material expression of resistance to normative power. This is because, in itself, an act of stylistic resistance affirms the extant *in*capacity of disciplinary forces to totally control the will of the individual. By the very fact of an individual's *not* following the norm, one can see that the norm lacks the power to dictate that individual's behavior (Foucault 1990a). Does this act of resistance win new autonomy for the resisting subject? Or does it testify to an autonomy that already existed? The fact that stylistic resistance is sometimes described in terms of "insubordination" (Hebdige 1997: 404; Butler 1997a) is telling. Colloquially, insubordination refers to an act of talking back to someone in a position of authority. In real life, such acts rarely result in a shift in power between the authority figure and the insubordinate. If anything, the acts may bring punishment upon the insubordinate, so as to reassert the superior power of the authority. The same goes for stylistic insubordination; by bucking mainstream norms, anarchists often invite punishment in the form of social scrutiny and even police surveillance. Resistance may thus result in a reinforcement of hegemonic power, rather than a sustained disruption of it.

Consider Minty's forearm tattoos once again. They visibly demonstrate the fact that mainstream social norms were impotent to dictate her behavior, or else she could not even have made the choice to get the tattoos. Minty was quite conscious of the social forces which *would* still be at work on her after getting her tattoos, such as the withholding of certain forms of employment based on her appearance. This consciousness, in fact, informed her decision to get the tattoos; recall that she saw them as "a really great way to, like, communicate I'm not joining your world, you know?" Yet, though her tattoos symbolized a hostility (i.e. a "fuck you") toward the social norms which would lead others to judge her employability based on such a thing, it's unclear that she is able to do more than offer an angry gesture in response to that judgment. The fact of her getting the tattoos does not change the fact that she *will* probably become less employable as a result. It does not then challenge the systemic disciplinary power of conformity, which works precisely through such mechanisms as employment standards. Minty's refusal to conform does not deprive hegemonic forces of the power to proscribe her social opportunities based on that refusal. As Bourdieu (1989) explains, official institutions and other social elites carry immense symbolic capital, which allows them to enforce the standards of which cultural tastes will be deemed widely acceptable, status worthy, and deserving of economic and political rewards. While Minty's tattoos communicate to her anarchist peers and others that she is committed to living a different kind of life (one in which traditional status and rewards may be less important), this is, again, merely a *representation* of difference and not a material alteration to existing power relations. In other words, she holds little power to make her "vision of the world" (Bourdieu 1989: 10) more socially valued, such that anarchist beliefs or lifestyles become more attractive on a broad scale.

According to Hebdige's reading of spectacular subcultures, what anarchists like Minty and Miles *are* able to do is "contradict the myth of consensus," by showing that not everyone subscribes to the dominant definitions of the world and that it is possible to resist the forces of social conformity (Hebdige 1981: 18). This may be an important step for oppositional movements, since, in order to win broad support, hegemonic discourses of power must present themselves as simply reflecting a reality that pre-existed them (Gramsci 1971). Hebdige understands spectacular subcultures as subversive of hegemony because they expose social norms as constructed rather than natural. Furthermore, because hegemony in liberal societies is maintained by convincing everyone that a silent majority has consented to the present system, highly visible forms of dissent falsify the putatively democratic legitimacy that upholds that system. In this way, anarchists, through their visible presence, may point out that there are cracks in the façade of liberal capitalist ideology, that not everyone buys into the status quo, that alternative philosophies and lifestyles are available, and that at least some people find them preferable.

However, the question remains whether anarchists' stylistic deviations are *read* as signifying such a substantive ideological critique. In other words, if spectacular subcultural style is intended to disrupt the myth of consensus, which specific kinds of consensus does anarchist style effectively disrupt? Do mainstream members of society actually interpret the anarchists they see as offering a critical campaign against hierarchical power structures? Is it possible, or indeed likely, that stylistic dissent is readable as dissent only against *stylistic* conformity and nothing further? Where a subculture's concern is with stylistic conformity, then contradicting a myth of consensus around fashion norms is a significant act of resistance. But anarchists are *not* primarily concerned with style—their political issues run much deeper. Recall for example that Miles maintained that his stylistic practices are only "tangentially" an enactment of his anarchist politics. It seems clear that where style is not the sole site of oppression, it cannot be the sole means of liberation. Anarchists are concerned with many expressions of power, not just those associated with stylistic conformity. They may thus find that resistance in the form of stylistic non-conformity is entirely inadequate to address the breadth of social problems that anarchists concern themselves with. As John Clarke et al. (2005) and others argue, style cannot alter political structure. Though they may symbolize a deeper commitment to political resistance, acts of stylistic resistance "'solve' but in an imaginary way, problems which at the concrete level remain unresolved" (48). Yes, Minty and Miles show us that they have been able to liberate their bodies from certain repressive standards of mainstream society, but the freedom to have tattoos and odd hairstyles is certainly not an end goal for either of them. Beyond this, the question remains whether, having effectively disrupted a myth of consensus, stylistic performances can do anything to promote the substantive political alternatives espoused by the performers.[9]

What then is at stake *politically* when anarchists adopt spectacularly non-conformist modes of self-presentation? Returning to two concepts discussed in Chapter 1, "prefigurative politics" and "propaganda by the deed" are commonly invoked by activists to make sense of their own small-scale acts of resistance (Gordon 2008). Both ideas imply that individual acts can serve as positive examples that will ideally inspire resistance among others. Yet, in my observation, there is little sustained attention given to the precise process by which resistance is inspired. That is, while a lot of attention is paid to the production side of radical spectacles, less is paid to the consumption of these spectacles by those who observe them. Something must happen *after* the act of symbolic resistance for it to gain value as a political intervention; namely, the message of resistance produced by the anarchist activist must be consumed and responded to in some way by others.

If the point of performed resistance is to inspire collective resistance at a deeper level than that of personal style, then the strategic question for anarchists is whether individual and subcultural practices of self-presentation are up to the task. As a representative form of communication, style relies on a chain of semiotic linkages between visual signifiers and more abstract concepts, in order for meaning to be conveyed. For any kind of intended reaction to be incited in observers—including identification and political sympathy—those observers must first be able to reconstruct the chain of signification as it was intended by the creator of the message. If Person A visually presents themself as an anarchist by adopting the practices described above, Person B must be able to see "black clothing" or "tattoos" or make the connection between those symbols and anarchist identity. Person B may then react by thinking "yes, I am an anarchist too," thus fulfilling the social identification function of anarchist style. But say Person B is not an anarchist—the more likely circumstance. In order for anarchist style to operate as a political critique, Person B must further be able to connect the signifiers of anarchist identity with the ideological content of anarchist philosophy. Beyond that, Person B must be disposed to be agreeable to the ideological content that he or she is able to associate with the stylistic presentation that he or she is witnessing, and take up the cause himself or herself. The process of communication involved in the deployment of style as political critique is largely located in the mind of Person B, although the self-presentation of Person A is the initiator of that process. The meaning that Person A intends may not be the meaning that Person B produces when making sense of Person A's performance.

As cultural theorist Stuart Hall (2006) explains, both the encoding of messages and their decoding take place within ideologically structured contexts, but these contexts may be "asymmetrical." By asymmetry, Hall is referring to the ideological mismatch that may exist between encoders and decoders which results in audiences making a different meaning than the one intended by the producers of a text. When Person B tries to understand what Person A's personal style means, Person B will have to fit Person A's look into whatever discourses Person B already has at his or her disposal. Kobena Mercer (1987: 42), in his discussion of the hairstyles of radical Black activists, notes that "for 'style' to be socially intelligible as an expression of conflicting values, each cultural nucleus or articulation of signs must share access to a common stock or resource of signifying elements." As an anarchist activist, Person A has likely constructed his or her look within the context of extensive and sophisticated critiques of capitalism, patriarchy, and other systems of domination. Yet, unless Person B is similarly versed in these critiques, the symbolic connections between Person A's self-presentation and those political discourses will be unmade. As Jeffrey Juris (2008b: 89) points out in his study of theatrical anarchist activism, "although the meaning of specific actions may be evident to activists, they are often difficult to interpret for an outside audience."

It's not just that outside audiences don't know what to make of anarchists' style. Non-anarchists who don't have the discursive resources at their disposal to interpret anarchist modes of self-presentation as substantive, valid political critiques may write anarchist activists off as weirdos, troublemakers, criminals, and so on (Morley 1983). In the parlance of J.

L. Austin's (1975) speech act theory, if one sees anarchist style as a kind of speech act of resistance, then one has to acknowledge that it is often an infelicitous one. While it may be felicitous to the extent that observers will recognize it as resistance of some form, it will often be infelicitous in that they won't understand quite what is being critiqued. Sally, an interviewee, acknowledged that people outside of anarchist subcultures can be unaware of the beliefs that underlie, for example, a freegan anarchist's choice to wear old, "grungy" clothes out of a desire not to contribute to the harmful cycle of consumption and waste. Sally bemoaned the fact that outsiders are likely to view these anarchists as "hipsters" whose style of dress is a mere "image," rather than a material manifestation of their beliefs. This misinterpretation precludes any possibility that observers might be persuaded by the performance to adopt their own critical stance toward consumer culture.

All radicals face this difficulty of asymmetry since they are, by nature, mounting a radical critique and departure from hegemonic ideological premises and the discourses that are most accessible to the mainstream. But the difficulty outsiders have in correctly interpreting the intended meaning of anarchist practices is further compounded by the "systematic distortion" (Hall 2006: 170) of radical messages within mainstream media culture. The intended meaning of any given lifestyle practice may be obscured by dominant discursive frameworks which position alternative lifestyles as unserious, immature, apolitical, or even dangerous. As radical dissenters, anarchists are working from a deficit of symbolic capital: their vision of the world is inherently at odds with that held by those whose vision is most commonly accepted; they will thus have to struggle to have their critique even receive a fair hearing, let alone be received positively as an accurate indictment of political conditions (Bourdieu 1987, 1989). As Herbert Marcuse (1972) observed of the 1960s radical counterculture, it can be hard to protest "the Establishment" and be taken seriously since the establishment is by definition mature—the politics of the establishment come off as realistic because they *are* the ideology of the existing reality. In Marcuse's analysis, "the quality of clownishness and childishness easily appears to adhere to authentic acts of protest in situations where the radical opposition is isolated and outrageously weak while the Enemy is almost everywhere and outrageously strong" (51). By this logic, any symbolic act of protest against the status quo is at a disadvantage to be received positively, precisely because it contradicts the ideological basis of the discursive framework within which the vast majority of people will interpret that act of resistance (Hall 1977). Indeed, one commenter on a *New York Times* blog article about anarchists' efforts to create visual spectacle at protest events described them as, "a bunch of 20-something children that think they understand the world, parading around so that all can see how wonderfully liberal they are. What we need are answers and solutions, not drama."[10]

Another problem of communication that anarchists face is that the aesthetic characteristics of their style may just as likely disgust observers as appeal to them, particularly where they violate established social norms. Dave Laing (1997), drawing on theories of avant-garde art, discusses this with respect to punk, pointing out that there may be a difficulty in communicating social criticism through radical aesthetic forms. Because the aesthetic expression is found to be distasteful, "the resistance of the audience to the music or other art-work makes it impossible for any meaning to be registered. The viewer or listener turns off" (414). This rings true with mainstream responses to anarchist style. The same commenter to the *New York Times* post quoted above said, "The costumes of some participants just confirm that their efforts are as meaningless as their message. Mardi Gras ended a few weeks ago." A freakish appearance may inspire confusion, dismissal, or distaste, rather than interest or acceptance. This is not to say that anarchists have some responsibility not to disgust people, but it should be no surprise if, having been disgusted, people are not very amenable to the underlying political message.

Marcuse (1972) also suggests that lifestyle practices that deviate from the mainstream may alienate those who (correctly) read them as a criticism of their own mainstream cultural mores. Whether anarchists intend to or not, they may give the impression that their rejection of norms is done to demonstrate their intellectual superiority to the masses who aren't sophisticated enough to have developed a political critique of mainstream popular culture. Consumption scholar Douglas Holt (2002) discusses this idea using the term "ideational difficulty," meaning that people may fetishize subcultural, ascetic lifestyles precisely because most people find them difficult to understand, access, and adopt. Here, mainstream lifestyles and popular culture are rejected not so much for their detrimental political effects, but more so on the basis that they *are* mainstream and popular. This is hardly likely to endear anarchists to those people who feel strongly attached to their own mainstream, popular cultural tastes. The challenge for anarchists is to produce a message through which people can accept a critique of mainstream culture without feeling that they themselves are being accused of willfully unethical behavior—or perhaps worse, unconsciously stupid behavior—through their adherence to some of its practices. Marcuse (1972: 79) argued in the 1970s that there was a "need for an effective *communication* of the indictment of the established reality and of the goals of liberation." The problems of communication experienced by anarchists indicate that it continues to be important to go beyond stylistic performance in order to provide a discursive context in which people can situate lifestyle practices *as* ethically motivated acts, and thus understand and perhaps empathize with why they are politically valuable.

Misinterpretation and dismissal are not the only unintended consequences incurred by anarchists' modes of self-presentation. Co-optation and commodification loom as nearly inevitable threats to spectacular subcultures. Because the ideological dissent represented by anarchists' style is oblique and often unregistered by observers, the style can quite easily be co-opted for purposes inimical to the movement that spawned it. Images and styles of rebellion are, in fact, often fetishized in the mainstream for their "edge" and other aesthetic characteristics. This is an issue that has consistently plagued radical movements in consumer society.[11] In her discussion of "commodity lesbianism" (the process by which images of lesbians are taken up as edgy fashions and sold to straight consumers), Danae Clark (1991: 193) makes the point that, "Because style is a cultural construction, it is easily appropriated, reconstructed and divested of its original political or subcultural signification. Style as resistance becomes commodifiable as chic when it leaves the political realm and enters the fashion world." Commercial entities have an interest in decoupling resistant style from resistant projects— the consumer base for the aesthetic forms of a movement is always far larger than the base of strict adherents to its oppositional ideologies.

People who are intrigued by the anarchist symbol far outnumber people who subscribe to anarchist political philosophy. Thus, commodification generally involves a conscious effort to drain away the political ideas that are signified by movement symbols while retaining the surface image, as in the example of a recent line of scented personal hygiene products with the word "anarchy" splashed across its labels and advertisements.[12] One can see from this example how commodification often necessarily involves the decoupling of the symbols of radicalism from its material practices— clearly, the marketers of these products do not wish to evoke the actual scent of anarchists' bodies, which often smell of unadulterated body odor in overt protest of the personal hygiene industry. One possible consequence of commodification is that the meanings of difference and non-conformity eventually no longer attach to the subcultural images at all, thus symbols that once marked an individual as an anarchist (to those in the know) no longer serve even that function. A second consequence is that commercial entities profit through the exploitation of groups whose voices continue to be unheard while their images are circulated at will. Insult is added to injury when the voice that is silenced is one that is explicitly ideologically opposed to the capitalist system itself, as in the case of anarchism.

Indeed, as anti-capitalists, many anarchists find it particularly offensive that commercial entities might profit from consumers' aesthetic attraction to anarchist style, thus integrating anarchist lifestyle practices into the capitalist system so as to strengthen the system itself. The style and symbols of anarchism are frequently used to appeal to youth consumers who may have a vague attraction to the rebelliousness it signifies, though they may not be familiar with the deeper ideological content of anarchist philosophy. Symbolic aspects of anarchist style have been co-opted by entities who do not necessarily share the core values of anarchism. Imagine, for example, circle-A t-shirts produced in a sweatshop and sold by a multinational corporation in a store that pays its workers minimum wage and quashes unionization. Think also of the dynamic discussed in Chapter 2, in which alternative dietary choices are folded into the marketing schemes of commercial entities and branded as hip. CrimethInc. succinctly expresses the dismay felt by anarchists when such processes occur: "Our rage against the machine is sold for the benefit of the machine! We're fucked!" (CrimethInc. 2000: 159).[13] This process is akin to what John Clarke (2005) calls the "defusion of style." Like a bomb squad disarming an incendiary device, aestheticization—often accompanied by commodification—is seen to render nascent forms of political resistance unthreatening to its targets. It does so by tricking consumers into believing—or by exploiting their existing belief—that the symbolic expression of dissatisfaction is equivalent to or directly causal of the material subversion of the forces they oppose. Resistance thus gets enacted through forms of consumption that are in fact profitable for those forces (or their corporate allies).

The ultimate strategic question for activists is whether style can function as a rhetorical tool that can be used to win support for anarchists' projects of social change. As a communicative performance, does subcultural style have the capacity to serve as propaganda that persuades outsiders as to the correctness of the subculture's underlying philosophy? As I've shown in the previous section, there are significant factors that work against such communicative potential, as far as anarchists' self-presentation is concerned. However, there are other functions served by the stylistic practices discussed in this chapter. Style makes visible forms of identity which would otherwise be unrepresented on the body. This can be useful for political subjects who wish to make their dissident identities known, for the purposes of self-construction and social bonding. At the same time, style can work to create aesthetic boundaries, as well as to reinforce social distinctions along lines that replicate existing structural hierarchies. The question for anarchists is ultimately what they hope to achieve through stylistic performance. As with any political tactic, style can be deployed strategically. The communicative ramifications of lifestyle, as discussed in this chapter, are some, among many, of the issues that must be taken into account in the full exploration of activist practice and movement strategy.

4

"You gotta check yourself": Lifestyle as a site of identification and discipline

I've been looking forward to my interview with Josef. He's a regular fixture in the Southern California anarchist scene—I've seen him around at events for years. He looks the part, with his black combat boots and keffiyeh wrapped around his neck. He's well connected, it seems like everyone I've interviewed in Los Angeles knows him. When we sit down to chat in February 2009, it's on the large porch of a communal house where the Downtown LA Food Not Bombs group prepares food every Sunday, to transport on bicycles to Skid Row, to feed the homeless there. We talk for a long time about his history in the punk and activist communities, and about what anarchism means to him. He speaks in exclamations and vivid language, at one point describing himself as an "anarchist Los Angeles pirate" because he chooses not to have a stable home and to navigate the city only on his bicycle. For Josef, as for many of the individuals I spoke with, anarchism is more than an abstract set of political philosophies; it provides direction for his behavior, and even his thoughts:

> As an anarchist I struggle for a better self. It's like I want my thoughts to be golden, I want my thoughts to be pure, like free of hate, full of love, you know, that as an anarchist ... I don't want to think patriarchy, I don't wanna think racism, I don't wanna think consumer[ism], you know, I wanna live autonomy.

Josef's use of the word "struggle" is telling: conscious effort is involved in keeping one's self and behavior in line with anarchist norms. Recall too Josef's imperative, as quoted in Chapter 2, "if you're an anarchist but you're like, gonna go eat at McDonalds, you gotta check yourself right there, you know?" The language Josef uses here alludes to the productive power of anarchist identity—the capacity for anarchist identity, as a discursive concept, to get subjects to think and act in ways other than they might have done, to "check" themselves and adjust their behavior if necessary. It also shows the difficulty of resisting the hegemonic systems that every individual, even an anarchist like Josef, is also implicated in: patriarchy, racism, consumerism, and so on.

There's a commonly expressed sentiment that a "real" anarchist behaves in particular ways. This might include "not pulling authoritarian shit," as Josef's friend Tina said. It also frequently includes lifestyle practices. For example, Josef bluntly told me, "I'm vegan because I think that's what real anarchists should be, you know." Orlando was another interviewee who had adopted many lifestyle practices that might be identifiable as anarchist—he biked everywhere, only wore second-hand clothing, and lived in a group house with other activists. He acknowledged to me that it was difficult, if not impossible, to live wholly according to anarchist principles, but that he was trying to become an "actual" anarchist despite the obstacles. I also heard the inverse of statements like this—individuals apologetically saying that because they drive a car or eat dairy, for example, that they aren't really anarchists. Miranda said that "I can't really consider myself a total anarcho-cyclist because in fact I have a car." Emily confessed, "I gotta admit, I'm a bad anarchist. I watch a lot of TV." I then asked her, "does that make you a bad anarchist, to watch TV?" She explained, "It does, it makes me a perfectly impure anarchist to be as addicted to television as I am."

One is quite clearly not "born" an anarchist. No, one must construct oneself as one, drawing on the symbolic tools available. Despite its constructed character, "anarchist" is a powerful identity around which many kinds of individuals can mobilize to become "collective agents of social change" (Castells 2003: 70). The subjectivity of a political radical may be shaped in part by a personal experience of oppression, but more crucially it involves interpretation of experience—one's own *or* that of others—which recognizes and strongly critiques an existing system of power. Because its political philosophy does not specify a "minoritarian subject"—a particular kind of person on whose behalf it claims to struggle (Warner 1993)—the "anarchist" would seem to be an identity open to all to adopt. In other words, they are explicitly united on the basis of shared ideas and goals instead of a pre-existing shared condition such as geographical location, class status, gender, or ethnicity (Gemie 1994; Curran 2007; Williams 2007). In this way, contemporary anarchism would seem to be "a politics of articulation," in which individuals who unite under the sign "anarchist" bring various investments and backgrounds to an activist community whose values and projects are continually contested, negotiated, and always in process (Hall 1993; Reed 2005: 127).

On the other hand, the identity "anarchist" may not be as open in reality as it is in the hypothetical. Identification with anarchism in the contemporary United States is often strongly associated with maleness, whiteness, straightness, and middle classness.[1] By not being connected to a *specific* experience of social oppression, anarchism perhaps disproportionately attracts those whose political critique is not grounded in their own personal experiences of oppression. This is not intrinsically undesirable—radical political causes need as many participants as they can get; however, one of the consequences is that forms of their own privilege to which individuals are not attuned may follow them into the activist spaces they form and join. The result may be that the movement feels as closed to "outsiders" as conventional identity-based movements do. And in the case of contemporary anarchism, the "outsiders" just may be people of color, women, queer people, and people who are poor or working class. The exclusion of such people is a problem for a movement committed to combating hierarchy and oppression.

How is lifestyle implicated in these questions of political identity and movement belongingness? Historically, radical political movements have cultivated particular pictures of the proper or normative activist subject; often, these pictures include certain lifestyle practices which are coded as political, such as diet, self-presentation, and so on.[2] These pictures serve to discipline participants' behaviors. Individuals internalize these pictures, drawing on them in disciplining themselves, both consciously and unconsciously. Furthermore, ideals of the proper activist lifestyle are, at times, used as grounds for boundary policing around the borders of the group: individuals are sometimes literally "called out" or ostracized when they are perceived as not upholding the ideals of the movement. In this way, even activist identities that are not tied to a minoritarian subject position evince some the features of "identity politics" associated with more conventionally identity-based social movements, including endless infighting about who has the right to claim membership in identity categories and who has the right to speak on behalf of the oppressed. As a result, identity can prove to be as troubling within anarchist movements as anywhere else. Identities and subcultural cultural norms can be productive, but also limiting, for political activists. In this chapter, I subject the idea of anarchist identification itself to scrutiny, in order to expose how it is achieved, how it is understood by individual activists, and what effects it has within their everyday lives.

In a way, anarchism is a frustrating case for thinking about identity and authenticity since one can't really *be* an anarchist all the way. Given that present conditions prevent any of us from stepping outside of hierarchical relations of power—both materially and ideologically—it's hard to say how one could genuinely and completely "live" anarchy. Indeed, this is a vexing problem for anarchist activists themselves, who sometimes evince anxiety about really living their beliefs, proving to themselves and others that they truly *are* anarchists. But that's what makes this a terrifically fruitful case to explore. Post-structuralists, suggest that all identities are, in fact, always fictions that are forever threatening to be undone, exposed as not being fixed or natural (Hall 1996b). And so, perhaps the ways anarchists cope with that fiction (i.e. turning to lifestyle practices in their attempts to authenticate identity) can shed light on why and how lifestyle and authenticity become significant for many contemporary subjects, not just radical activists.

Defining and performing anarchist identity

Few of the individuals I interviewed felt that the identity "anarchist" was straightforward to define. Like so many identity labels, "anarchist" is a floating signifier, in that it means different things to different people in different contexts. Yet, there must be some value in the label, since most of the individuals I interviewed used the word to describe their political identity, at one time or another.[3] When I asked interviewees to explain what anarchism meant to them, I got a variety of answers. An anarchist would seem to be someone who believes that anarchy—or a lack of hierarchy—is the ideal organizational relationship among social beings and institutions, and that collective cooperation can ensure individual well-being while preserving personal autonomy. But an individual's definition can also entail many nuanced facets. Take Emily's response when I asked if she had a working definition of anarchism:

> Well, what I like about anarchism and the way that I envision anarchism is that we sort of live in this big kind of constantly shifting power matrix and there's all different kinds of powers and all different kinds of oppressions. And what I think is good about anarchism is anarchism really looks at the way those structures and occurrences and all manifestations kind of interact with one another for the benefit of some and to the detriment of many many more. And so, um, the way that I look at anarchism is that it's a way of, like, you want to have the kind of economic equality that you would get from sort of a socialism, of course, but you want to have it through mutually cooperative groups of people coming together to solve through consensus their own community problems and issues and find collaborative means towards that kind of equality as opposed to having it be imposed by a government institution. And then also having also an understanding that, you know, economic equality isn't just the only thing, wanting to have respect and equality for people, for all races, genders, ethnicities, sexualities, and I think it's also about kind of having a love for that kind of diversity too . . . .

Emily's definition (which actually went on for several more minutes) is emblematic because of its complexity. For her, rejecting hierarchy involves very specific, intentional analyses and tactics, each of which must be enumerated to capture what anarchism means to her. Joel remarked that the number of positions with which anarchists may find themselves in solidarity means that "you can't have a political platform . . . and so that makes the term ambiguous." While Jeremy acknowledged that "there's certainly some semblance of a discernible, geographically-dispersed group of people who self-identity as anarchists," and he ventured to guess that "they all define anarchism as the interrogation and transformation of hierarchical social relations," he was in agreement with Joel that "there's not really a coherent ethical trajectory to be found, there; even where relatively consistent aesthetics can be located across geographies." Jeremy was quick to add that he didn't think this incoherence was "necessarily a bad thing" but he wondered if anarchism as an identity was really the most accurate way of describing the realities of anarchist communities and practices.

Why do some activists retain the label then? For many, the identity "anarchist" is not just a descriptor of abstract *principles* held—it is a predictive signifier that indicates the type of *behavior* a person can be expected to exhibit. As Matthew put it, "Anarchist . . . describes my attitude toward other people, what I want for them and for myself." Raychel explained that when she "actually learned what anarchism really was," she realized, "it wasn't just something that you call yourself to be rebellious and then just sit down and not do anything. I learned that, you know, anarchism was a lifestyle, it was changing things through the way that you lived alternatively to what, you know, what this society is." Tina also felt that a person's using the label anarchist for themselves would indicate something about the way they lived their lives. She said, "I like it when people call themselves anarchist," because she felt that meant she could trust them "not to pull, like, authoritarian, like, shit . . . . I feel like I don't have to have my guard up for someone's say[ing] things that are probably ignorant or authoritarian which happens a lot." In situations like the ones Tina alludes to, identification as an anarchist serves as a symbol that facilitates social interaction, in that it provides a set of expectations about how one will behave.

Joel said that his identity as an anarchist indicates the ideological principles he currently espouses *and* the material practices he *would like* to embrace. So, while Joel often explicitly identifies himself as an anarchist, he thinks of anarchism as something to be aspired to through his daily activity, rather than a fixed characteristic of himself or other individuals. Picking up on a performative understanding of identity, Joel felt that merely agreeing with "all the tenets of anarchism" was not enough to make him or anyone else an anarchist. He felt that, similarly to how within post-structuralist philosophy language is thought to construct the subject (a theory he referenced explicitly), "practice constructs the anarchist. And so, like, you become more anarchist, if you want to even call it that, or you become more of a political being who identifies as anarchist, legitimately anarchist, as you work in the frames that promote the ethics that anarchism entails."

"Identity work" is a concept sometimes used to refer to the self-reflexive project in which an individual seeks "to achieve congruence between their emergent social identity" and "their subjective sense of self" (Stein 1999). The ongoing practice of "checking oneself" (as Josef put it) in order to make sure that one's behaviors are in line with one's political beliefs is a kind of labor undertaken by the individual subject. In Foucaultian terms, this is the labor of self-care, calling on the subject to apply "attention, knowledge, and technique" to one's everyday activities (Foucault 1984a: 360). When individuals adopt a set of lifestyle practices, they don't just decide "how to act but who to be," as Anthony Giddens puts it (1991: 81). In a striking example of this, interviewee Emily told me that when she was younger and imagined the "kind of person that [she] wanted to be," she "kind of figured that the kind of person [she] wanted to be would be a vegetarian." She elaborated, "I guess I just sort of figured it went along with the lifestyle so I actually just started telling everybody that I was a vegetarian." Although Emily didn't yet identify as an anarchist at this time in her life, she was already shaping her lifestyle in such a way that it ended up being compatible with a typical narrative of anarchist self-identity. Not only did she adopt vegetarianism, but she also chose to avoid driving a car and embraced a non-conformist style of self-presentation. When she became acquainted with an anarchist community during college, it was a smooth transition to fit in with that scene based on the lifestyle narrative she had already constructed for herself.

Even seemingly innocuous settings such as potlucks or workshops can bring up occasions on which anarchist individuals are called upon, either implicitly or explicitly, to account for their identities and practices. I attended more than one event in which everyone in attendance was asked to introduce themselves and more or less offer an account of what anarchism meant to them. This usually involved everyone sitting in a circle, and going around the circle saying our names and briefly saying "why I'm an anarchist" or "what I find valuable about anarchism." Instances such as this are clear incitements to do what Butler (2005) calls "giving an account of oneself" as an anarchist-identified individual. For Butler, when one gives an account of oneself, one accomplishes three things: (1) one relates the content of one's life to another person; (2) one makes oneself into the kind of person who would give that account; and (3) one establishes a relationship between oneself and the others to whom one gives the account. This relationship is one of power, in which the one giving the account feels bound to do so in the face of the other's expectation. It may not be a power relationship in the sense of one person dominating another, but it is a form of animating power in that it motivates the subject to act and respond in particular ways that they might not do otherwise.

The answers given during these go-around-the-circle activities seemed to indicate the implicit pressure the participants felt to give a satisfactory performance of anarchist identity. People often named historical activists, movements, and theorists they identified with, and listed the current organizations and projects with which they were active. I myself felt anxiety on these occasions, as I attempted to formulate an introduction for myself that would satisfy the group and prove my legitimacy as an attendee. While my situation (as a researcher and a participant) may have been unique in that there were different stakes in my presence being accepted by the group, I do think that the feeling that the introduction was a compulsory "opportunity" to prove myself could have been a common one.

The lifestyle practices associated with authentic anarchist identity do not emerge in a vacuum; there are no pure, ideal expressions of anarchist political philosophy. Rather, what is deemed appropriate for anarchists to do in their everyday lives is entirely a product of context and culture. This poses a problem for the use of "anarchist" as a descriptive signifier of identity, since what constitutes an authentic performance of anarchist identity may vary across social contexts. As we will see in Chapter 5 for example, a practice like polyamory may be taken for granted as an element of anarchist lifestyle in one community, whereas in another, monogamy would be the default. Someone identifying as an anarchist in the first community would be expected to perform a commitment to polyamory, and not doing so would jeopardize one's claim to an authentic anarchist identity, whereas in the second this would be less of an issue. "Scripts" of identity are so complex that it may be impractical or impossible for any single individual to keep up an authentic performance of anarchist identity at every turn, with every action (Appiah 1996: 99). As sincere as one's own commitment to anarchy might be,[4] one might find oneself not measuring up to someone else's assumptions about what it means to be a real anarchist.

Despite people's seeming awareness that anarchist identity is hard to define, the social dynamics of anarchist scenes often operate as if sincerity can be readily observed through an individual's behaviors, including lifestyle practices. Lifestyle is seen to be a place where one demonstrates the degree to which one has sincerely disidentified with capitalism, patriarchy, and all the other oppressive systems that characterize mainstream culture. Sometimes this can mean that the more "normal" or "bourgeois" one's lifestyle is, the less sincere an anarchist one is taken to be. I'll give more concrete examples of this shortly.

Miranda, the one interviewee I spoke to who does not self-identify as an anarchist, observed, "I don't know anyone who identifies as an anarchist. It's a funny term because you feel like it's an impossibility . . . . You feel like there's a bar that's set really super high and you can never really be that so why even bother identifying yourself that way." In fact, identity labels may be particularly significant in contexts where one's beliefs are radically incompatible with the constraints of one's material situation. That is, under circumstances where anarchism is difficult to put into one's lifestyle practice, it may become even more important to call oneself an anarchist. In other words, the structural conditions of capitalist, statist, patriarchal culture work to prohibit the complete enactment of anarchist values, as much as one might wish to live like an "actual" anarchist (to quote Orlando, an interviewee). If you are simply unable to materially perform your anarchist beliefs, it may become all the more important to use symbolic representations—like identity labels—to communicate those beliefs.

Minty offered a defense for the usefulness of identity to convey ethical orientations, even if they don't fully correspond to material reality: "that's kind of like the funny thing about identity categories, they really don't capture who you are but right now they kind of are the only language that we have to speak to, like, our beliefs." We live in conditions that, for a variety of reasons, make it truly impossible to perform perfectly authentic anarchism. In such circumstances, sincerity has to stand in for authenticity; there is no other choice. This may explain why anarchists place such investments in lifestyle practices, since those are the indices of sincerity. The present impossibility of a truly anarchist society on a broad scale may account for individuals investing heavily in their microscopic everyday lifestyle practices, since it may only be in this limited capacity that they are able to achieve the realization of anarchist principles. When even this realization is difficult, symbolic representations of identity may come to the fore, above or alongside material enactments, as a way of demonstrating one's sincere commitment to the cause.

Disclaiming anarchist identity

People may just back off claiming the label of "anarchist" entirely, in part to avoid being called out for inauthenticity. Miranda—the one interviewee who emphatically rejected the label anarchist for herself—said "I'm probably ideologically like these people, but I like to shower." When I followed up by asking, "so you don't identify with anarchism?" She said, "I definitely identify with it but I would never consider myself an anarchist." While Miranda's affinity for anarchist philosophical principles may well be sincere, the fact that she adopts certain "bourgeois" lifestyle habits such as showering every day, owning a home, and having a legal marriage calls the extent of her commitment to anarchism into question, for herself, and potentially for others. In Miranda's case, the label comes to represent a division, based not on abstract political beliefs but on material performances of authenticity.

For some, this dualism is a needless "construction of boundaries around an anarchist identity [which] excludes people based on their status, rather than their (potential) political views" (Heckert 2004: 114). Anarchist scholar and activist Jamie Heckert does not like the idea that people may choose not to work together based on whether they identify as anarchists, rather than on the compatibility of their political projects. Uri Gordon also observes that "an explicit reference to anarchism might be seen as exclusive, one which does not admit many of the individuals and movements that activists cooperate with and with whom they have solidarity" (Gordon 2008: 40). Indeed, several interviewees expressed wariness about the potential for their identification as anarchists to alienate potential activist allies, particularly those who are unfamiliar with the discourse of anarchism or hold negative conceptions about it. To deal with this situation, several interviewees remarked that they would identify as an anarchist or not depending on whom they were talking with. For example, Pritha said that she calls herself an anarchist, but that she is less likely to do so when working with activists of color, like herself, who have historically felt unwelcome in anarchist movements (more on this issue below). Mark explained that when he was younger and less experienced with political organizing he had been "a lot more quick to . . . let people know, 'hey, I'm an anarchist,'" but he had since changed his approach:

> I don't find myself jumping to let them know that I'm an anarchist like right off the bat . . . . I think more[so] I try to . . . develop relationships, like have a practice, principles, and politics, and then at a point that it might be relevant, talk to people in specific terms about anarchism. But it's not like a first priority for me as far as organizing is concerned.

Alma also related that, in her experience with community organizations which were not explicitly anarchist-identified, "there was a fear of calling yourself an anarchist because then you would be alienated or sort of laughed at or something." Joel, too, said that in situations where he felt the term anarchist was likely to be misunderstood, it would be disadvantageous to identify himself that way. He said that he had observed people in his activist communities turning away from calling themselves anarchists because it can be seen as "affronting" or "combative" even to identify in this way. Especially since anarchist philosophy is commonly mischaracterized and misunderstood, there is a danger that the label could turn people away before they even had a chance to establish common political ground.

Even among themselves, anarchists may not know what their peers mean when they use the label to categorize themselves. Leo recognized that an "excess" of connotations meant that the signifier "anarchist" was associated with a multiplicity of signified meanings, saying "I don't even sometimes call myself an anarchist because it's such a, such an excessive word." In other words, different anarchists may define the identity label in many different ways, even though they use the same word to refer to themselves. There is always an inherent slippage between a representation and its intended material content, thus it is not always accurate to judge someone's commitments based on the label they use for themselves. As Branch put it, "whenever someone's labeled an anarchist you shouldn't just automatically assume their politics are agreeable." This separation between anarchist as identity label and anarchist as political philosophy is vexing for some. Sally was hesitant to identify herself as an anarchist because she didn't "know what in particular [she]'d be advocating" by categorizing herself that way. Others said that it was more important to look at people's material practices than the terms they used to identify themselves. As Jerome put it, "I don't care what people call themselves as long as they're doing good stuff in life that effects change."

Alyssa observed that the looseness of the identity means that there are "various sorts of people" whom she would recognize as anarchists but whose political theories and practices she doesn't particularly like. Aaron noted in an online chat, "the thing about anarchism is that it's a really big tent, b/c a central concept [of anarchism] is that there isn't one authority on what it is. Which is unfortunate, b/c it means some anarchists are literally almost so different as to be enemies. So in some ways, it means very little. For me." Emily took a similar view, saying, "There's probably so many people out there who identify as anarchists that I couldn't even have any hope of identifying [with]." She felt that,

> That's the joy and the curse of anarchism as a concept because you can almost define it in any way, along with a few basic tenets you can almost make it anything. I think that's really great but then it also can take something that is really, like, charged and sort of de-charge it, if the problem is everything, of, you know, I can see how people could be focusing on completely different things and thinking about the world in completely different ways.

The diversity of beliefs and practices that fall under the "big tent" of anarchism is probably also what accounts for the seemingly endless list of sub-identities within anarchism: there are anarcha-feminists, anarcho-communists, green anarchists, primitivist anarchists, and so on. Branch pointed out "there's so many different kinds of anarchism or concepts or takes on anarchism— the classics still get debated to this day—same with Marxism, same with socialism, communism, any isms. [And] um you know it depends if you're an anarcho-syndicalist, what era you're from, if you're theoretically-based. . . ." Tom noted, with bemusement, "it's really hard to define a word like anarchism because, like, so man, people have their own, like, 'Well, I'm a nihilistic anarchist,' or 'I'm an anarcho capitalist, anarcho-fascist, anarcho-anarchist.' You can just make up all this shit." These subdivisions of identity play out socially too: as Emily pointed out, even within the same geographical location, such as Phoenix where she was from, "there'll be whole different groups of anarchism that don't even interact . . . they could be working on totally different things or having totally different ideas." This was why Branch felt that "a large majority of today's activists don't have a definition" and why he "take[s] it differently at different times . . . . It's not a closed, defined thing as far as I'm concerned." One interviewee, Tom, expressed his belief that "all categories of identification . . . are kind of silly," but he also conceded, "I will identify as an anarchist if it's necessary for certain means." Tom was similar to many of the other individuals I interviewed, in that the degree to which they claimed and performed anarchist identity depended on the context in which they found themselves at any particular moment.

According to Stuart Hall (1996b), the absence of definitive claims about the content of identities is what may characterize effective political movements in postmodern society. Hall offers the notion of "arbitrary closure" to describe the way in which social groups temporarily accept particular meanings as defining themselves and motivating political actions. Because meaning is open to endless shift and contestation, individuals' self-definitions of identity and politics are contingent and "necessarily fictional" (Ibid.). This resonates with the way Branch conceptualized his identification with anarchism:

> It's a constant learning process that you develop over time, your living conditions change, your understanding of the world changes, and so for me I see anarchism as, like, an ongoing thing that grows with me and my understanding of it grows and my conception of how it should operate or what it means changes and grows.

A political identity constituted through everyday practice is inherently contingent; it is repetitively reconstituted through performance. The fact that it must be continually performed leaves room for the evolution of the performance as anarchist politics are discursively struggled over and thus transformed and tailored to specific times and locations. Political identities like anarchism can be seen as signs, which carry meaningful content but are still open to "play" (Butler 1993). Identity signs can be strategically deployed for the purposes of collective struggle, but the "signifiers" and "signifieds" of those identities do not have to remain fixed for all time (Butler 1997a; Spivak 1987). Though the interviewees quoted here recognize that the meaning of the identity anarchist shifts across individuals and contexts, they can unite under the sign when expedient.

However, some individuals may also be morally opposed to the very notion of anarchism as a unitary identity, even for strategic purposes. As anarchist anthropologist David Graeber (2002: 62) succinctly puts it, "there are some who take anarchist principles of anti-sectarianism and open-endedness so seriously that they are sometimes reluctant to call themselves 'anarchists' for that very reason." In this view, even to identify as an anarchist is to contradict anarchist philosophy. Tom seemed to agree with this, "Like to me, words are bullshit. . . words could be used as like a box to define your identity and a lot of people do that and that's what makes me sad, like, in a lot of the anarchist scenes I've been a part of you always get the people that are like kind of scared to just let themselves actually be free . . . ." Miranda extended this skepticism of identity to other forms of self-representation: "I don't like the idea of anarchism in terms of uniform, in terms of, like, you have to be a certain way and, like 'this is cool' and 'this is not cool.' It's like, I thought this was all supposed to be about blowing up these ideas of what's cool, like even when I went to the anarchist book fair in LA it's like, ok, there's uniforms [because everyone was dressed alike]. Like what kind of anarchists are you, you know?" She felt that the uniformity of appearance among anarchists at this particular event exposed a misunderstanding of anarchist philosophy among the participants. Opinions like Miranda and Tom's are ultimately at odds with the notion of there being an "authentic" anarchist identity. Yet, dressing in a particular way, along with the adoption of other lifestyle habits, may be important for expressing the sincerity of one's identification with a defined community. Without drawing on performative markers of political identity, those who wish to communicate to others that they are committed to the principles of anarchy may find themselves in a tough spot.

Social identities, discipline, and accountability

As implied by the examples given above, identity performances are constituted socially rather than purely individually. To say that you identify as something is to recognize that this something exists in a larger discursive sense that is available to others as well (Spivak 1997). The labor of self-care may be experienced as the effort of an individual subject, but it always involves others who serve as witnesses, interlocutors, and supporters. This network of others is both real—in that one may attend events where one comes face to face with others who ask one to account for oneself—and imagined, as when the discourse of "authentic anarchism" is activated in the mind of the individual. Josef's struggle for "a better self," one that resists patriarchy, racism, and consumerism, is a prime example of the power of normative discourse to bring ethical practices and subjects into being. The identity "anarchist" has disciplinary power, in that individuals who claim the label are subject to the norms associated with it; they feel compelled to take personal responsibility for conducting themselves in a way that will be deemed appropriate. In Foucault's model of disciplinary power, the subjectifying capacity of discourse works precisely through getting individuals to take personal responsibility for their own conduct; subjection is recognizing the ethically correct thing to do and attempting to do it (Foucault 1990b: 92). The anarchist-identified subject is created and recreated in the moments of ethical discipline along the imagined journey to "a better self."

The capacity of radical movement discourses to win allegiance and direct individual behavior can be understood through Stuart Hall's (1996a, 1996b) reading and reworking of both Foucault's theory of subjection and Louis Althusser's (2006) theory of interpellation. Hall offers an analysis that can incorporate the active investment in oppositional ideologies by resistant subjects. Hall argues that the "suturing of the subject to a subject-position" is a two-sided process, involving not only the hailing of the subject by discourse but also the recognition by the subject of a shared ideal in common between themselves and the content of the discourse (Hall 1996b: 6, 2). In line with Antonio Gramsci's understanding of hegemony as being built on "the consent of the governed" through the appeal of "common sense," Hall believes that identification, solidarity, and allegiance are established on the foundation of a felt affinity between subject and discourse (Hall 1996a, 1996b). Radical movements can thus constitute their own hegemonic spheres, in which subjects come to identify themselves with a particular resistant political ideology (such as anarchism). As Jorge Larrain (1996: 49) puts it, "individuals are not necessarily recruited and constituted as subjects obedient to the ruling class, the same mechanism of interpellation operates when individuals are recruited by revolutionary ideologies." Historian Michael Denning (1997: 63) argues that the culture of radical movements constitutes an "alternative hegemony," through which "political sentiments and opinions are transformed into ways of living and ways of seeing."

The "ethically correct" behaviors set forth by cultural discourses of anarchist identity—what anarchists have collectively decided on as the markers of authentic anarchism—will become necessary for the subject to adopt, in order to make oneself recognizable as an anarchist. Examples of these behaviors include: having a vegan diet, getting around by bicycle, resisting mainstream norms of hygiene and self-presentation, and being sexually non-monogamous, just to name a few. Individuals may well feel as if they are making autonomous choices in how to behave—but the way lifestyle gets communicated about within anarchist movements also works to produce regular patterns of behavior. Participants in movement cultures may even take pleasure in the practices through which they constitute themselves as authentic members. Rather than feeling as if their natural desires have been constrained or violated by the group, they are in relationships of "consensual discipline," not domination (Foucault 1984b: 380).

Discourses that circulate within and across anarchist movements—in the form of written documents, formal presentations, and informal conversations—establish what is accepted as "normal" behavior for individuals who identify as anarchists (Foucault 1990a; Haenfler 2006: 197). Norms may not be explicitly stated: they work by recommending themselves as natural and reflective of a desirable state of affairs. Certain confluences of disciplinary power work to produce a coherent, *resistant* subject, one who consciously and consistently positions oneself against dominant institutions such as the state and conducts one's behavior accordingly.[5] Within political movements, norms can often be justified on the basis that they are expedient for the goals of the movement (though the nature of a norm is that it may never actually require justification). One might "optimize" one's lifestyle so as to be most "useful" to an activist project.[6] Behavior according to movement norms may even be seen as being ethically mandated. By conforming to these group norms, or "ethical repertoires" (Rose 1999: 265), on an everyday basis, individuals win acceptance within the community. Failing to adhere to norms, however, can bring shame upon the individual, and even draw explicit rebuke from their peers. If an individual commits a large enough transgression of movement norms, they face social ostracism and may even be formally banned from participating in political organizing activities.

Aaron spoke of this in terms of "accountable community," saying that living and organizing closely with other anarchists works to bolster one's adherence to shared lifestyle practices:

> You literally live with other people who call themselves anarchists, who have a similar frugal punk-y lifestyle, and you put a lot of time into creative projects, and into discussions about what it means to live out your politics, etc. You're in close proximity, and if anybody suddenly stops being vegan it's a big deal. And I think the same is true as far as political identity. It's easier to maintain a very abstract identity like 'anarchist' when you have other people to orient yourself around, other compass points.

In Aaron's experience, it's not just a matter of having other people present "to orient yourself around" although this is part of it. It's also about people actively holding others in their community "accountable," expecting one's peers to answer for their personal practices, even in such matters as diet. One anarchist will often tell another when they witness them do or say something that they deem to be inconsistent with anarchist ethical principles; this is known colloquially as "calling someone out." The ostensible purpose of this is to raise consciousness among one's fellow anarchists and to encourage each other to stay committed to their shared political project.

Revbaker, in describing his experience with the anarchist scene in Denver, said that, "Political correctness was followed to a T. If you dared express any characteristics of 'dominant' culture through actions or words, it would be quickly pointed out." Even if an individual never personally experiences being called out, the expectations for normative anarchist behavior work to incite such behavior before the fact of any direct communicative exchange about it. After enough time and exposure to the social norms of anarchists, habits are reified to the point where they become naturalized ways of life for the individuals who claim identification with anarchism. The anarchist lifestyle or "habitus" (Bourdieu 1984) eventually appears to be second nature to those who have adopted it. The extensive discipline involved fades from notice for those who most easily pull off the performance, though newcomers, outsiders, and people who are less readily able to adopt the accepted lifestyle practices may be more cognizant of the substantial effort that goes into fulfilling the standards of authentic anarchist identity.

Alternative communities of activists can feel like "home" for those who are accustomed to and experience a desire for alternative ways of life. Emily felt that the anarchist scene was a place that welcomed her and made it possible for her to sustain her identity and lifestyle in communion with others:

> I think that a lot of the anarchist cultures that exist are almost like support cultures. They're great social networks, they're great for feeling like you have a place in the world and it can help to alleviate some of that kind of pain that comes with being an anarchist, and frustration.

Branch articulated a similar feeling:

> It's always like anything, it's harder when you're on your own; as soon as you start finding like-minded people or a community it becomes a support base . . . and mak[es] it feel maybe like a bit more of a norm when you're surrounded by a culture that says it's not the norm—that's always incredibly helpful.

There are clear parallels here to Chandra Mohanty's (2003) discussion of the "politics of struggle." In the politics of struggle, individuals unite with others on the basis of common ideologies and goals, without making claims to any essential traits or even shared experiences. In political struggle, individuals may find an epistemic and emotional "home," which Mohanty explains is "home, not as a comfortable, stable, inherited, and familiar space but instead as an imaginative, politically charged space in which the familiarity and sense of affection and commitment lay in shared collective analysis of social injustice, as well as a vision of radical transformation" (128). In Mohanty's view, solidarity and shared struggle need not come from shared identity. However, it is the case that anarchism is a sign that invites identification from many individuals, who then act and form community in its name. Branch and Emily's comments speak to the particular importance of community support within movements whose ideals and practices are marginal within society at large. Opportunities for collective enactment of anarchist lifestyles are especially important for the production of radical subcultural identities because of the lack of validation by the narrative resources available in mainstream popular culture. With other anarchists around, one is reminded that one's lifestyle choices are envisioned as part of a shared political struggle. The anarchist lifestyle thus connects one to a collective activist identity that is reiteratively constituted on a daily basis. When the efforts and pressure of living like a real anarchist are noticed at all, they may seem like a small price to pay for membership in an idealistic community of activists.

Policing the boundaries of anarchist identity

The notion of authenticity is often marshaled as the premise upon which anarchists actively call each other to account for their lifestyle practices. At times, it seems to matter less what the practices are and what material outcome they may have in a given particular situation, than it does that those practices have been symbolically equated with "real" anarchism. Jeremy described this as "a current toward indulging the widely-held truisms of the 'anarchist community,' usually eschewing evidence or critical examination altogether, in favor of policing a particular ideological or aesthetic line." In other words, while people could be called out because their actions can be shown to have a detrimental impact upon others, they are called out for not doing what "real" anarchists do. One of the problems introduced by this, which I will discuss more below, is that there may be competing ideas about what real anarchists do. Without a critical interrogation of what defines "real" anarchism, and why any given definition is ideologically and strategically sound, holding people accountable can easily be mistaken for (or actually devolve into) self-righteous moralism and arbitrary boundary policing.

For indications of some of the specific operations of normative, disciplinary power among anarchists, take for example the way interviewees spoke of the standards of dress they had encountered in anarchist communities. Matthew, in describing the "anarchist suit" he wore at one time said, "All the clothes had to be very faded and dirty and gross and vaguely militaristic." His wording here is crucial—it was not that his aesthetic style just happened to match a uniform look adopted by others in his community—his feeling was that his clothing "had to" conform to a particular style. Joel used a similar turn of phrase in describing the pressure he felt to look a certain way among members of his local Food Not Bombs group in Washington, DC. As he put it, "you always had to kind of signify yourself in a way that was appropriate . . . you had to kind of follow the norms." He went on to explain, "you couldn't fit in [with the mainstream]—you couldn't wear like a button shirt. Not that you couldn't, but people didn't." His final comment is important;

people didn't necessarily feel directly *prohibited* from dressing in certain ways, but the outcome of the social norms was that they *didn't* dress in those ways. By getting called out oneself, or even just witnessing others get called out or refused entry into the community on the basis of performances like these (a phenomenon I will discuss more below), individuals learn which lifestyle practices are accepted as authentically anarchist and which are likely to call into question their identification as an anarchist. While occasions on which one is called to perform or narrativize self-identity may be seen by some as positive opportunities for self-fashioning, social discourses of normativity also create a context in which one is always at risk of being judged and rejected when one's performances fail to measure up to cultural norms.

Recall Emily's comment that the amount of television she watched made her an "impure" anarchist in the eyes of others. When I asked if people called her out on her taste for television, she said, "People look a little weird when I say how much TV I watch." I don't think Emily genuinely believed that she was unethical or a "bad anarchist" despite those being the words she used; she was just extremely conscious of the fact that she could be perceived as such by others in her circles. Emily explained it in the following terms:

> I think anarchists, there is sort of like . . . there's a judgment about how you live your lifestyle, like what you consume, how you consume, how you interact with media, what your, you know, to a much lesser extent what your sexual practices are, what kind of music you listen to.

Similarly, when Revbaker talked about the enforcement of political correctness within the anarchist scene, he observed that the movement could seem "closed off, cliquey, dogmatic or even elitist—at least it was to a wide-eyed, naive and socially awkward 19 year old" like himself. Mark, too, noticed what he called a "sectarian attitude" among anarchists he'd tried to organize with, "like this notion of, like, what we're trying to do is the authentic [anarchism] and what other anarchists are doing is like a waste of time or something."

Although Mark was speaking in terms of organizing tactics, this attitude can also extend to lifestyle "tactics" as well. Alyssa perceived that some of the anarchists she knew in Santa Cruz held the attitude that they were "better than other people" due to their adoption of certain lifestyle habits, such as, "being vegan/being freegan; living in the woods; having a 'purer' form of anarchism than anyone with a job; riding bikes." Miles too described becoming disillusioned with some people's "holier-than-thouism against other anarchists." Such dynamics are cause for concern for some anarchists, who are frustrated by what they perceive to be "an arms race to the bottom of who can be more radical, and who can 'out' other 'anarchists' as not really living up to their principles" ("Anarchism and Decadence" 2008).

When I asked Aaron what he thought it meant to identify as an anarchist, he replied fliply, "to unnecessarily subject yourself to a lot of judgment."[7]

The judgment of people's political sincerity based on how closely their expressed tastes match an accepted image of authentic anarchist identity can have real consequences for who is welcomed in the movement and who is actively excluded. Rilla recalled the experience of a woman she had met while doing labor organizing in Los Angeles, who came from a wealthy family and dressed "preppy" ("she actually tied her sweater around her shoulders and stuff") but became politicized through her work with the labor union. When the woman moved to Philadelphia, Rilla put her in contact with some anarchists she knew there, but when the woman tried to attend one of their organizing meetings, Rilla had heard that they "wouldn't let her in and said that they thought she was like a cop or something. The group wouldn't let her join and turned her away at the door." The preppy woman's taste and appearance signaled that she didn't truly belong, and thus that she must have had an ulterior, inauthentic motive for wanting to get involved in anarchist organizing. Given that radical organizations are regularly targeted and infiltrated by law enforcement personnel, it's not entirely irrational to be suspicious of those who don't signal their belonging through the common signifiers of anarchist identity. Although the way someone is dressed may seem like a superficial basis for assessing their legitimacy, it can be a giveaway that someone doesn't even know enough about the scene to realize that they will mark themselves as not belonging by dressing in particular ways. Dressing "like an anarchist," with all the subtle stylistic cues that might involve, can communicate that one has spent a significant enough amount of time in the scene to cultivate what Pierre Bourdieu (1984: 66) calls "competence" through "slow familiarization," and thus has proven their commitment to its political project through this sustained involvement.

It is possible that someone could be in solidarity with anarchist politics and have valuable contributions to make without being aware of or wanting to adopt the particular tastes of anarchist subcultures. Matthew, via email, related his experience of trying to get involved with anarchist organizing in Philadelphia while he was attending graduate school there: "The Philly anarchists were suspicious of me because I was a graduate student at Penn. They said I was 'bourgeois.' One said I could 'work with them' but that I couldn't 'BE one of them' (!!)." Even though Matthew had spent several years in the anarchist scene in Chicago and could presumably establish his credibility as an experienced political organizer, his choice (and ability) to pursue graduate education at a prestigious private university jeopardized his perceived legitimacy as a true anarchist. Minty also said that she had gotten "shit" from some anarchists about her job at a non-profit organization, which often involves her working with state agencies and on electoral campaigns. She said that people had called her a "professional activist," and a "tool" of the system for doing paid work of this nature. Anarchists often position themselves in opposition to "liberals," "reformists," and other political orientations which are seen as less radical. To partake in lifestyle practices—like going to graduate school or holding a job in the non-profit sector—which are seen as "bourgeois" may signify (accurately or not) that a person's beliefs more closely align them with such undesirables than with authentic anarchists.

It is important to point out here that sectarian divisions are not seen as arbitrary or petty or unnecessary by those who attempt to enforce them. On the contrary, they are understood as real and meaningful differences in political philosophy and goals. This is why sectarian divisions are generally positioned as having moral justifications, or as being about political "correctness." There is an implicit assumption that the level of an individual's sincerity of commitment to anarchist politics can be rather straightforwardly read in one's personal habits. An attribution made in passing by a participant in a discussion session at a conference I attended was quite telling on this point—a woman was posing a question to a roomful of people about how they, as anarchists, could productively work with "people who don't share our values." She used the term "SUV drivers" as shorthand for the people who don't share anarchists' values; the implication was that driving an SUV is antithetical to anarchist ethics and detrimental to anarchist projects, and thus this speaker assumed a shared perception that anyone who drives an SUV does not hold anarchist values. It could be that all anarchists truly find SUVs to be ethically objectionable, or that all anarchists realize that if they want to be accepted as a true anarchist they had better not be seen driving an SUV. Either way, it clearly made sense to the woman speaking to assume that SUV ownership is not likely to correlate with aspirations to anarchist identification.

But another participant in the discussion pressed the point, responding to the first comment, asking whether SUV drivers do not "share our values" or do they just "live a lifestyle that we don't think of as *expressing* our values?" Along these lines, one blog post argues that anarchists ought to "take revolution seriously and realize that people who take to the streets are our allies, even if they wear nike shoes, eat meat, and drive SUVs" ("Anarchism and Decadence" 2008). Certainly, people may share political philosophies while their personal ethics play out differently in their tastes and lifestyles. There is a tension to be worked through here, between the need for anarchists to be able to recognize and connect with each other through performances of identity, and the desire not to fetishize lifestyle practices to the point that they are reified as the only legitimate manifestation of anarchist sincerity.

The fact that anarchist is fundamentally a constructed identity could be a point of possibility for activist communities. The borders of the community are endlessly permeable, since what anarchism is can grow and change with the conditions and problems at hand. That there is no final definition of what it is to be a true anarchist allows for productive fluidity, which might respond to situational specificity in the deployment of lifestyle-based tactics and the enforcement of lifestyle norms among claimants to community membership. If the contextually specific character of all anarchist lifestyle practices could be more fully exposed and embraced, there might be less of a tendency among anarchists to enforce particular tastes and habits as the be-all and end-all of authentic anarchism. The fact remains though that the many contextual factors that enter into an individual's performance of anarchist identity are often invisible, particularly to those whose structural privilege enables them to easily adopt the accepted trappings of anarchist authenticity. Despite the lack of "necessary or essential correspondence" (Hall 1996b) of anarchist identity and ethics with other identity categories such as age, gender, or race, it is the case that actually existing constructions of anarchist authenticity may favor, or at least be perceived to favor, some subjects over others. The question to ask in any particular context is, do the lifestyle practices most strongly associated with authentic anarchist identity inherently exclude certain types of individuals from achieving a convincing claim to anarchist identity? The next section addresses this question, and in the process offers a sociological explanation for why anarchism has earned a reputation for being a movement of the privileged.

Lifestyle and the re-centering of privileged subjects

Anarchist *philosophy* does not favor the structurally privileged; in fact, it aims to dismantle structures of power and privilege. Yet, a major external (and internal) critique of contemporary anarchist movements is that they are homogeneous and unwelcoming to the marginalized subjects they claim to best serve. Lifestyle politics may contribute to the conditions that this critique responds to. Lifestyle practices, especially consumption habits, are widely perceived as being open to personal choice. This perception is aided by the mythologies of neoliberalism that posit a completely autonomous subject unconstrained by discrimination and acting purely in the interest of creatively cultivating a desired narrative of the self. Under this assumption, it may seem quite logical to judge the sincerity of a person's anarchist politics by looking at one's lifestyle choices. For instance, to some extent, the woman who made the comment about SUV drivers was not completely out of line; in my observation, anarchists do not tend to drive SUVs. Yet, is it possible that there are anarchists who *do* drive SUVs, but go unrecognized as anarchists due to the assumption that an authentic anarchist *wouldn't* drive an SUV? Furthermore, might SUV drivers be more easily viewed as potential allies in activism if it was not assumed ahead of time that they could not possibly have a sincere investment in anarchist principles?

The decision to not drive an SUV is a fairly autonomous one—there is little in the way of an economic barrier or cultural bias to prevent someone from choosing to live a non-SUV-driving lifestyle. Insofar as "not driving an SUV" is a mark of authentic anarchism, it's a lifestyle choice available to pretty much anyone. But let's take another typical lifestyle practice that is used as a mark of authenticity, one that is commonly debated in anarchist communities for precisely the reasons I'm concerned with here: veganism. Does the fact that veganism is strongly associated with anarchist lifestyles make the anarchist community always already unwelcoming to people from particular cultural backgrounds in which meat is central to the cuisine? For example, there is a commonly voiced assumption that people of color are less likely to find veganism appealing as a lifestyle practice (this is not to say that such an assumption is empirically validated, but it's one that comes up often). If veganism is used as a measure of someone's sincerity and authenticity as an anarchist, are non-vegans then marginalized within anarchist movements? And *if* people of color are unlikely to be vegans and vegans are more valued as members of anarchist movements, then are people of color less likely to be valued as anarchists? We could substitute any lifestyle practice for "veganism" here, asking whether the regular practices of anarchism are more or less accessible to people of different races, ethnicities, genders, ages, class backgrounds, disability statuses, etc. Bicycling as a preferred mode of transportation, for example, excludes people with certain disabilities from performing that expression of anarchist sincerity.

An intersectional analysis that considers anarchist lifestyle practices in light of other categories of identity can help to assess the regular ways in which the normativity of anarchist subcultures exerts its disciplinary force on different kinds of subjects. It can also help to show why many critics of lifestyle anarchism assert that the accessibility and appeal of some anarchist lifestyle practices is disproportionately skewed toward young, white, middle-class males. I argue that this perception grows out of the fact that some of the practices that are most recognized as authentic or legitimate expressions of anarchist identity may also be perceived as being most accessible to those coming from the most privileged social positions. In other words, the lines of exclusion around anarchist identity often, in fact, mirror mainstream patterns of social division and domination. There is a fear that this cultivates homogeneity within anarchist movements, which limits the scope of both its analysis and its reach.

In Bourdieu's (1984) study of lifestyle and taste, he showed that distinction tends to break down along lines of class status and educational background: the most cultural capital accrues to those from affluent backgrounds and who have had advanced education. Thus, social privilege begets further social privilege when certain choices are made, and hierarchical social divisions are reinforced. The subcultural capital associated with certain anarchist lifestyle practices can work in a similar way. Some subcultural lifestyle practices— and by extension the winning of subcultural capital associated with them— are more practicable for some participants than others (Carrington and Wilson 2004). Being that authentic anarchist identity is constituted through some of these practices, this has consequences for who is most likely to be recognized (including *by themselves*) as *being* an authentic anarchist. Individuals with certain forms of privilege in mainstream society may be best equipped to conform to some of the norms of anarchist culture as well. Emily, who is white and in her twenties, observed that anarchists' awarding of cultural capital to certain lifestyle practices could work to exclude many potential allies:

> It limits anarchism and what is considered legitimate within some anarchist circles, to this one mold of being like a hippie vegan. Like, people don't buy new clothes, people don't watch TV, that stuff isn't, most people in society aren't necessarily like that, and I don't think it's, like, the best means of, like, attracting people that aren't already in that kind of subculture you know . . . . I think a lot of ways anarchists present themselves is not necessarily positive in terms of having a diverse anarchism, and I think a lot of the lifestyle constraints are sort of, can be kind of exclusionary.

Though Emily admitted to sharing many of the stereotypical lifestyle practices of anarchists, such as being vegetarian and not owning a car, she reflected, "you're not necessarily inclusive of all communities if you're this strict on what your affectations are." Like all forms of disciplinarity, anarchist norms are repressive as well as productive, and may be particularly so at different times for different people. Norms that are productive and empowering for some people may prove unduly restrictive for others (Butler 2004a: 8). When I asked Aaron, a white man in his twenties, if he felt there was a community of people who would identify themselves as anarchists, he speculated that "I think if you did a survey, the folks who respond 'yes' without caveats to that question are younger, middle class, white men." Note that Aaron was not making a claim about the anarchist community actually being comprised only of younger, middle-class white men; rather he was pointing out that such individuals would be the most likely to unreflexively or unproblematically use the term anarchist to refer to themselves and the political communities of which they count themselves a part.

Interviewees like Aaron also felt that anarchist identity could be problematic in that people may "hide behind" the label "anarchist" in order to avoid the "stickier work" of actively confronting their own role in perpetuating systems of oppression, such as patriarchy, white supremacy, and class hierarchy. This dynamic works to obscure real structural inequalities that are carried over from mainstream culture into anarchist subcultures. When white men who identify as anarchists hold their own lifestyle practices as the ideal expression of anarchist sincerity, and don't have a critical analysis that recognizes the privileges they bring to their implementation of anarchist lifestyle practices, they (perhaps unwittingly) perpetuate subcultural norms that make others feel excluded. This creates a vicious cycle in which already marginal subjects, particularly women and people of color, feel both unprepared to adopt anarchist lifestyle practices and disinclined to see the appeal of doing so. The response to this lack of participation by marginal subjects is often "how can we get more women and people of color involved in our activist community?" rather than, "what about the subcultural norms of our community may be failing to appeal to women and people of color?" and "are our norms worth rethinking?"

As with many other subcultures, age is a central factor affecting the nature of individuals' participation in anarchist lifestyles practices. Many of the older (over age 30) people I interviewed had at one time engaged in the typical anarchist lifestyle practices but had since abandoned them. One reason for this is simple burn out—years of living under certain conditions can take their physical and emotional toll. Lifestyles characterized by extreme precarity, such as squatting, traveling, dumpstering, and shoplifting, may prove unsustainable in the long term, particularly when more stable options are available. Also, the tightness of anarchist communities, which may involve living in close-quarters in group houses, and sometimes distancing oneself from one's non-anarchist family and community, can take an emotional toll after years of living that way. The departure of older people from the scene ends up being self-reinforcing. Although Jeremy cited several reasons why he had distanced himself from anarchist communities, based on carefully considered ideological and strategic concerns, he also added, "it often feels creepy being the only person over 30 in the room."

Several interviewees expressed frustration with what Minty called the "fucked up misogynist ideas and practices" that result in women feeling silenced and therefore unwelcome within anarchist scenes. Mark traced the "posturing" that goes on within anarchist communities (both at events and in online forums) to a "certain kind of macho, like, way of relating to politics" which he said was characterized by "shooting everything else down and then propping yourself up." Tina noted that women feel hesitant to speak at meetings or to take on leadership roles in the movement because they are insecure about "sound[ing] smart enough" or being accepted as a "really true anarchist." Adam Tinnell (2008) notes that this dynamic is due to "a big problem with the way radical men conceptualize their masculinity," implying that what many men see as an ideal performance of anarchist identity is troublingly characterized by behaviors that may be alienating to women. Leo pointed out that women are not the only ones alienated by these performances; he observed that expressions of "machismo" in activist communities also work against men who aren't comfortable with a stereotypically masculine gender performance for themselves.

Manarchism is a term used within anarchist circles to identify the tendency for some individuals and scenes to make women feel marginalized or excluded. So-called manarchists are not necessarily intentional in their marginalization of women, but rather they perpetuate sexist dynamics through their failure to examine and challenge their own male privilege. Minty said that some women still feel that they are treated like "accessories" to men within activist communities. The imposition of this role is reinforced by their fellow activists hitting on them or holding them to dominant beauty standards—reminding women that despite their radical activist identities, they can still be implicated in patriarchal gender dynamics. Pritha explained manarchism to me this way:

> I guess what I meant by 'manarchist' (and the context in which we use it here in DC) is men who claim to have radical politics but when it comes to interpersonal relationships, are often patriarchal and heavily assert their male privilege. You know when you're in a meeting for an anarchist org[anization], and there's that one guy who dominates the conversation, never lets anyone (much less a woman) get her say nor does he listen— he's a manarchist. Full of dude-liness that he never bothered to unpack though he thought he did.

Manarchism may perpetuate male privilege in multiple ways. One is by valorizing lifestyle practices that are, for whatever reason, more appealing or practicable by men than by women. Aggressive styles of dress and sexual promiscuity are typical anarchist lifestyle practices that may carry graver consequences for women than men. It's not that men are essentially more able to dress aggressively or engage in polyamorous relationships, but there are real social factors that might disproportionately deter women from these practices.

Another way manarchists perpetuate their privilege is by failing to acknowledge women's participation in subcultural lifestyle practices, often because these men assume that women are less knowledgeable or skilled than men are in particular areas. For example, Sally, an experienced cyclist, expressed frustration with male friends who assumed that she wouldn't know how to repair her bicycle or that she would be uncomfortable riding on busy streets. Though she herself had never let this frustration deter her from cycling, she wondered if it had affected other women in the scene. Tinnell (2009) expresses a similar frustration with the bike culture in Denver, lamenting that "there is nothing radical about the way bike culture is performed right now," since "everywhere you look, women are either being objectified to sell some bike event or product or are being put down through misogynistic language or posturing." Tinnell goes on to observe that within this scene which is supposedly aligned with a radical political critique of mainstream culture, "all of a sudden it is okay to reenact the type of dominant patriarchal culture that you might find in [a] frat house."

Rilla described a conflict within an anarchist collective house she had lived in, in which a male resident was upset about one of the female roommate's public displays of affection with other women on the front porch and her occupation as a sex worker. He argued that she should be kicked out of the collective house due to her not being enough of an activist. The woman was, in fact, part of a sex worker's union, and thus was involved in her own form of activism, though it may not have taken a form preferred by the male resident. Rilla suspected that his discomfort stemmed more from her wardrobe and sexuality than her activist credentials. The discomfort experienced by the male resident—which mirrored mainstream attitudes toward women's sexuality—was expressed by minimizing the female resident's activist practice as less authentic and thus she was portrayed as less deserving of membership in the anarchist community.

The demands of family may also disproportionately affect the capacities of certain people, especially women, to devote time to anarchist projects and leisure activities. During a discussion at an anarcha-feminist picnic I attended, one woman said that it was hard for her to get away from home to attend such social gatherings unless her husband was available to watch their child. Alma, who does not have children but lives in close proximity to her parents and grandparents, said that she feels the stresses of trying to live up to the demands of organizing and activism while looking after her family's needs. Compounding her feeling of responsibility to her family was the fact that they are all immigrants from Mexico who rely on her to help them navigate life in the United States. Alma expressed a bit of resentment toward fellow activists who are more easily able to conform to the "more than human" norms of political organization cultures:

> You're always expected to produce to a certain degree, to a certain level, and I think it's irrational to try to push people to be more than human and of course if you don't live up to that expectation then you're lazy or you're a flake and it's like no. Like I mean some people might detach entirely from their families, I know plenty of student organizers at UCLA whose parents live in New York City and they don't have to get called by their grandma to like, translate [between Spanish and English].

Alma recognized that her position as a woman and an immigrant put her at a disadvantage for proving her commitment, compared to others who may not have to balance the demands of family with their activist identities. These are just a few examples to illustrate how privileges in the mainstream are carried through to anarchist subcultures—there is no shortage of similar incidents to be found in nearly every activist community.

Anarcha-feminists have struggled to bring these gendered dynamics to the attention of their comrades, and indeed many organizations have tried to actively address conditions which marginalize women in the scene. For example, the Bicycle Kitchen in Los Angeles has devoted one evening a week to a woman/trans-only night in its workshop, in order to provide an environment where women won't feel intimidated to learn about bicycle repair. By helping women to build skills and gain confidence in this setting, the Bike Kitchen may alleviate some of the apprehension that women feel about getting involved in the often male-dominated anarcho-cyclist community. An anarcha-feminist organization that Tina, Minty, and other interviewees were involved with, has made it a priority to create a welcoming atmosphere for people with children in the Southern California anarchist community. For example, they spearheaded an effort to organize free childcare at the Southern California Anarchist Conference in order to facilitate parents' participation in conference sessions.

Yet, these kinds of efforts by organizations can only go so far toward changing the social dynamics of the subculture. With regard to the childcare issue, Emily commented that, while people in the anarchist scene in Phoenix were quite accepting of parents being involved, the social heart of the scene was the parties that occurred after organizing meetings. Because people really got to know each other and form bonds at these late-night parties where drinking and drug use were common, parents could be unintentionally excluded from building collegial relationships. Leo related that he had been "shocked" by the outpouring of interest when the anarchist-feminist collective was started in Los Angeles. He saw this as an indication that while there may have been "rhetoric and words" of support for feminist perspectives within the anarchist scene up until that point, people weren't "really dealing with the complexities of what it means." Without proactive, structural efforts to make the movement welcoming and attractive to people who may not be able to seamlessly reconcile their lifestyles with those of most anarchists, such people will be effectively excluded, though that may not be anyone's desire or intention. Also, without an active redefinition of what it means to perform "authentic" anarchist identity, the norms may still systematically favor those more comfortable behaving and relating in masculine ways.

Just as anarcha-feminists have made critiques of male privilege within anarchist scenes, anarchist people of color (APOC) have voiced frustration with white anarchists' perpetuation of systemic racism and ethnocentricity. As an article written by two APOC asserts, "There is this idea that once someone pronounces themselves 'anti-racist' then they assume that they are an ally of people without their privileges, immune from critique. Even if they take criticism in a positive guilt-free manner, they too often neglect to see that they are part of a whole racist system" (Musuta and Hickey 2008). One concern often raised is white anarchists' seeming ignorance of and subsequent disregard for issues that disproportionately affect people of color. For example, several typical anarchist practices put their practitioners in the position of drawing police scrutiny and possibly harassment. Given the established pattern of police violence against and over-criminalization of people of color in the United States, these individuals have more to lose by adopting even mildly rebellious practices than do their white counterparts. For example, shoplifting may be much more easily adopted as a lifestyle practice when one isn't automatically targeted by security staff, a daily occurrence for people of color. A zine called *Shoplifting: The Art and the Science* (n.d.) recognizes this limitation, urging readers, "Because you shoplift, or can shoplift, [it] doesn't mean you are radder or a better anti-capitalist than the rest of us. It may just mean you have privileges which play into everything you do including stealing."

People of color who are potentially interested in anarchist politics may also be deterred by the common perception that the movement is a white scene, and thus the perception may become self-fulfilling. Minty, who identifies as white but whose job involves doing organizing work with many people of color, struggles with trying to reach out to different communities so that "you're not just having the same white kids come to your events." Though it is probably not ever the intention of event organizers to actively exclude non-white participants, racial homogeneity in the scene can be self-perpetuating. For example, Minty said that she invited her co-workers to an anarchist event she helped organize, and that "they came out and it was like all white kids [*laughs*] and they were like 'ummmm,' so they stayed for like five minutes and left, you know . . . ." The supposed lack of connection that people of color feel with certain "subcultural" aspects of anarchism is also frequently cited as the reason for the putative whiteness of anarchist movements. As one APOC writer summarizes, "Many people of color in the U.S. today do not wish to be associated with what has become the stereotypical white North American anarchist movement that is less about community and more about creating a lifestyle out of anarchism" (Stepp 2008). Another APOC echoes the concern, saying, "a significant part of the problem lies in the subcultural lifestyle of many anarchists, including myself" (Nomous 2007). This writer, going by the pseudonym Otto Nomous (sounds like "autonomous"), asserts that the association between anarchism and "'punk' or other 'alternative' persuasions" is alienating rather than inviting for most people. He points out the fact that,

> the general tendencies of most white/punk anarchists tend to be to settle for the symbolic, and fail to support the real struggles of people to change the world precisely because they have a choice as opposed to people who have to struggle for their livelihood.

In this view, the identities and interests of people of color are assumed to be at odds with the taste preferences associated with anarchist subcultural identities, since these are merely symbolic.

While it is crucial to be alert to the ways in which subcultural tastes may draw unofficial boundaries around activist scenes, it is also important to be careful when making assumptions about who feels excluded and why. Rilla pointed out that, in Los Angeles, both the punk and the anarchist scenes regularly included people of color, particularly immigrants or children of immigrants from Central America. Yet, due to dominant assumptions about the whiteness of those scenes (which may be more accurate in other regions of the United States), this involvement by people of color was sometimes overlooked even in narratives that were specifically about the Los Angeles context. Rilla explained that such oversights were aided by assumptions that, when people of color were involved in activism around immigration issues, for example, they were doing so from some essentialized racial position and not from an anarchist analysis. To give one example from my research that illustrates Rilla's point, Josef traced his political radicalization to two different sources—the punk scene on the one hand, and his experience of oppression as an immigrant from Nicaragua on the other. Yet, if one were looking at Josef with the assumption that punk anarchism is a white thing, it would be easy to read his political identity as being more tied to his ethnicity than to his subcultural tastes. On the other hand, a white anarchist who was involved in the punk scene would receive a less ambiguous reading, tracing his political identity directly to his subcultural practices. Over time, one can see how this could reproduce the stereotype that the subcultural aspects of anarchist identity are a "white thing."

Rilla's point was that, if one assumed that people of color were not likely to be anarchists, one could easily make one's observations about their activist causes fit with one's preconceived notions about what anarchist activism entails. The same goes for people's subcultural tastes. I interviewed multiple women and people of color who had been exposed to anarchist politics through their participation in punk scenes, for example, so I am wary of too quickly assuming that such tastes necessarily make women and people of color feel excluded from identifying with anarchism. It is more responsible to try to recognize the ways that all of these scenes can reproduce the misogyny and racism of the dominant culture, rather than to conflate involvement in those scenes with particular essentialized subject positions. While it is important to consider the ways in which taste-based markers of authenticity may work in advance to exclude people of particular structural locations, it is also important to consider the specifics of context and to examine the lived experience of the participants in that context. Without doing so, one may reproduce certain strands of conventional wisdom about subcultural tastes that play into essentialist understandings of identity categories.

But, regardless of whether the lines are as neatly drawn as some critics would claim, it is quite clear that performing an authentic anarchist identity is never as simple as just believing in anarchist philosophical principles and then automatically adopting all the attendant lifestyle practices. For various reasons outlined in this chapter, the label anarchist may be problematic to identify with. The responsible move by a critic would be to examine the specific ways in which people experience conflicts between their different social identities and anarchist subcultural practices and to be attentive to how the collective experience of participants in any given context may be reproducing larger patterns of oppression such as sexism or racism.

Ironic sincerity

Anarchists are not naïve about any of the issues I described above. As should be clear from several of the quotations included in this chapter, self-identified anarchists are, in fact, engaged in a great deal of reflection and self-criticism about many aspects of their movements and culture. The way many approach their identity as anarchists is self-reflexive and cognizant of the very issues discussed above, resulting in a sort of ambivalent identification with the category itself. Jeremy, for example, offered the thoughtful critique that, "anarchism as a way of representing experience allows and disallows certain things; it's more pliable for some than others. I don't think it's terribly helpful to hold people's experience up to one particular vocabulary." Yet, moments later, when I asked him "do you call yourself an anarchist?" Jeremy answered with a resounding "Absolutely." There was both irony and sincerity in this response. Since he had just finished offering a sophisticated reflection on the shortcomings of identity categories, he was clearly aware that his own commitment to such a category would be ironic, yet he embraced the label for himself anyway. Other interviewees conveyed similarly ambivalent attitudes. When I asked Alma whether it was important to her that she call herself an anarchist, she replied, laughing, "Not at all. Sometimes." Like Jeremy, she was aware of the limitations introduced by identifying as an anarchist, but was still committed to the utility of the term—and she was able to find humor in the contradictions therein.

We might say then that some anarchists deploy a kind of "ironic sincerity" in their use of the term as a descriptor of identity and a motivator for action. The irony stems from an awareness—based in self-reflexive critique—that the term "anarchist" has no fixed or "authentic" referent. This lack of fixity comes from several sources: the impossibility of truly achieving anarchy within the context of long-standing structures of hierarchy and oppression; the many ways of defining and practicing anarchism; and contextual factors that shape how different kinds of people put their anarchist beliefs into practice. Despite the ironic self-awareness of the limitations of authenticity for anarchist identity, many anarchists hold a commitment to sincerity when evaluating their own or others' identification with anarchism. This investment in sincerity results in discourses of "accountability" which attempt to motivate individuals toward those lifestyle practices that are seen as indicative of anarchist sincerity. At times, accountability is perceived as boundary policing, which, for many, seems to be at odds with the anti-hierarchy ethos of anarchist philosophy. For anarchists, the question remains then, whether lifestyle norms are politically and ethically defensible, or whether "authenticity" should be redefined away from lifestyle in order to achieve an effective anarchist movement.

These questions have resonance beyond the anarchist context. In many circles, the labels people use for themselves and the habits they take up in their everyday lives are seen as important. Labels of identity, and to some extent even material practices, are important for what they *represent*, not necessarily for what they *are*. For the activists discussed here, the identity anarchist may be incidental; the key thing is that individuals are able to come together and recognize in each other the collective analyses, ethics, and interests that will allow them to struggle together for a political project. Recognition of the "incidentalness" of identity labels could be helpful in that it could relieve activists—and others—of the obligation to police each other's labels and lifestyle practices. This is not to minimize the ethical significance of some lifestyle practices. To the extent that they have some material effects, they may continue to serve as useful indicators of political commitment. However, there are contextual factors that shape what counts as a legitimate expression of commitment and who has the capacity to express themselves in that way. To deploy the discipline of lifestyle norms productively, rather than oppressively, requires endless critique and redefinition—a static image of anarchist authenticity could not respond to all of the intersecting forces in any given context, as we have seen. But while the content of anarchist authenticity might change, the sign of "anarchist" could remain as an identity under which to unite with sincere commitment. This potential is what many activists understand as being useful about retaining an identification with anarchism, even while they recognize some of the problems it poses.

5

Strategic sexuality: Polyamory, queer self-identification, and consent-seeking as activist interventions

One of my earliest personal exposures to anarchist philosophy came in 2004, when I was a college student in Michigan. I'd heard vaguely of anarchism before, of course—I had friends who played in punk bands and listened to the Sex Pistols (a band whose most famous single is "Anarchy in the UK"). But, as I became immersed in feminist theory in college, I decided to write a paper on critiques of marriage, and the name Emma Goldman began surfacing in my research. Coincidentally, while I was working on that paper, I went to see a friend's band play at an anarchist infoshop in Lansing. Like most infoshops, the space was used for multiple purposes. It housed a small library of books and pamphlets, but to pay the rent it put on shows by local musical acts. While watching the bands play, a rack of photocopied booklets caught my eye, particularly one with the title "Marriage and Love" by Emma Goldman.

The pamphlet was a reproduction of Goldman's essay written in the early years of the twentieth century. Though the phrase "the personal is the political" would not become widely familiar until several decades later with the burgeoning of the women's liberation movement in the 1960s and 1970s, Goldman's views expressed a deep belief in the close relationship between the personal and the political. She argued that the institution of marriage was a tool of capitalism, patriarchy, and the state, and that these structures were contributing to the oppression of women by controlling them in the most intimate spheres of their lives. Goldman advocated the practice of "free love" in which women's bodies would not be "owned" by their male partners, but rather would be under the autonomous control of women themselves. Free love was a way of subverting the oppressive ideologies of monogamy and marriage and helping all emotional and sexual relationships to be experienced more anarchistically, that is, apart from hierarchical power. The practice would not only free individual women (and men) from hierarchical relations, but would also serve as a symbolic challenge to the hegemony of ideologies that linked love with the marriage institution.[1]

A century later, Goldman's ideal endures in some contemporary anarchists' embrace of polyamory as an ideal structure for romantic relationships. Anarchists also bring their political principles into other aspects of their sexuality. Like their forerunners in previous anarchist and radical feminist movements, many of today's anarchists militantly hew to the idea that even the most personal of one's practices can be—even must be—used as sites of political expression and action (Greenway 2009; Kissack 2008). Sexual "preferences" may be problematized—or subjected to self-reflection and ethical scrutiny (Foucault 1990b: 10)—much as are the other aspects of lifestyle I've discussed in this book. Sexuality is a unique aspect of lifestyle to consider in the context of political strategy however, because it is less widely understood as a matter of choice in the way that other aspects of lifestyle (such as dress or consumption patterns) might be. While sexuality is experienced as intensely personal, sexual practices also have multidimensional motivations and implications, including moral, activist, identificatory, and social ones (to invoke the categories I developed in Chapter 2). This chapter explicitly documents and analyzes some of these dimensions of sexuality among anarchists, by focusing on three expressions of anarchist sexuality: polyamory, queer self-identification, and consent-seeking.

Polyamory

At the 2010 Los Angeles Anarchist Book Fair, I picked up a pamphlet titled *Complicated Relationships: Conversations on Polyamory and Anarchy* (Ardent Press 2008). The back cover of this publication asserts that "Anarchists have always challenged whatever seemed rigid and assumed in daily life within an authoritarian system, and relationships have certainly been up for debate." As described in the pamphlet, one of the "rigid and assumed" aspects of daily life debated by anarchists is participation in institutionalized monogamy. Polyamory, as used by contemporary practitioners, describes a romantic or sexual relationship in which partners have an open and conscious agreement not to be romantically or sexually exclusive. In other words, sex and romantic attachments are permissible outside the couple. It may even be that the individuals involved do not think of themselves as a couple at all, but are involved in a triad or other larger group.[2] In some cases, a couple may be "primary partners" with each other, but sleep with other individuals who are known as "secondary" partners. In other cases, an individual may have sex with several people without considering oneself to be in a committed relationship with any of them. As the *Complicated Relationships* pamphlet explains, polyamorists are, "people who expect to get their intimacy and sexual needs met by many people, who have lives more independent of their partners, both temporally and spatially" (Ardent Press 2008: 5). In short, having a sexual or romantic relationship with one person does not preclude maintaining ongoing sexual and romantic relationships with others. An essential element of polyamory is the awareness and consent of all involved. Polyamorists are very clear on the point that polyamory is not cheating or infidelity or adultery, which would imply deception and violation of the terms of an exclusive partnership. This is why polyamory is sometimes also referred to as "ethical non-monogamy."

The critique of monogamy remains prominent in contemporary anarchist discourse, as evidenced, for example, by the recent publication and distribution of the *Complicated Relationships* pamphlet. Consider also that there is a chapter on how to maintain non-monogamous relationships in CrimethInc.'s (2005a) book, *Recipes for Disaster: An Anarchist Cookbook*, which is an instruction manual of sorts for many of the most common practices taken up within anarchist subcultures (other chapters initiate readers in the arts of dumpster diving, bicycle collectives, and shoplifting). Polyamory also came up frequently during my interviews: when prompted by me to talk about their dating practices, interviewees commonly brought up polyamory, taking it as a given element of anarchist lifestyle politics, whether or not they practiced it themselves. Interviewees found it salient to specify whether they were or were not monogamous without me explicitly asking for this piece of information. They thus seemed to take for granted a generally accepted connection between anarchist politics and polyamorous dating practices.

Importantly, non-monogamy is often approached as an identity or orientation, rather than a straightforward description of actual sexual practice. Polyamory can be "used as a descriptive term by people who are open to more than one relationship even if they are not currently involved in more than one" (Ardent Press 2008: 8). Thus, a relationship may be characterized as polyamorous even if, in practice, the individuals never have sex outside the partnership. In these cases, the understanding and intent of the partners is that sex outside the partnership is permitted. For example, interviewee Joel's relationship with his long-term partner was for a time technically monogamous in practice, insofar as neither of them had sex outside the relationship. But, he said, "we always identified ourselves as open because it was like, we understand that that's a good thing to do." By the same token, an individual may identify as polyamorous even if they are not currently involved in any sexual relationship. As the "Nonmonogamous Relationships" chapter of CrimethInc.'s (2005: 404) *Recipes for Disaster* puts it, "there's nothing that says you have to go to bed with more than one person at a time to be non-monogamous." Just as one can identify as gay or straight even when one is not currently sexually active, the identity "polyamorist" indicates an individual's stable preference or need or ideological commitment to become involved in polyamorous relationships.

What does polyamory have to do with anarchism? Certainly, not all polyamorists are anarchists, nor do most non-anarchist practitioners of polyamory see the practice as being political. The vast majority of literature on polyamory does not invoke explicitly political themes, in the sense of associating the practice with specific political philosophies such as anarchism. However, as I mentioned above, there is a long-standing affinity between anarchism and the rejection of compulsory monogamy. Goldman (1977: 73) opposed monogamy because she felt it mirrored the relation of private property within capitalism: in monogamous relationships, people are "possessed" by their partners, to the exclusion of all others. Thus, monogamy treats the individual's body, love, and sexual intimacy as if they are exclusive economic goods, whose exchange values are depleted or negated when they are accessible to multiple partners. Gayle Rubin (1997) in an article titled "The Traffic in Women" (the title of which is borrowed from a Goldman essay), points out that the cultural injunction to monogamy is a side effect of the capitalist division of gendered labor, in which men and women are trained for different types of work and are thus dependent on each other and encouraged to form paired bonds (Rubin 1997). Furthermore, the critique of monogamy is also often informed by a feminist analysis that recognizes the ways in which monogamy has historically shored up arrangements in which men exercise ownership or control over female bodies (who may effectively be treated as sexual chattel, hence the "traffic in women" referenced by Goldman and later Rubin). To reject monogamy, therefore, is to challenge the legitimacy of patriarchy, capitalism, and the state.

Many contemporary anarchists espouse a critique of monogamy that encompasses all these factors. For example, an interviewee named Grant, a twenty-something man who lives in Washington, DC, articulated the connections he sees between his practice of polyamory and his commitment to an anarchist society:

> I think polyamory for me has to do with anarchism being more than just a non-state solution to state capitalism, but a complete assessment of all forms of hierarchy . . . . it has personally helped me address aspects of my patriarchal socialization. It's a tangible way to express that I really don't feel ownership over my partners, and it contributes to a level of openness and honesty you often don't find in monogamous relationships. Additionally it helps me avoid codependent relationships which I think contributes to one of the great successes of capitalism, namely dividing people from each other.

If monogamy is seen to support capitalism and patriarchy, then state-sanctioned marriage is perceived even more negatively by anarchists, since it further institutionalizes hierarchical relationships and reinforces the power of the state. Interviewee Josef stated the case emphatically: "I think, like, being married and all that is, like, that's just a whole 'nother prescribed, uh, uh, subscription to patriarchy and it's bullshit, it's like property management, and I don't, I don't believe in that, you know?" Grant also expressed frustration that "the ultimate individual goal in a capitalist society is to find a husband or wife and sequester yourselves off from the rest of society in a toxic family unit," offering this as one of the reasons he practices polyamory.

The anarchist response to the contemporary gay marriage debate further illustrates the anarchist position on marriage in general. A zine put out by queer anarchist network Bash Back! argues that, "For queers to appeal for marriage is to desire assimilation into a heteronormative conception of sexuality, gender, and relationships, things which the state should have no business regulating or legislating in the first place" (BAMF! Productionz 2009). The Bash Back! zine goes on to say that, "State recognition in the form of oppressive institutions such as marriage and militarism are not steps toward liberation but rather towards heteronormative assimilation." Elsewhere, anarchist essayist Ruthann Robson (1996: 325) asserts, "For anarchists, the issue of homosexual marriage is akin to the issue of conscripting women. No, homosexuals should not 'be allowed' to marry, but then neither should heterosexuals . . . . Sorry, but 'living together contracts' are also impolitic."

In theory, anarchists' opposition to institutionalized monogamy is less about advocating for particular sexual desires (for multiple partners, say) than it is about a radical commitment to the individual's freedom to determine the nature of one's own sexual practice, without coercion by the market or the state. Within the discourse of polyamory, "free love" expresses the idea that sexual activity should not be constrained by repressive social conventions, particularly not when those conventions are simply an ideological product of capitalist and patriarchal conditions. Proponents of free love argue that sexual partnering ought to be undertaken only in pursuit of mutual pleasure, not as a means of attaining power (either institutional or interpersonal power). Polyamorists often advocate the ideal that sexual practice should express one's true or natural desires rather than those that have been imposed by repressive ideological systems. As a participant in one discussion of non-monogamy put it in the *Complicated Relationships* pamphlet:

> [people] are most often too willing to adjust their lives to some idealized way of living that they think is right but that isn't how they really feel. Conforming to what is socially imposed. People are so confused and have never had a chance to grow up in a normal environment. Normal in the

sense of not being restricted and having to go through all the authoritarian institutions of sexuality. They don't have the opportunity to freely relate to other people and freely be sexual. (Ardent Press 2008: 3)

The practice of free love is supposed to create a social environment in which people can learn to cultivate sexual relationships free of coercive, hegemonic values.

Some of the anarchists I spoke with alluded to the fact that monogamy didn't feel right or just "didn't work" for them at a personal level. Minty, for example, said she has "never been monogamous" because "it's not in my blood." Importantly, though, Minty did not necessarily use "blood" to invoke a naturalizing defense of polyamory—she followed up her comment by acknowledging that her reasons for not being monogamous are "both personal and political." This is where anarchist polyamorists depart somewhat from most advocates of polyamory. While many defenses of polyamory make recourse to evolutionary arguments about the nature of human sexuality (e.g. Ryan and Jethá 2010), anarchists perceive ideological dimensions of sexual experience and explicitly recognize their sexuality as a medium through which to struggle against oppressive, hegemonic forces. In this, polyamory is constructed similarly to other anarchist lifestyle practices, as a way of unsettling one of the many social and cultural norms "we might be taking for granted" (Ardent Press 2008: 6) due to our interpellation within ideological discourses. The project of destabilizing cultural norms of sexuality is what aligns polyamory with queer critique, a discourse whose relationship to anarchism I will now discuss.

Queer self-identification

Institutionalized monogamy is just one dimension of hegemonic sexuality which anarchists oppose. State- and market-sanctioned marriage is one of a whole "network of norms" that works to privilege heterosexuality (Jakobsen 1998: 518; Berlant and Warner 1998). As opponents of social hierarchy of all kinds, anarchists are against this social privileging of heterosexuality. This brings them into alliance with the queer political project, which is committed to radically critiquing and subverting the hegemony of heterosexuality. The identity designation *queer*, once a derogatory term used to mark the deviance of homosexuality, was reclaimed by homosexual activists by the early 1990s, in the wake of the gay liberation movement of the 1970s and gay men and lesbians' radical response to the AIDS crisis in the 1980s.[3] The concept of heteronormativity describes the normative order in which individuals are interpellated and often coerced into conformity with practices that maintain the dominance of heterosexuality (Warner 1993). Activists who take on the label of queer take their political project to be the radical destabilization of heteronormativity, which, given that heterosexuality is "deeply embedded by now in an indescribably wide range of social institutions" (xiii), involves their challenging mainstream institutions and discourses at nearly every turn. Anarchist sexuality, insofar as it can be thought of as a coherent type of sexuality at all, is itself usefully understood as a kind of queerness, since it shares a commitment to challenging a wide range of normative institutions.

The discursive articulation of anarchist politics and queer sexuality is probably owed in large part to the work of activist groups which identify themselves explicitly as both anarchist and queer, an identification sometimes contracted to "anarcha-queer." The group Gay Shame, for example, advances a radical alternative to the liberal discourse of gay rights and gay pride, suggesting that queer sexuality is best nurtured not by assimilation to mainstream culture or the winning of privileges through consumerism and statist campaigns, but by direct actions that aim at more autonomy and a better quality of life for queer people (Sycamore 2008). United more by a networked, multi-sited ethos than by an official organizational structure, Gay Shame activists explicitly position themselves against capitalism and engage in creative, spectacular demonstrations that attempt to shatter the myth of heteronormative (and homonormative)[4] consensus.

Since the inception of Gay Shame in 1998, other anarcha-queer actions, organizations, and publications have emerged with similar missions and tactics. A recent example is Bash Back!, which formed in 2007 in preparation for protests at the 2008 mainstream political party conventions in the United States, and has spawned the formation of active local chapters across the country as well as a recurring Radical Queer Conference. A zine about Bash Back! states, "We oppose heteronormativity, assimilation, capitalism, the state, and all other oppressions," and defines queer as "a threat to authority and hierarchy everywhere" (BAMF! Productionz). There are many other organizations, zines, blogs, and message boards that advance similar viewpoints.[5] As one anarchist blog puts it:

> Queer-anarchism is a happy marriage of two philosophies that break down barriers in pursuit of freedom and liberation. As both anarchist-communists and as individuals oppressed by larger heteronormative culture we believe that coming outside of sexual and gender binaries is inherently political. (Anarchist Federation 2009)

We can see queer sexuality as a democratic or libertarian kind of sexuality, one in which the individual's autonomy is valued above all other factors, including social mores. Interviewee Miles' experience with his female partner offers an example of the valorization of the transgression of repressive social binaries: "what was best about our relationship was just how non-gendered it was. Not that we shared each others clothes and called each other 'ze/hir'[6] or anything, but just that it wasn't caught up in what seemed to be the same patterns and habits of the world at large in our practices of heterosexuality." Though the hegemonic discourse of sexual identity would categorize Miles and his partner as having a "straight" relationship, they experienced it as something other than this, since straightness would imply conformity with dominant patterns of heterosexual relating, which Miles did not feel they were in conformity with.[7]

A key way that the discursive and political alliance between anarchism and queer is manifested is through the tendency for some self-identified anarchists to also personally identify with queer sexuality. The use of the term queer to describe one's sexual identity is, for many, a means of resisting the way that sexuality has, for ideological reasons, been parceled out into discrete categories which are assumed to be fixed and essential characteristics of individuals (Jagose 1996: 125). When taken as a self-claimed identity label, queer is a dramatization of one's resistance to hegemonic narratives of sexual identity. To illustrate the way that queer identification troubles the dominant assumption of a straightforward and determinate relationship between the gender of one's partners and one's sexual identity, consider my experience with two interviewees in particular. Both Alyssa and Minty told me that they identified as queer. Both also refrained from providing a definitive designation of the gender identity of their sexual partners, though the opportunity to do so presented itself during our interviews. In Alyssa's case, she implied that she was sexually attracted to women and explicitly referred to one former lover using a feminine pronoun and name. In the months following our interview, I learned that Alyssa had had both male and transgender partners. Based only on what she shared during our interview, a logical assumption might have been that Alyssa's sexual activity was confined to women. Certainly, Alyssa was under no obligation to specify the gender identity of each of her former and current partners, but I think it is telling that she only explicitly made mention of her attraction to women. In the context of our interview, the heterosexual aspects of Alyssa's sexuality were "closeted," though I can't say whether this was intentional on Alyssa's part. As a researcher, I cannot make claims as to why Alyssa's own account of her sexuality included some details and not others. I can only point out that it might be consistent with a practice of linguistic activism that attempts to privilege and make visible queerness, as a subversive move against conditions in which queer desires and practices are normally suppressed or not talked of, even when they exist. This would be an inversion of the more conventional practice of "covering," in which an individual obfuscates the aspects of one's identity that might signify queerness, in order to allow a heterosexual identity narrative to be assumed by his or her audience (Yoshino 2007).

In Minty's case, her response when I asked, via email, if and how her sexual identity was related to her anarchism was: "My gender identity as queer is not a recent development. I knew from a very young age that I loved womyn and [this] is very tied to my sense of self."[8] Other than this statement, she did not provide any direct information about her sexual identity, though she did on several other occasions throughout the interview mention former partners and lovers. Interestingly, she always used gender-neutral pronouns to refer to these individuals. Further complicating her statement that she "loved womyn," I later ran into Minty at an anarchist event she helped organize, where she was publicly kissing and holding hands with someone who visually presented as a man (though not knowing this individual personally, I do not know if "he" self-identified as such). The tactic of evading the specification of one's sexuality is a common one in queer cultures; one linguistic theorist, in describing her circumlocutions to avoid identifying herself as a lesbian by neturalizing the gendered pronouns referring to her female partner, calls this the "recognizably gay tactic of avoiding pronominalizing anaphora" (Morrish 2002: 186). Morrish notes that this "recognizable tactic" works to indicate her gayness to those in the know (who have experience with this tactic) and keeps her sexuality indeterminate for everyone else. I would argue that Minty and Alyssa's avoidance of "pronominalizing anaphora" functions analogously though not identically: by circumlocuting the identification of partners whose gender might imply a heteronormative identity, Minty and Alyssa avoid reifying the dominant assumption of heterosexuality. Just as, in certain repressive contexts, the mere mention of homosexuality is taken as "promoting" a queer lifestyle, it could be that Minty and Alyssa, and other anarchists who don't identify themselves as straight, believe that by mentioning their heterosexual practices and relationships they might be seen as promoting or privileging heterosexuality above the queer alternatives, which, as anarchists, they do not wish to do.

I offer these observations not in order to call into question the authenticity or sincerity of Alyssa and Minty's self-narratives, but rather to recognize their self-narratives as moments of *production* of a non-normative sexual identity. While it is possible to see their accounts of their own sexuality as a repression of practices and desires which do not fit a particular queer narrative (a queer narrative that conflates queerness with homosexual orientation), I prefer to see their accounts as actually corresponding to a different queer narrative (a queer narrative that embraces the indeterminacy of identity categories). Their own accounts, in combination with my observations, "dramatize incoherencies" (Jagose 1996: 3) in the often taken for granted relationship between sexual orientation, practice, and identity. These anecdotes about Alyssa and Minty illustrate that there is no simple way to characterize their sexual identifications, nor did either woman attempt to offer me a straightforward representation of their erotic desires through their assumed identity categories. The closest either came to labeling their sexual identity was to use the term queer, which no doubt they understood to be an inherently indeterminate category. That they identified as queer actually told me very little about the precise nature of their romantic partnerships.

Indeed, their ambiguous identity performances enact the idea(l) that sexual identification is not a simple representation of desire or activity. This is in keeping with the queer project of troubling fixed and determinate identity labels (Butler 1990).

Queer, for all its erotic indeterminacy, is not *politically* indeterminate for the anarchists who identify themselves with it. Queer may be an "anti-identity" as far as sexuality is concerned (and even that is debatable) but it is most certainly a coherent, if not fixed or essentialist, political identity (Jagose 1996, Seidman 1993). Queer definitely refers to a specific and well-defined political project (albeit a fluid and historically contingent one), and thus there is little question that anarchists, by identifying themselves as queer, wish to ally themselves with that project. Alyssa, for example, was clear about the fact that her queerness is a political orientation in addition to being a sexual identification:

> I've identified as queer on and off since high school, or maybe junior high, depending on whether you track queerness alongside desire/sex with women. But I think that I began to think of myself as queer in a more settled way maybe ten years ago, and that is definitely political—not just about desire and who I have sex with but also about an orientation against capitalist heteropatriarchy.

Many anarchists are similarly explicit on the point that they identify themselves as queer for self-consciously political reasons.

Alyssa's insinuation that queerness doesn't necessarily track with her homosexual desires and practices is particularly important for thinking about the complex relationship between practice on the one hand and identity on the other. One anarchist essayist poses a similar distinction between practice and identity: "Being bisexual does not mean that we [anarchists] engage in sexual relations with everyone; it just means that we recognize the potential to so engage" (Robson 1996: 325).[9] Anarchist sexuality in this respect is not about having sex with particular kinds of people, but rather entails an openness to the queer notions that erotic desire is and ought to be fluid, and that sexual identity ought to reflect and allow for that fluidity. For example, when asked to talk about her sexual identity, Tina responded, "I identify as no preference. Um, I think I lean towards, like, um, heterosexual, like, relationships because that's what I've been primarily involved with, but I don't like to identify as straight. I find it oppressive." Indeed, the majority of interviewees indicated that they had been mostly involved in heterosexual romantic relationships. Yet, even those who were mostly or exclusively involved in heterosexual *activity* showed a reluctance to completely identify themselves as heterosexual *people*.

Recall that a similar dynamic of disidentification often plays out in relation to monogamy. Even those anarchists who are currently monogamous voice support for the idea of polyamory or have practiced polyamory in the past. Rilla, for example, was an interviewee who said that she always "ends up being monogamous" though she understood the political motivations behind polyamory: "If I think about it critically, I could see why people advocate it [polyamory], you know? It sounds good but I just, I tend to always end up in monogamous relationships with men." I think Rilla's language here is important. By describing her habit of having monogamous relationships with men as something she "just ends up doing," she does not imply that monogamy (or heterosexuality for that matter) is any more natural or justifiable than polyamory. She puts herself at a critical distance from hegemonic sexual normativity. Similarly, Leo expressed support—and even longing—for polyamory, but admitted that in practice he tends to be monogamous: "I wish I was polyamorous. I wish I could psychologically cope with polyamory [*laughs*] but, um, I probably couldn't, so instead I'm a very reluctant monogamist." The anarchist understanding of queer identity and the anarchist understanding of polyamory are similar, in that both are not so much about material actions as about ethical orientations and the importance of symbolically representing those orientations. In this, they are similar to other aspects of anarchist lifestyle which depend heavily on discourse to construct them as radical political interventions. There is an important analytical distinction to be made between the material and symbolic consequences of personal sexual practice. Within the norms of a culture or subculture, some practices are valued for what they *represent*, whereas others are valued as material goods in themselves. This distinction is relevant to consider when assessing the strategic suitability of a given tactic in a particular situation. Where representation is of political significance, questions of visibility, audience, and discursive framing are crucial to assessments of a practice's strategic utility.

Subcultural norms of sexuality

I will consider the broader political implications of these sexual practices as they travel beyond the anarchist subcultural milieu, but for now I want to hold my analysis for a moment at the subcultural level, to consider the effects of normative lifestyle discourses on individuals *within* anarchist subcultures. One interviewee, Emily, listed sexual practices among the things anarchists used to pass judgment on each other (though she did say that sexual practices were less of a factor than consumption habits and aesthetic tastes). By articulating authentic anarchist identity with non-hegemonic sexualities, the subcultural discourses of sexuality circulated by anarchists work to discipline self-identified anarchists into adopting particular practices as a means of demonstrating the authenticity of their commitment to anarchist politics. One effect of this construction of authentic anarchist identity is the experience of internal dissonance and unease when felt personal desires conflict with subcultural norms. For example, Joel observed that individuals who attempted to practice polyamory were ashamed when they found themselves experiencing feelings of possessiveness or jealousy, as if these emotional reactions jeopardized their identities as "good" anarchists. The CrimethInc. essay on non-monogamous relationships also posits that, "it's probably just as common for lovers in a non-monogamous relationship to feel insecure about their longing for monogamy, or at least some of the reassurances it professes to offer, as it is for them to feel ashamed of their desires for others" (CrimethInc. 2005a: 398). Orlando said that he had seen his friends get "stressed out" about their own desires, putting pressure on themselves to be in open relationships, even though they did not personally find the arrangement pleasurable. Leo made a similar observation, that people (himself included) feel pressure to practice polyamory because it is seen as ideologically preferable to monogamy:

> Ideologically, I thought it was fine, but I was really trying to force the ideology on my reality . . . . Some people want to be polyamorous but they just can't cope with it, like [on] their own psychological level. But you can tell they suffer at it and they're making everybody else suffer, and . . . like, some people don't want it, but yet they're taking that position.

Anarchist scenes evidently have the potential to reproduce the dominant culture's "lack of a concept of benign sexual variation," in Rubin's terminology (1984: 282), only in the opposite direction to mainstream society. Among some anarchists, straight identity and monogamy are positioned as morally inferior to queerness and polyamory.

This "hierarchical valuation" of sexualities—to borrow another phrase from Rubin (1984: 279)—is used as a mechanism of discipline within anarchist communities. At times, the disciplinary effects of subcultural norms may reproduce patterns of domination for which anarchist sexuality was supposed to be a remedy. For example, some women feel quite strongly that the anarchist emphasis on polyamory ends up reproducing sexual domination and exploitation of women within the anarchist scene. In an essay titled "Polyamory on the Left: Liberatory or Predatory?" one anarchist woman expresses her belief that "having multiple partners at any given time is not liberating for women," that "being open to the fuck, as all polyamorous women are supposed to be, is *men's* definition of liberated female sexuality" (Kreutzer 2004, emphasis mine). In Kimberley Kreutzer's view, the normalization of polyamory does not reflect the sexual desires of most anarchist women, but is rather a means of rendering them "sexual chattel to be passed back and forth between brothers in arms." One interviewee, Melissa, seemed to share this view, when she argued to me that polyamory has nothing to do with feminist politics, that it is merely a justification that anarchist guys use to get away with cheating on their partners.

In an anarchist's ideal, anarchic world, perhaps individuals would have the wherewithal and autonomy to refrain from sexual arrangements they don't find personally pleasurable or liberating. Yet, in our present context, subcultural norms can be powerful sources of discipline, particularly when questions of political authenticity and commitment are at stake. Kreutzer argues, for instance, that women who do not prefer to be in polyamorous relationships are disciplined into submission by the equation of authentic anarchist identity with polyamorous sexuality. That is, Kreutzer and other women suggest that if a woman expresses a personal desire not to be polyamorous, she is perceived as unserious in her commitment to anarchist politics. The disciplinary power of authenticity comes into stark focus when women actively refuse polyamory: "When we decide we aren't polyamorous, given the male defined terms and standards, we are called 'old-fashioned' a term that by leftist standards is degrading and humiliating" (Kreutzer 2004). In order to avoid such marginalization, women may adopt polyamory even though they do not personally desire it: "Because of the views towards non-polyamorous relationships I have seen many unwilling women sleep with other men in order to prove that they are not 'old-fashioned,' but that they are in fact new, 'liberated' women" (Ibid.). In the eyes of those who see polyamory as an expression of male privilege, using the practice of polyamory as a gauge of anarchist authenticity risks disproportionately marginalizing women within activist communities, or even disciplining their sexual behavior in ways that seem to mirror traditional patterns of gendered domination.[10]

Even if we set aside the issue of whether subcultural norms have the effect of replicating mainstream hierarchies, the fact that they instantiate any kind of hierarchy is unsettling for many anarchists. From a practical perspective, the institution of any kind of moral hierarchy around sexual practices can spawn drama that may prove detrimental to a unified atmosphere within the movement. The CrimethInc. essay on non-monogamous relationships points out a tendency for some polyamorists to be "insistent or even confrontational" about the correctness of polyamory as a political practice, yet it asserts the importance of not "making others feel they must live up to some standard around you" (CrimethInc. 2005a: 399). The essay also asserts that, "It is important that we avoid developing a competitive culture of non-monogamy, in which people must feel shame for wanting anything 'bourgeois' or 'traditional'" (CrimethInc. 2005a: 398). The solution for these writers is to do away with normative standards altogether: "*Everything*, every desire and need, has to be respected, or else this is no revolution after all, just the establishing of a different norm" (CrimethInc. 2005a: 398). But clearly, not "*every* desire and need" ought to be respected—what of the patriarchally perpetuated desire by some men to assert sexual dominance over women?

Where people are drawing on hegemonic histories of oppression in their own personal behavior, shouldn't they be held responsible for doing so, when they might do otherwise?

A puristic anti-normativity position risks reproducing the liberal model of free choice that treats individual acts as pure expressions of personal agency, even though systemic power relations are always at work in structuring those acts. To invoke this discourse is both to dismiss the real obstacles that work against the adoption of oppositional identifications and practices and to excuse people when their choices happen to replicate traditional oppressive relationships. The likely effect of a movement purporting to reject norms altogether is the invisible conservation of dominant norms from within and beyond that movement.[11] Philosophically, it might make sense to oppose the way that norms, both mainstream and subcultural, constrain personal autonomy. Yet, unless anarchism is to stand for a kind of moral relativism, standards of ethical authenticity, and the dynamics of disciplinarity they generate, *are* politically defensible for anarchists in the interest of social transformation.

Consent-seeking

To illustrate this point, I want to look at another sexual practice that is strongly associated with contemporary anarchism—that of consent-seeking. One CrimethInc. article asserts that "the first and most important matter in bed (or the stairwell of the parking deck, or wherever you are) is the question of consent" (CrimethInc. 2005a: 474). Just as anarchist organizations are often actively structured to facilitate decision making by consensus, the seeking of consent is advocated as a prerequisite for sexual activity between individuals. A document disseminated by organizers of the 2009 G20 protests in Pittsburg in advance of the summit provides one example of anarchists' attempts to define sexual consensuality:

> Consent is actively and voluntarily expressed agreement . . . . The following do not qualify as consent: silence, passivity, and coerced acquiescence. Body movements, non-verbal responses such as moans, or the appearance of physical arousal do not, necessarily, constitute consent. Further, if someone is intoxicated, they may not be in a position to give you consent. Consent is required each and every time there is sexual activity, regardless of the parties' relationship, prior sexual history, or current activity.[12]

Discussions of consensuality and its importance to anarchists can be found in many other places as well. The Slingshot Collective is a publishing entity that puts out a popular radical-themed calendar/organizer each year. Several of its annual editions have included an article entitled "Will You Go Down on Me?," which extols the virtues of open communication between sexual partners as a means to non-coercive sexual exploration. The guidelines for the 2009 Bash Back! Convergence included points on "practicing active consent," such as, "Always ask for explicit verbal consent before engaging or touching someone" (BAMF! Productionz 2009). At the 2008 BASTARD (Berkeley Anarchist Students of Theory and Research & Development) Conference, I attended a panel discussion on the links between anarchism and BDSM,[13] in which all of the presenters cited the central role of consensuality for both traditions.

The ethical basis for this position within anarchist philosophy is that consent-seeking is understood as a way to consciously counteract the dynamics of domination and hierarchy that may manifest themselves in personal interactions. An anonymous contributor to the magazine *Rolling Thunder* puts it this way: "Non-hierarchical, consensual relationships are the substance of anarchy, and we need to prioritize seeking and promoting consent in all our interactions" (CrimethInc. 2005b: 41). The distributors of the "Sexual Consent Guidelines" document quoted above similarly argued that "Doing personal work to consistently seek consent and respect the times when it is not given helps to combat rape culture, and informed consent, sexual and otherwise, is necessary in the building of strong, healthy anti-authoritarian communities." As the distribution of this document attests, there has been a marked effort to make anarchist convergences into spaces where people feel safe from sexual assault at the hands of comrades.

The method of "calling people out" is commonly used to address instances of sexual assault or harassment when they happen within the movement.[14] Sometimes, the term is phrased as "calling someone out on their shit," meaning the person has a consistent issue of ethical failure that they are perceived as needing to work through in order to have integrity as an anarchist. The purpose of calling someone out on their shit is ostensibly to motivate them to alter their behavior so that it is more aligned with ethical standards. It may also be to communicate to others in the scene that this individual's anarchist credentials are not to be trusted. For example, in light of the fact that some anarchist men may use the discourse of polyamory to justify dishonesty and infidelity to their female partners, Joel informed me that "guys who are players under the auspices of anarchism are called out really quickly." Those who egregiously violate anarchist ethical standards, for instance by perpetrating sexual assault on a comrade, may even be banned from participation in organizations and events, effectively stripping them of their social identities as members of the anarchist movement.

The issue of consensuality can shed light on the productivity of disciplinarity around ethical commitments within anarchist subcultures, given its near-universal status as an absolute ethical good. Even staunch sex radicals insist that "the absence of coercion" ought to be a universal criterion for judging the moral acceptability of sexual practices (Rubin 1984). Consensuality makes an interesting case for exploring an anarchist critique of normativity, since it's hard to imagine how the universalization of consent-seeking could play into an oppressive power dynamic that anarchists might ethically oppose (this could be a failure of imagination on my part, though). A "hierarchical valuation of sexualities"—in Rubin's terms (1984)—that values consent-seeking above coercion would be just what anarchists would desire, though the use of the word hierarchical might make them squeamish. This squeamishness might be alleviated by recognizing that there is an analytical difference between the practice of consent-seeking on the one hand, and the practices of polyamory or queer self-identification on the other.

To seek consent is to materially enact a social relationship in which the individual recognizes another as horizontally positioned in relation to oneself and treats the other accordingly. The act carries ethical value in itself. By contrast, to identify oneself or one's relationship as queer or polyamorous is not to *enact* a particular power arrangement. For one thing, these identities don't necessarily correspond to a given material reality, and even if they did, there is nothing intrinsically immoral (within the values system of most anarchists) about an individual's tendency to have sex with a particular gender of person versus another, or with one person versus many people. Thus, as a political practice, identification as queer or polyamorous is an *expression* or *representation* of dissent against a macrosocial system of power in which some types of subjects are able to dominate others by virtue of their subject positions. To have erotic desires that are heterosexual or monogamous is not an ethical lapse in itself. Within an anarchist ethical framework, it may be consistent to try to discipline subjects into practices of consent-seeking, and inconsistent to try to discipline subjects into practices of self-identification, which are not in and of themselves oppressive or liberating. Yet, in spite of this, my research shows that, among anarchists, identifying in such a way as to potentially *imply* one's support for the hegemony of heterosexuality and monogamy can be seen as politically unpalatable. Recall Tina's claim that I quoted above: "I don't like to identify as straight. I find it oppressive." So there must be something at stake beyond the material enactment of power relations – why does Tina feel uncomfortable merely identifying with a hegemonic sexual category, regardless of whether or not she actually wields illegitimate power over others in her own life?

Identification as contestation

I want to further clarify here what is at stake for individuals who "don't like to identify as straight" or as monogamous. Many anarchist activists position their very self-identification as a site of contestation against hegemonic (or "straight") constructions of sexuality. For anarchists, like many other sex radicals, to adopt the label of queer is not to foreclose heterosexual activities, but rather to symbolically disavow the social coercion involved in enforcing what Adrienne Rich (1980) calls "compulsory heterosexuality." Coming out as queer is not, in these cases, an act of exposing one's "true" or "inner" identity. Rather it's "a voluntaristic and reflexive act" which is "accessible to anyone who possesse[s] the right political convictions" (Stein 1997: 48). What is at issue here is less an objection to heterosexual desire and more an objection to heteronormativity, or the idea that sex between so-called opposite sex partners is normal, natural, and correct (Berlant and Warner 1998: 548). Ideally, as Annette Schlichter explains, "the object of the critique is neither heterosexual desire nor the subject desiring another gender but the *sociocultural system*, which inscribes a heterosexual identity as a hegemonic position" (Schlichter 2004: 546, emphasis mine). Similarly, the anarchist critique of monogamy is usually, in theory, a critique of *compulsory* monogamy, rather than a critique of any particular couple's actual habit of sexual exclusivity.

There are multiple scales of operation here: whereas normativity is intrinsically macrosocial, personal behaviors are intrinsically microsocial. There is a distinction to be made between the "cultural system that produces and regulates sexual identities" and the individual subjects who end up taking on identities within that system (Schlichter 2004: 546). Yet, proponents of a kind of micropolitical sexual resistance often fail to make this distinction; on one side, straight subjects are held accountable for the perpetuation of an oppressive cultural system (which they cannot, as individuals, reasonably be held responsible for); on the other side, queer subjects are attributed the capacity to resist or subvert an entire system by their performance of a non-hegemonic identity position. While there is convincing theoretical and empirical support for the ways that macrosocial phenomena like norms have microlevel effects through their work on individual subjects (as elaborated in the work of Foucault, for example), the opposite operation is less well supported. In other words, while norms have identifiable effects on individual bodies, individual bodies are less clearly shown to be able to make a material impact on social norms.

Despite this lacuna of evidence, somewhat grandiose claims for the assumed effects of individual actions on the social order are often made by proponents of queer identity and practice. For example, a leaflet circulated by self-identified queers at New York City's gay pride march in 1990 proclaimed, "Every time we fuck, we win" (Anonymous Queers 1999: 589).[15] It's true that by engaging in queer sex, individuals succeed in doing something that bigots don't want them to do. But does the act of queer sex undermine the power of those who would prohibit it? If anything, it exposes the bigots' already existing lack of power to completely control queer sexuality. It is unclear how precisely the exposure contributes to the project of winning *more* power for queers in society. Diana Fuss (1989: 101) is worth quoting at length on this point:

While I do believe that living as a gay or lesbian person in a post-industrial heterosexist society has certain political effects (whether I wish my sexuality to be so politically invested or not), I also believe that simply *being* gay or lesbian is not sufficient to constitute political activism. A severe reduction of the political to the personal leads to a telescoping of goals, a limiting of revolutionary activity to the project of self-discovery and personal transformation. 'The personal is political' re-privatizes social experience, to the degree that one can be engaged in political praxis without ever leaving the confines of the bedroom. Sexual desire itself becomes invested with macropolitical significance. The personal, I am arguing, is *not* political, in any literal or equivalent fashion.

Following Fuss, it's arguable that personal acts may have political significance, in the sense that they carry political meaning, but that doesn't necessarily ensure their efficacy in radically subverting *systems* of domination. There is no necessary relationship between gestures that are imagined to *represent* a desire for subversion (e.g. calling oneself queer), and *actual* subversion of a network of power (e.g. overturning heteronormativity).[16]

We can see the parallels here between sexual practices and other lifestyle practices discussed in earlier chapters. All, as the acts of individuals, perhaps undertaken in private, are limited in the impact they can possibly make on the norms of mainstream society. Furthermore, many of the privileges of normative sexual identity are discursive and unquantifiable, such as pervasive cultural validation and familial acceptance of one's romantic partners. Thus, these privileges cannot simply be renounced on an individual basis, discarded along with the hetero identity label. To be fair, anarcha-queers do tend to renounce many elements of the "network of norms" that comprise the "complex field" of operations that upholds heterosexuality as a privileged social position (Jakobsen 1998), state-recognized marriage being a major example. But even here, we have to be critical about the idea that an individual's personal rejection of marriage matters for the dismantling of heteronormative hegemony. As Lauren Berlant and Elizabeth Freeman (1993: 219–20) point out:

> Butler's metropolitan polymorphous solution to the politics of spectacle recognizes local, urban, consumer-oriented spaces as crucial sites of political transformation; but her imagined 'gender performances' never link the politics of repeated contact between individual and visible bodies to collective forms of political affect or agency.

In order to see an individual act of "trouble-making" as something other than a trivial gesture, we have to return to the idea of performance as a theatrical act. Within the logic of performance, there is an actor *and* an audience, and that which is performed attains its social force through its effect on that audience. Within this logic, resistant sexuality must in some way be a public performance (even if the public in question is very small); individual transgressions do not, in themselves, subvert relations of oppression. (This is why closeted queerness does not even have the potential to generate social change, no matter how much it is experienced as rebellious by the individual queer subject. To again invoke the typology of effects I presented in Chapter 2, there may be personal outcomes to private queerness, but not activist ones). I would argue that anarchist scenes, as subcultural spaces in which activism and socializing are inseparable, do provide a sort of sphere of publicity in which alternative sexualities may be performed for others. Furthermore, subcultures in which particular performances are contextualized within a discourse of politicized sexuality just might offer the kind of link between individual performances and collective affect and agency that Berlant and Freeman call for. Resistant sexual practices are positioned by anarchists, not as random choices, but as recognizable expressions of anarchist politics. As certain practices are consistently valued and promoted within anarchist scenes and discourses, they take on a collective character.

Take the way that sexuality is performed within the anarchist community in Washington, DC, for example. According to interviewees such as Joel and Gabby (and several others who had lived there), both polyamory and queer identification were part of normal sexuality for DC anarchists. Such normalization had come about as the groundbreaking performances of certain visible individuals were taken up by others within the scene. Joel observed, "What happened is that, cuz, it enters the sexual vocabulary of people I think, it enters the sexual vocabulary through someone else, like someone has the idea, 'oh we could have open relationships, let's think about this.'" Joel went on to talk about one well-known and well-liked couple in the DC anarchist community who had an open relationship, which he felt paved the way for others to try out the practice. As he put it, "A lot of people fell into that, 'if they can do it maybe we can do it.'" As more people "fall into" the practice of polyamory, it becomes all the more visible and even commonplace within the social spaces of the scene.

Anarchists in DC tend to live together in communal housing arrangements, and their group houses become gathering places for members of the local anarchist community (as well as visiting travelers). People thus have opportunities to witness others' lifestyle practices that might otherwise remain sequestered in private domestic spaces. Even the most intimate expressions of sexuality are on display for others to observe and emulate—everyone can see (and hear) how many and what kinds of people someone is bringing home on a regular basis, and who disappears with whom into whose bedroom. In the context of the dominant culture where sexuality—especially alternative, resistant forms of sexuality—is often encouraged to remain hidden, semi-public alternative spaces create the feeling that it is perfectly acceptable—even normal—to be openly queer, polyamorous, etc.

In this kind of community setting, the promise offered by one CrimethInc. essay, "Look around and you'll see that there *are* alternatives . . . to the traditional ways of making love and being sexual that mainstream culture offers us," actually rings true (CrimethInc. 2000: 203). Once non-hegemonic sexuality becomes a subcultural norm, the performances have transcended individual bodies, though of course they may remain marginal in relation to the larger social order.

Certain practices are normalized more so in some settings than in others. Polyamory, for example, was matter-of-factly accepted as a normal relationship structure by interviewees from Washington, DC. Interviewees from other places demonstrated an *awareness* of polyamory as a typical anarchist lifestyle practice, but were less likely to have practiced it themselves; for them it was not so important as a marker of their anarchist identity. Gabby had spent several years in the anarchist scene in DC, but at the time of our interview she was living in Los Angeles, where she had grown up. She explained that in DC, polyamory is "the main relationship type that everybody's in" and the refusal of monogamy is taken for granted, whereas in Los Angeles, Gabby felt that she was more likely to be met with opposition if she proposed having an open relationship with a potential partner. Gabby speculated that one reason for this was the stronger tendency toward what she called "machoness" among men in the LA anarchist scene. This difference between the two subcultural environments points to one of the important factors in the capacity for performative resistance to be effective: a resistant performance must resonate (at least somewhat) with existing discursive, cultural, and personal values, or it will not even make sense as "a good thing to do" (to invoke Joel's understanding of polyamory quoted above). It also highlights that while sexuality, like other lifestyle practices, may be an individual practice, it is not a solitary one—it relies on the understanding and cooperation of others. A collective commitment to oppositional expressions of sexuality is thus crucial for sustaining even individual practices of resistance.

Miles' experience with his partner is testament to this. Miles was initially optimistic about his ability to have a marriage that preserved the radical, non-heteronormative nature of his relationship with his partner. In an email exchange with me, he described his disappointment at finding this optimism to be unfounded:

When I got married I was relatively young, and even though I 'never believed' in marriage, I thought it was such a trivial thing that I could participate in the institution without it having any effect on me or our relationship. I have learned the power of these structures in how they shape your world and how others deal with you (and you with them), and don't like it. This so-called intimate relationship has become an interest of others (and, of course, the state). I guess I used to think that you could turn these things against themselves from the inside and it didn't make any difference if you had the right attitude. I don't believe that now . . . . So the 'marriage experiment' is a failure, from my point of view, but now, as I contemplate what it would mean to move to another stage, I realize how caught up I am in the state (I have to ask permission from others to change my relationship), as well as the inertia of not only our relationship, but the 'tradition' of marriage and all the cultural baggage that brings.

Miles did express to me that he does not really feel himself to be a part of an active anarchist community. It is tempting to speculate that if he and his wife had, in fact, been surrounded by others who reimagined intimate relationships in the same way Miles would like to (had they lived in collective houses in DC for example), they would have been able to sustain a more "radical" partnership, even as a married couple. But as it was, merely understanding that there are other anarchists out there who share his attitudes toward marriage was clearly not enough to protect Miles and his wife from the material effects imposed on them by the institution itself and the "cultural baggage" that goes along with it.

In addition to cultural pressures, the structural incentives to monogamy and marriage thrown up by the state and the capitalist economy are significant enough that they may outweigh even strong desires to resist such practices in one's own life. Even assuming one has the support of an alternative subculture, the pressure exerted by dominant ideologies and structures still works against the adoption of resistant lifestyles. Heteronormativity is deeply entrenched in mainstream culture, and particularly for those individuals who do not experience a felt, erotic desire for non-heterosexual sex, there may seem to be little material incentive for renouncing the privilege of heterosexual identity, though they may see the symbolic political value of doing so. Take as an illustration the exchange I had with Miranda about her and her husband's practice of monogamy:

LPS: Are you guys monogamous? Do you believe in monogamy?
Miranda: Do I believe in it or are we?
LPS: Either, both.
Miranda: Um, I don't believe in it, but yes we are [*laughs*].
LPS: Does he [your husband] believe in it, is that why you are?
Miranda: I don't think so . . . . yeah, theoretically we're anarchists who don't believe in monogamy, but practically we're married because he has health insurance on his job.

The fact that Miranda insists on a distinction between whether she "believes in" monogamy and whether she "is" monogamous, as well as the reason she gave for being married (health benefits), epitomizes the disconnect between political ideals and what may be practically feasible for individuals to do in their personal lives. Contestatory identification with polyamory may not make sense as a tactic of resistance when basic, immediate concerns like health care are involved. In situations such as these, personal motivations may trump ethical, activist, and other considerations.

Both Miles and Miranda's experiences illustrate the point that radical, systemic change may be a prerequisite to individuals' even having the capacity to choose alternative lifestyles. Heterosexism, statism, capitalism, exploitative sexual power dynamics, etc., do not go away for anarchists simply because they try not to engage with them in their own personal practices. However, the production of a strong subculture in which individuals share commitments to avoid pernicious forms of sexuality can certainly foster different and more appealing experiences of sexuality for those individuals than can be found in mainstream culture. As alternatives become normalized in anarchist communities, new kinds of desires, relationships, and even selves are produced.

A diversity of sexual tactics?

Resistant sexual practices are not solely undertaken for the direct personal benefit of the practitioners. Like other politicized lifestyle practices, polyamory and queer self-identification are also often imagined to have activist effects. What then might be the broader social ramifications of these individual or even collective subcultural performances of resistance in the form of queer, polyamorous identity? By assuming an identification that positions them as non-straight and non-monogamous—by disidentifying with normative sexuality—these individuals are enacting resistance to the process of normalization or "distribution around a statistically imagined norm" (Berlant and Warner 1998: 557). Statistically imagined norms are often used in normative projects—that is, the supposed fact of something's occurring most often in a society is advanced as justification for that thing's dominance and privilege over other things (Jakobsen 1998: 518). By proliferating instances that deviate from the norm, disidentifiers might imagine that they can effect a statistical shift such that the norm moves to the left of where it once was. The logic is, the fewer people who publicly identify as straight, the less "normal" straightness will be, and ultimately, the less normative power the ideology of straightness will have.[17]

The displacement of non-conformity away from actual, physical sexual activity and onto symbolic representations of sexuality (i.e. identity labels) rather ingeniously sidesteps debates about whether sexual desire is biological or cultural, rational or instinctual, agentic or determined, politically innocent or politically valent. Within the anarchist discourse of queer identification, at issue is not what kind of people one has sex with, but rather whether, by specifying that information through one's identification, one participates in a system that awards or withdraws social power based on this information. While people can perhaps not be held ethically accountable for what they desire (if we assume that desires are somehow below the level of consciousness, that they are "governed by some internal necessity" [Fuss 1989: 2]), people can, it would seem, be held accountable for whether they discursively position their desires as aligned with a privileged sexual subjectivity.

Yet, whether or not an individual can be held ethically accountable for their public identity is perhaps beside the point. The mere presence of queer people does not qualitatively subvert the dominance of heteronormativity, though it may offer an alternative that quantitatively chips away at the numerical dominance of straightness by attracting away adherents. Furthermore, as I discussed in the previous two chapters, simply exposing people to alternatives will not be enough to attract them to a non-dominant position. Some ideological realignment must take place for formerly privileged practices to be displaced by more liberated forms of sexuality. Such realignment depends, at least in part, on the circulation of rhetorically effective arguments in defense of these more liberated forms. This circulation may be a realistic proposition within the anarchist subcultural milieu, given the subculture's discursive infrastructure; ideas are rather easily spread to very receptive audiences via electronic and print media as well as conferences and other physical meetings. Yet, beyond the limits of the subculture (i.e. in the realm of broad social transformation), resistant sexuality befalls the same trouble as all other forms of lifestyle politics. It is simply invisible or, more to the point, illegible as a political intervention. In fact, individual transgressions may serve to restabilize the very normalcy of the norms they transgress, if they are read as mere whims or worse, as pathological deviance.

What is needed is a discursive context in which alternatives can be made to resonate with other values. This may have been partially achieved within anarchist subcultures, in which anarchist political philosophy has been aligned with queer sexuality, in ways described above. But can broader social transformation really be generated by anarchists' personal practices of sexual resistance? While it seems clear that individual practices of sexuality can contribute to the subversion of mainstream norms *within* the subcultural spaces of anarchist movements, it is less clear that these acts have an impact on anyone not already operating within the anarchist political framework. For those who are heavily invested in heterosexuality, monogamy, and marriage, the knowledge that there are people out there who are not so invested will do little to unsettle their own personal investments. For people who don't share the ideological commitments upon which anarchist practices of sexuality are based, these practices may well lack appeal, and, in fact, may just as easily disgust and alienate as attract and inspire.

This is one reason why some anarchists feel it is strategically ill-advised to be too insistent on non-conformist performances of sexuality, just as some feel that it may be detrimental to dress in distinctive styles. Melissa, for example, voiced frustration with anarchists being insensitive to the fact that working-class communities of color may not be comfortable with the forms of sexuality practiced by anarchists (whom she seemed to position as not claiming membership in those communities—that is she seemed to be referring only to white, middle-class anarchists). She thought that openly embracing queerness and polyamory had foreclosed potential relationships of solidarity and had posed an unnecessary obstacle to collaboration between anarchists and non-anarchists in urban St Louis, where she had been an activist. Melissa's perception of the dynamics in St Louis may indeed be accurate. However, it seems problematic to assume that inner-city people of color are predisposed to be alienated by oppositional sexual practices. Indeed, although I cannot make statistical generalizations from my small interview pool, I observed no obvious correlation between interviewees' sexual practices and their class statuses or racial identities. That is, interviewees who identified as middle class and/or white did not strike me as any more or less likely to practice or support polyamory and queer self-identification than other interviewees. Of course, the one thing all my interviewees had in common, across their various class and racial identities, was their identification with anarchism. So, setting aside Melissa's potentially problematic assumptions about class and race determining attitudes about sexuality, she is onto an important point, which is that people who are not operating with a baseline openness to non-dominant sexualities may be best communicated with in other ways than embodied performances of sexual resistance.

In line with this, many interviewees mentioned the importance of "meeting people where they're at," meaning they saw the value of accepting and working with people who do not (yet) share their goals, values, identities, and lifestyles. The willingness to meet people where they're at is, at times, a strategic effort to forge alliances in recognition of the cultural differences that may account for differing attitudes toward sexuality. For example, Mark reflected that he often encounters homophobia among the working-class laborers he tries to do organizing work with. For him, this highlighted the importance of cultivating strong personal relationships based on points of political solidarity, so that he could feel comfortable challenging comments and attitudes he finds offensive. For Mark, it was important not to alienate people he is trying to do political work with, but it was also important to him that he not "let shit fly" when he felt it was inappropriate.

It's worth noting that it may have only been possible for Mark to keep this kind of attitude because of his own identity and position of privilege with respect to hegemonic sexuality—had he identified as queer, and visibly presented himself as such, he may have found it much more difficult even to establish productive personal relationships in the face of vocal homophobia.

Mark was able to make a strategic choice about how he communicated about his anti-hierarchical politics, based on his own subject position and relationship to the people he was talking to. It may not be a choice that is available to all other anarchists, nor a viable tactic for promoting anti-hierarchical values in all situations, but it has its utility in this particular context. Given my above argument that whether Mark *personally identifies* as queer or not is not directly material to the project of subverting the *social privileging* of straightness, I think anarchists can find value in the way he exploits his position of privilege in order to facilitate dialogue with people who would likely be unreceptive to queer political performances. Importantly, tactics like Mark's can coexist with embodied performances by those anarchists for whom queerness and polyamory are internally felt *needs* and not solely *representations* of political dissent.

A catchphrase among anarchist organizers of large-scale protests is "diversity of tactics." When anarchist organizers use this phrase, they are stating that they recognize the legitimacy of a range of modes of resistance, from whimsical theatrics to combative confrontation with police to violent destruction of property. Each bloc involved in the protest is accorded the autonomy to freely decide which tactics it will employ. This decision can take into account the social positionality—membership in various, intersecting social categories with each posing their own constraints and possibilities— of the protesters. For example, there are often individuals who identify as "unarrestable" due to factors like not possessing the requisite documentation for their presence in the United States or having to support young children. Unarrestables may thus try to refrain from tactics that involve illegal activities. Tactical decisions can also be tailored to the desired outcome of the action. In any specific instance, protesters may consider whether their aim is to win public support for a cause, to forge unity among themselves, or to have an immediate material effect on an unjust situation, each of which is a valid reason for action but each of which might call for a different tactical approach.

The case of anarchist sexuality shows that the diversity of tactics principle can be productively applied to lifestyle politics as well. What this principle requires, in any case, is a fundamental commitment to reflexive critique. That is, activists must be constantly vigilant about considering the ramifications—both intended and unintended, both direct and indirect—of any given instance of a practice. For example, if one is considering one's own practice of polyamory, one has to ask whether it satisfies one's personal desires and needs, whether it loosens the grip of capitalism and patriarchy on one's own personal experience, whether it communicates an indictment of capitalism and patriarchy to others, whether it effectively demonstrates to others that polyamory is a viable alternative to monogamy, and so on. And one has to ask these questions in any given situation, with the under-standing that the answers will change depending on who is involved, where they are, and who is watching.

This kind of commitment to contextual reflexivity requires that specific tactics not be fetishized for themselves. A given tactic may not work for some people, in some places, at some times. Boundaries of authenticity thus cannot be drawn based purely on the adoption of a tactic. Moral righteousness cannot be claimed on the basis of a lifestyle choice, since that choice may only be politically efficacious in certain contexts. Lifestyle politics makes most sense when its practices are approached as provisional and subjected to situational critique (in a way that mirrors the ironization of anarchist identity described in Chapter 4). Situational critique provides an alternative to purism, which is a trap that frustrates many activists and in some cases even drives individuals away from activist movement cultures. The minute problematization and discipline engendered by movement cultures can be taxing and ultimately exhaust the reserves of commitment that individuals have toward the movement. Purism goes hand in hand with the aestheticization of politics in that it refers to the judgment and policing of individual habits to the extent that they fail to line up with subcultural norms about what is acceptable anarchist practice and what is not. These judgments are supposedly based in the substantive ideological differences that motivate subcultural deviations from dominant ways of life. But because everyone can be called out at some point for not living up to anarchist principles—to live in contemporary society is to be complicit with capitalism and other forms of exploitation—the search for purity is a trap in which everyone is doomed to fail. In the most generous reading, purism comes from an ethical place—it is supposed to point out where people are not being consistent with their values and hopefully to bring them in line. But besides playing into a dynamic of normativity that would seem to be at odds with anarchist philosophy, purism may have a paradoxical effect of driving people away from activist movements rather than actually spurring them to bring their behavior in line with anarchist ideals.

Ethical critique that attends to the specific conditions of any given situation—including the structural constraints experienced by the individuals involved—offers a way to retain accountability without devolving into puristic moralism. It makes more sense for lifestyle practices to be assessed on the basis of their practicability and observable effects in particular contexts, rather than activists making a wholesale embrace or rejection of a given lifestyle or lifestyle practice.

6

Bridging the chasm: The contradictions of radical lifestyle politics in neoliberal context

Several years ago, I sent a brief message to an email list for anarchist academics. It seemed innocuous enough to me—I was just inquiring whether anyone was aware of the first appearance of the term "lifestyle anarchism" in writing, as I wanted to be sure to cite it properly. Lifestyle anarchism is a term, often used pejoratively, to refer to a mode of relating to or identifying with anarchism that involves a preoccupation with many of the practices I've described in this book: self-identifying, consuming, and styling oneself in particular ways that differ from the mainstream and mark one's membership in an activist subculture. While I was aware that the discourse of lifestyle politics is a source of anxiety and tension for many anarchist activists— as I've demonstrated throughout this book—I did not expect the reaction that followed. While a few people attempted to answer my question, many others took the opportunity to debate the concept of lifestyle anarchism itself. Over the span of a few days, dozens of emails were exchanged in which various individuals (with varying degrees of nuance and civility) offered their own definitions of lifestyle anarchism, shared relevant personal experiences from their own involvement in anarchist activist communities, and argued for varying levels of investment in lifestyle politics, ranging from intense commitment to measured ambivalence to biting disdain for lifestyle anarchism. At times, the conversation became hostile—there was even a bit of name-calling! I was starting to see why, on another anarchist message board, the topic of lifestylism has proven so incendiary that it is explicitly forbidden to bring it up.[1] As might be expected, no unanimous conclusion was arrived at by the email list participants about the proper role of lifestyle within contemporary anarchist movements. But what became clear to me from this episode was that, at least for the kind of people who are invested enough in the project of anarchism to participate in an email list about it, the subject of lifestyle carries high stakes. Clearly, some anarchists feel there is value in defining, defending, and debating the place of lifestyle-based tactics within their political projects.

Though I never was able to locate a definitive source for the origin of the term, it probably first came into use during the 1980s, within critiques of the tendency for some self-identified anarchists to become preoccupied with lifestyle practices to the exclusion of other activist work. At this time, anarchism was being taken up by members of punk subcultures, under the influence of politically outspoken bands such as Crass and the Dead Kennedys (Thompson 2004). Many youth in the United States and Europe were motivated by radical, anti-capitalist critique to establish communes, renounce consumerism, and vocally oppose the state and its violence. They were basically doing as their forerunners in the hippie counterculture had done, but with the hard-edged aesthetic introduced by punk music and style. Many of the practices examined in this book became explicitly imbricated with anarchism in this era. Yet, the fact that many who became involved in punk scenes lacked a deep understanding of anarchist history or political philosophy meant that their enactment of anarchist principles could, at times, be fairly limited, remaining at the "shallow" level of their individual lifestyle choices. This was what earned them the pejorative labels of lifestyle anarchist or lifestylist. Since that time, lifestylism has retained its connotative associations with the anarchopunk sector of the broad anarchist movement, but the label may be extended to include anyone who attempts to resist or evade "the system" in some capacity in their everyday lives (Molyneux 2011: 55).

A central focus of this book has been the relationship between lifestyle practices and the constitution of anarchism as a political identity and activist project. While each chapter has somewhat addressed some of the internal tensions around the specific lifestyle practices discussed, these tensions must be situated amid a larger discourse within anarchist movements that questions the very legitimacy of lifestyle as an arena of activism. This discourse also questions the authenticity and sincerity of individuals who adopt lifestyle-based tactics as part of their identification with the anarchist project. This may seem contrary to what I argued in Chapter 4, where I said that engaging in particular lifestyle practices can be an index of one's authentic and sincere commitment to anarchism. In the contrary position I am addressing here, critics of lifestyle anarchism assert that a commitment to lifestyle politics may belie a *lack* of political seriousness since it is a misguided approach to radical activism. In fact, this contradiction—that commitment to anarchist lifestyle practices is simultaneously used as a marker of sincerity and inauthenticity—is not easily resolved, and seems to generate no end of controversy and debate among anarchist activists. It seems that there are no winners in the "anarchist realness" contest—you might seem insincere if you don't adopt certain practices in your everyday life, but if you are seen to be too invested in those practices, your authenticity as a serious activist comes into question.

In this chapter, I examine the meta-discourse about lifestylism as an authentic or inauthentic mode of activist engagement among anarchists, with a particular focus on the function of the rhetorical figure of the lifestyle anarchist within this discourse. In doing so, I hope to cast light backwards over the content of the previous chapters, to help illuminate what exactly *is* at stake in activists' practices of lifestyle politics. As I will argue, there is no clear-cut line to be drawn that would separate "real" anarchists from lifestyle anarchists, despite what some critics may claim. Drawing on the evidence marshaled by previous chapters, I reiterate a central argument of this book—that lifestyle is a major site for the constitution of radical activist identity and community in addition to being the site of many tactical interventions. An individual or group's adoption of lifestyle tactics thus always *does* more than even its practitioners may intend or be conscious of. The multifaceted—and sometimes even self-contradictory—effects of lifestyle practices complicate any straightforward judgment about their place in the activist toolkit.

Radical lifestyle tactics are so problematic as a form of activism because they are a product of neoliberal conditions while at the same time representing resistance *against* many of the political projects of neoliberalism. The ideology of neoliberalism interpellates individuals as self-interested, self-reflexive subjects who monitor and regulate their own conduct in the pursuit of various goals (usually those of the market and/or the state). It is common sense, in this context, for the individual to be an important (even primary) unit of political participation. Because of this, an activist strategy based on lifestyle tactics can appear immanently appropriate since it mobilizes individuals to exercise power in their immediate situation and to achieve observable results in that sphere. Yet, at the same time, radicals object to the principle of possessive individualism, which goes hand in hand with neoliberalism's capitalist logic, and to the delegitimation of collective social formations, which is inherent to neoliberal ideology. An activist strategy based on lifestyle tactics can thus appear disturbingly inadequate for the contemporary radical leftist project, which seeks broader social reorganization.

This chapter will further delineate some of the contradictions contained within and invoked by lifestyle politics within radical activist frameworks. As the presence of these contradictions should make clear, any pursuit of purity or total identity with the radical ideal through lifestyle is bound to fail. This inevitable failure suggests the necessity of a reflexive critique that takes into account the limitations of any given tactic in any given situation, while noting the specific conditions under which certain tactics are appropriate and effective, and keeping in mind that any effects will be multiple and inflected by many intersecting factors. My concluding thoughts attempt to enlarge the scope of the discussion to consider what the contradiction-riddled case of lifestyle anarchism can illustrate about the nature of radical critique under conditions of a neoliberal postmodernity that seems both to enable and to always foreclose complete identity with the radical political project.

The discourse around lifestyle anarchism

James Purkis and Jonathan Bowen (2004: 8) use the term lifestyle anarchism to describe the "living [of] one's life in accordance to particular principles" which grow out of anarchist critique. By this simple definition, to talk about lifestyle anarchism is to discuss the set of everyday activities, tastes, and consumption habits enacted by anarchists *qua* anarchists. Since, as one interviewee told me, "anarchism is always about how one lives one's life," it would seem that lifestyle anarchism would be a fairly straightforward phenomenon. Yet, the term is actually much more loaded than this. As I said above, the labels lifestyle anarchist and lifestylist are frequently invoked within the anarchist scene to deride someone who is perceived to be more interested in cultivating their own personal liberation than in achieving social transformation. Lifestylists may be seen as selfish hedonists who are interested only in their own immediate interests. Or they may be seen as activists who perhaps mean well but whose interventions are misguided and ineffective because they fail to transcend individual experience. In the words of one webpage, lifestyle anarchism refers to "apolitical hangers-on in the movement. That is, people who dress the look or living in certain ways, but who don't really act on the basic tenets of anarchism."[2] A further nuance to the way lifestylism is used is that it is the kind of thing that everyone can point out but almost no one will admit to embracing themselves. So, while the individuals I've mentioned in this book certainly engage in some of the lifestyle practices and have some of the motivations associated with lifestyle anarchism, almost none of them would refer to themselves as lifestylists or appreciate being perceived as such. Supporting this, the entry for lifestyle anarchism on one anarchist website reads:

> Lifestyle anarchism is a term commonly used by those within the anarchist movement to criticize others who, they allege, practice anarchism as a lifestyle or fashion statement. The term is seldom used as a self-description and there are no anarchist organisations which describe themselves as lifestylist.[3]

Accusations of lifestylism can function rhetorically to designate a mode of activism that is less serious, or less effective, or less legitimate *than one's own*, whatever it may be. Invoking the specter of lifestylism is thus used in much the same way that lifestyle practices themselves are, as a tool for proving oneself as a serious, self-aware radical. Yet, as I pointed out above, one is pretty much damned if they do and damned if they don't when it comes to lifestyle politics. If one doesn't live the revolution in all the expected ways, one risks being illegible as holding a respectably radical critique. Yet, due to the anti-lifestylist rhetoric in some parts of the activist milieu, commitments to the anarchist lifestyle may put activists at risk of being identified with problematic expressions of privilege or subculturalism.

Murray Bookchin's (1995) essay, *Social Anarchism or Lifestyle Anarchism: An Unbridgable Chasm* is probably the authoritative source on the concept of lifestyle anarchism in its pejorative sense. As the title might suggest, the essay takes a binary view of anarchist orientations. It's based on a premise that there are two kinds of anarchists—those who are interested in radical social transformation and those who are interested only in their own lives—and that the activities of the second are detrimental to the effectiveness of the authentic anarchist movement. He argues, "These trendy posturings, nearly all of which follow current yuppie fashions, are individualistic in the important sense that they are antithetical to the development of serious organizations, a radical politics, a committed social movement, theoretical coherence, and programmatic relevance" (19). Bookchin situates lifestylism as being of a piece with "postmodernist" theories of power and subjectivity, advanced by Michel Foucault for example, that locate the realm of politics and oppression beyond the institutions of the state. For Bookchin, such an analysis is dangerous because he sees it as allowing radicals to displace their critiques and efforts away from the state, which, for him, ought to be anarchists' primary target. Through this displacement, according to Bookchin, lifestyle anarchists cease to be effective anarchists and no longer have any hope of achieving an anarchist society. Bookchin believes that radicals ought to take advantage of the failure of state institutions as an opportunity to promote revolutionary social transformations, but instead they cope with their dissatisfaction by withdrawing from social action into their own personal lifestyle practices, which often revolve around consumer choices and stylistic affectations. Thus, he sees lifestylism as a distraction from more effective forms of political activism, such as "institutionalized" coalitions "of the oppressed in popular assemblies, councils, and/or confederations" (10).

It should be noted here that Bookchin's stance in this essay seems to contradict his writings elsewhere, particularly in "Post-scarcity Anarchism" (1971) where he has been read as advocating a kind of lifestyle politics. In the later work, Bookchin was writing at a time when the countercultural movements of the 1960s and 1970s were seen to have been thoroughly co-opted or negated by the consumer culture of the 1980s. His perspective on punks, new agers, and other lifestylists is clearly informed by the unfortunate end met by earlier radical movements. Lifestyle politics had, in some ways, been critiqued by anarchists in earlier eras[4] but it took on new significance in the 1980s and 1990s because it was now solidly situated within consumer culture. Whereas a preoccupation with the individual could be critiqued from a strategic or philosophical point of view in earlier times, added to this critique was now a fear—based on first-hand observation and experience—that radical movements would be co-opted and defused by capitalist apparatuses.[5] Bookchin's critique of lifestylism was perhaps a bit polemical (one website describes it as a "bitter rant"),[6] but it did capture a real skepticism that continues to exist around lifestyle-based tactics.

In more contemporary expressions of this skepticism, a common target for accusations of lifestylism is CrimethInc., a publishing collective that puts out anarchist propaganda in the form of books, zines, pamphlets, posters, stickers, music, and videos. The CrimethInc. collective is intentionally evasive about revealing its exact makeup; its website describes it as "a decentralized anarchist collective composed of many cells which act independently in pursuit of a freer and more joyous world." By most accounts, its core consists of a small circle of individuals who publish anonymously or under pseudonyms and who oversee the production and distribution of the materials. But CrimethInc. is probably most usefully understood as the hub of a very loosely united community of readers who see their views and tastes reflected in the content of the collective's output and who may be mobized for actions and events organized under the CrimethInc. banner. Fans of CrimethInc. and those involved in the publishing collective were a recurrent target of criticism by people I interviewed in doing the research for this book. On several occasions, interviewees referred to CrimethInc. as a symbol of a concern with lifestyle, and used terms like "crimthinc kids" or "CT-ers" to stand in for the kind of people who seem to place a lot of stock in lifestyle practices. CrimethInc. has come to be associated with lifestylism because much of the content of its materials is related to practices of everyday life. An analysis of the corpus of CrimethInc.'s materials shows that these are not the only topics discussed—the books and zines also cover philosophy, social movements, international events, etc. The slick look of the materials (a combination of mass produced and DIY aesthetics) and the sophisticated distribution of them (they are ubiquitous at book fairs and radical book stores but are also available from mainstream commercial booksellers) associates them with a "branded" and "packaged" image of anarchism, to use the words of interviewee Miranda. This image and the way it makes radical ideas accessible to a broader audience of youthful consumers than might otherwise identify with anarchism reinforces the connotation that CrimethInc.'s fans are less than serious in their commitment to anarchist politics.

Some of the content of CrimethInc.'s materials supports the notion that some anarchists are more interested in their own personal experience of pleasure than in radical social transformation. For example, the writers of CrimethInc.'s most circulated book, *Days of War, Nights of Love* (2000: 39), claim to see a more socially oriented politics as futile because "it's difficult to imagine a whole different world order" and because none of us will live to experience a world without hierarchy. According to CrimethInc., "we should, rather, recognize the patterns of submission and domination in our own lives, and, to the best of our ability, break free of them. We should put the anarchist ideal—no masters, no slaves—into effect in our daily lives however we can" (39–40). Later in the same book, they argue, "we must seek first and foremost to alter the contents of our own lives in a revolutionary manner, rather than direct our struggle towards world-historical changes which we will not live to witness" (118). So, the emphasis here is less on building a collective movement that works toward a rearrangement of social power relations and more on "resurrecting anarchism as a personal approach to life" (34). Indeed, CrimethInc. proclaims in its "anarchist primer" pamphlet, *Fighting for Our Lives* (n.d.), that "the best reason to be a revolutionary is that it is simply a better way to live." Damningly, one critic asserts that "Crimethink's [sic] neo-Situationist exhortations to disentagle ourselves from commodity dependence read like lifestyle advice columns for the voluntarily poor and anticapitalist" (Kanouse 2006: 28). This critique is particularly interesting because the contemporary advice or self-help manual has been identified by many as the epitome of the neoliberal culture (Rose 1996; McGee 2005; Sender 2006; Ouellette 2004). The self-discipline exhorted by expert authorities in such manuals encapsulates the ideology of individual "responsibilization" in lieu of collective action aimed at solving social problems. This expression of neoliberal ideology maps quite well onto some of CrimethInc.'s tactical advice, as exemplified in the quotes above. Much as the underlying political ideology of neoliberalism assumes that all subjects have equal access to the law and the market, the advocacy of individualist tactics implies, erroneously, that everyone has equal access to those methods of resistance. By not taking a strong critical view of how structural conditions give some more wherewithal to pursue resistant lifestyles than others, the rhetoric of CrimethInc. may relieve the activists who subscribe to it from a feeling of collective responsibility for social welfare.

Some interviewees also expressed negative attitudes toward CrimethInc.-style activities and the anarchists who embrace them. Pritha, for instance, described (via email) lifestyle anarchists as the ones who don "black clothes, circle A tattoos etc." and said of them,

> I don't think 'lifestyle' anarchists (a la CrimethInc.) are really anarchists because I believe that anarchism is about cultivating community, hope and inspiration in an otherwise unjust and difficult world where capitalism

forces people to be competitive, cut-throat and isolated. For me, the resistance against capitalism and imperialism then isn't about hopping trains, stealing, or throwing pipe bombs at Starbucks but about working with all other marginalized communities to transform our society.[7]

Other interviewees criticized lifestyle anarchists for being too out of sync with "everyday people" (Emily) and for their "disconnection from larger communities that they might work with or help" (Rita). Matthew, who was in his thirties, noted that "CrimethInc. is very popular among people ten years younger than me" and admitted to having gone through a CrimethInc. "phase" of his own. He offered a reflection via email on some of the problems of lifestylism as encapsulated in CrimethInc.:

> My main beef with CrimethInc. is that it's intellectual rubbish. So far as I can make sense of it at all, the antidote to oppression is 'quit your job and join a squat.' CT's chief virtue is that they have some very, very talented writers and artists in their collective who make all of this seem very edgy and romantic and sophisticated, when in reality it's just adolescent self-indulgence, recycled 60s-era pseudo-revolution, etc. Most of all, it doesn't accomplish a damn thing for anybody - in the long term, not even for the CT'ers, most of whom end up getting tired of the life and going back to their parents or to school or work or whatever. Trainhopping and dumpstering and all that may be exciting and fun and so forth, but it's not anarchistic, it's not revolutionary. It's just shits and giggles. Those sorts of activities, even if pursued by a large number of people, wouldn't do much to promote the cause of anarchy or challenge the status quo.

When I asked Aaron (via online chat), who had cited Bookchin as one of his anarchist influences, what he thought of CrimethInc., he wryly remarked, "I think it's very sad that so many great resources are wasted on their (lack of) ideas. If I were in the FBI, and wanted to funnel alienated middle-class white kids away from being useful to radical movements, I would start CrimethInc."

As is implied in Aaron's comment, one of the major perceived problems with CrimethInc. and with lifestyle anarchism in general is its apparently disproportionate appeal to youth coming from positions of structural privilege. The concern here is that lifestyles which these anarchists recognize as appropriately resistant are actually exclusionary to, for example, women, people of color, and the working class, as discussed in the previous chapters of this book. Some activists worry that, by embracing subcultural lifestyles, anarchist movements self-select participants who may not have a deep awareness of the real, ill effects of capitalist exploitation, police power, immigration policy, sexual violence, and so on. There is a fear too that, when the "downward mobility" involved with many anarchist lifestyle practices becomes inconvenient, those who have the means to do so will just fall back on their economic, gender, and other forms of privilege, abandoning the cause of anarchist politics as well.

These are not problems that are *essential* to lifestyle activism. While specific dynamics like this may be objectionable, it's possible that there are conditions under which such negative consequences could be avoided, particularly if activists are thoughtful about doing so. For example, some of the tactics of anti-consumption described in Chapter 2 could be carefully articulated to the challenges faced by the poor and the working class. For instance, lifestylists embrace of bicycling could mobilize them to cultivate an infrastructure (such as repair collectives and safe bike lanes) that would hold value for many, even those outside the activist subculture, and could endure even if the more privileged bicyclists eventually moved on from the practice. But what makes many people uneasy about the idea of "white kids slumming it" (as Rilla put it) is the possibility that downward mobility is embraced because of a romanticization or fetishization of poverty that ignores the real, systematic struggles faced by poor people. One anonymous critique—titled "Rethinking Crimethinc" (W 2006) and circulated on various anarchist message boards—quotes a particularly disturbing sentiment found on a CrimethInc. book jacket: "Poverty, unemployment, homelessness—if you're not having fun, you're not doing it right!" The writer of the critique goes on to explain why statements like this are offensive:

> Condescending, privileged, middle class crap. The only people who could think that poverty is in any way fun are wealthy kids playing at being poor for a few years, the daily reality of poverty, unemployment and homelessness for the average person is very serious and something anarchists should always organize against rather than mock.

If one's experience of poverty happens in the context of a romanticized, "intentional living" situation, it could be that the privilege that one carries into that situation causes one to be less vulnerable to the harmful effects of poverty. Having this privilege is not unethical in itself, but if it blinds one to the systemic injustices that disadvantage others who don't have one's privileges, then one's personal downward mobility will be difficult to connect to broader social struggles. As Marcuse argues, retreating from mainstream culture may be a necessary step in the development of an alternative consciousness. But, he also cautions that such a retreat may also have the ill effect of reducing one's motivation to combat the objectionable parts of mainstream culture, since one might feel that one is both immune to them and innocent of perpetuating them (Marcuse 2001). Though the effects of oppression and privilege may be temporarily relieved or obscured through individual refusal, systems of oppression and privilege are not dismantled by such tactics. One may experience the effects of hierarchy less *in one's own life* but this doesn't necessarily mean that this benefit is shared by anyone else as a result of one's choices.

Bookchin's (1995) essay and some of the views expressed by interviewees illustrate the tension that endures among anarchists over the issue of lifestyle. The question of whether or how much lifestylism poses a threat to effective radical activist projects is one that still holds purchase. Some may believe, like Aaron, that tendencies like those represented by CrimethInc. are detrimental to radical movements because they distract bodies and resources away from more worthwhile projects. Others, like Matthew, believe that lifestylists are harmless, even if their activities don't "accomplish a damn thing for anybody." Yet, lifestyle-based tactics are widely embraced by some of the same people who are critical of lifestyle anarchism. In all my research, I didn't come across one person who thought that individual conduct was simply irrelevant to either anarchist identity or the political project of anarchism. Everyone accorded *some* importance to the way individual activists chose to live their lives, and activists who embrace practices associated with stereotypical lifestylism are, in reality, rarely motivated purely by individual self-interest. For the most part, the people I spoke with, observed, and read about, envisioned their actions as part of a larger movement and as components in a larger strategy. What this speaks to is that there may, in fact, not be any clear-cut criteria that could empirically distinguish between Bookchin's mutually exclusive categories of social anarchists and lifestyle anarchists. Lifestyle politics has traction beyond a restricted subcultural milieu of self-interested individualists. As a participant in the anarchist academics email exchange noted, "you don't have to be a CrimethInc. obsessed fuck you punk vegan bastard to think trying to live ethically is a good idea." The idea of trying to make a difference by living one's ideals has become near hegemonic, not just in activist movements, but also in consumer culture at large, as I argued in Chapter 1. Clearly, many parties feel it serves a useful purpose.

Rather than attempting to answer whether or not a commitment to lifestyle politics is a "good idea," a more appropriate pursuit would be to ascertain in what situations and for what goals is lifestyle activism an effective course of action. As the cases examined in this book have shown, it is not the case that lifestyle practices don't "accomplish a damn thing for anybody." They "accomplish" a great deal. That lifestyle choices do not immediately bring about large-scale revolution is obvious, but these choices do serve many functions within activist movements. They give expression to individual and collective identifications, they provide alternatives to hierarchical power relations on a small scale, and they symbolically prefigure larger goals. In a more negative vein, they may also serve to establish or reinforce social boundaries and hierarchies, within and beyond activist movements. Lifestyle practices may even generate money for corporate interests who are able to tap into activists' idealistic narratives. While people may disagree about whether the particular functions served are desirable or not, such assessments must be made in context, in consideration of the situational factors involved in any given case. Questions about the worthwhileness of lifestyle politics ought to be asked on a situational basis, for the sake of developing effective activist strategies. In the next section, I offer further considerations for the development of radical activist strategy against the backdrop of neoliberal, postmodern conditions.

Individualism and collectivism

The very complicated relationship between "the personal" and "the political" is a thread that runs throughout the discussions in this book. This relationship takes on a unique form within the conditions of neoliberalism. While activists such as those seeking women's liberation in the 1960s and 1970s were at pains to make the world acknowledge that their personal lives mattered in political ways, such an argument is, in some ways, obviated by the dominant logic of neoliberal society. It is now a hegemonic assumption that the individual is the privileged unit of political activity. Individuals are "responsibilized" into looking after not only themselves but also huge social and environmental problems, both by the state who abdicates responsibility for the welfare of its citizens and by the market which swoops in to fill the gaps, offering consumption-based "solutions" to the dilemmas individuals find themselves facing, thereby profiting off individual uncertainties and the desires they hold to do as much good as they possibly can (Rose 1999, Bauman 2001). The rise of "commodity activism" is just one indication of a shift from the conventional wisdom that political and social conditions are brought about through collective struggle to a state in which "political imaginaries and subjectivities are reshaped to fit the individualized ethos of neoliberal capitalism" (Banet-Weiser and Mukherjee 2012: 11). The logic of neoliberalism rests on assumptions that collective welfare—when collective welfare is the goal at all—can be ensured through the "invisible hand" made up of many subjects making their own individual choices about the "ethical" way to live their political values. There is, therefore, a new ideological terrain upon which radical activists must struggle to represent the connection between their personal experiences and broader relations of power, and upon which they must attempt to extend personal resistance out into the world beyond their own bodies and experiences. To claim *today* that "the personal is political" is to be met, metaphorically, with supportive nodding and a sales pitch for organic food. A radical critique will thus have to do more work to expose the workings of power and domination and to propose systemic change.

While the oppositional consciousness of radical activists such as anarchists certainly places them in an ideological position to recognize and critique the processes of neoliberalism, these activists are also caught squarely within those processes. Anarchist fantasies of living outside of capitalism, patriarchy, and the rest are nearly always frustrated by the overarching power of these systems. To transcend these systems as a society by disinvesting in them as individuals proves impossible, since each half of this strategy is a precondition for the other. The endurance of hegemonic ideologies of domination means that provisional practices of resistance, undertaken in the name of subverting domination as best one can, are subject to a kind of creeping in of dominant ideologies and power dynamics at every turn.[8]

As the examples offered throughout this book have shown, a practice undertaken with even the best intentions is always inflected by the oppressive conditions it was meant to combat. This introduces a kind of uncanniness into the struggles of those we might term "neoliberal radicals," a constant back and forth questioning about whether one is fighting the system or playing right into its hands. In assessing the motivations and effects of lifestyle politics, one is never quite able to decide what is authentic and what is inauthentic, what is resistance and what is recuperation.[9] Most advocates of anarchist lifestyle activism do imagine their personal practices to have an impact beyond their own experience. The major challenge for practitioners of lifestyle activism is to connect microscopic interventions to macroscopic struggles in a non-superficial way.[10] In the absence of such strong links, practices of lifestyle politics risk becoming the caricature of ineffectual individualism drawn by Bookchin. In the rest of this chapter, I want to detail further some of the ways that these traversals—from individual to collective, micro to macro—are negotiated by anarchist activists, and some of the inherent limitations that practices of lifestyle politics have in transcending the personal–political divide.

One of the most fundamental tensions highlighted by the debate around lifestylism is the tension between individualism and collectivism. While most anarchists agree that the preservation of individual autonomy and the collective pursuit of social justice are essential to any desirable political reality, there are disagreements as to how these two goals should be held in balance with each other and what are the best strategies for achieving them (Milstein 2010). The question of lifestylism within anarchist movements highlights this tension because it is a tactic that has both individualist and collectivist aspects. It seems to require the individual to take responsibility for one's own behavior and to attempt to generate change through personal habits. This goal of generating change may become unrecognizable when activists are perceived to be motivated by personal interest without an accompanying analysis or critique of the political structures that privilege some at the expense of others. In this way, lifestyle anarchists may seem indistinguishable (in form if not in content) from other subjects of contemporary neoliberal consumer culture who seek what Bookchin (1995: 11) calls "the sanctification of the self as a refuge from the existing social malaise." But lifestyle politics, as I've detailed in this book, also calls on activist communities to generate and cultivate cultural norms that encourage collective shifts in ways of living that both align with radical ideals and establish more just relations in the here and now. To invoke an example I discussed in Chapter 5, individuals don't just start rejecting monogamy on their own—they acquire "sexual vocabularies" from peers in their communities and they build networks in which the norm of monogamy is questioned so that others may feel empowered to reject it as well. In ways like this, so-called lifestyle anarchists blur the lines between "ideal-typical distinctions" that would categorize lifestyle tactics as either individualist or collectivist.[11] The categories of social anarchism and lifestyle anarchism are ideal types that cannot actually be found in the real world. Seen in this light, it becomes harder to dismiss lifestyle politics out of hand as Bookchin does.

Decentralized power and resistance

It is perhaps no coincidence that Bookchin's vitriolic critique of lifestylism goes hand in hand with his explicit dismissal of Foucaultian theories of power and resistance. Bookchin sees Foucault as advocating only disconnected acts of insurrection, and indeed sees lifestyle anarchism as a strategically untenable expression of this philosophy. Yet, there are alternative readings to be made of both Foucault and lifestyle politics. Foucault's understanding of power as decentralized and discursive need not preclude intentionality, cohesion, or the strategic mobilization of individual action. If anarchist lifestyle politics is read as a kind of *disciplined ethic*, it's possible to amend Bookchin's characterization of lifestyle anarchism as that in which "the sporadic, the unsystematic, the incoherent, the discontinuous, and the intuitive supplant the consistent, purposive, organized, and rational" (Bookchin 1995: 51). Whether such discipline is actually effective at meeting any of the strategic goals envisioned by the people who take on such lifestyle projects is hard to determine, particularly since the specific strategic goals may not be carefully staked out by activists themselves. What this book models is the utility of a contextualized analysis that examines the multiple consequences and motivations of specific tactical behaviors without assuming a "programmatic" standard for what counts as appropriate activism and what doesn't. Instead of assuming the end goals of a movement can be thoroughly determined in advance, along with which tactics are most appropriate for achieving those goals, it may make more sense to approach activism with what Jeremy Gilbert (2008) calls a "strategic *orientation*" (emphasis mine) that tends toward a common vision without claiming to know in advance how it must be achieved or what precisely it would look like once it is. Within such an approach, lifestyle activism makes sense as a space of trial and error, as a collection of moves that can be tweaked and reassessed according to the particular conditions at hand. This is not to say that lifestyle would offer an adequate solution to every problem, only that the ongoing and iterative nature of lifestyle politics—lifestyle practices by definition must be undertaken again and again, each day—makes the strategy open to "trouble" from within, trouble that employs critique for productive ends (Butler 1990).

When taking up a Foucaultian (1990b) interpretation of lifestyle politics, one important analytical distinction is to differentiate attention to the self from preoccupation with the self. Indeed, critics of lifestylism usually object not to the content or existence of anarchist lifestyle practices themselves, but to the extent to which those practices *preoccupy* both individual activists and activist groups. Preoccupation is problematic both because it may serve as a distraction from other activities and because if lifestyle practices are accorded disproportionate significance, the structural differences they play upon (such as gender, race, etc.) become an obstacle to coalition building rather than inconsequential differences in taste and background among potential allies. For example, a group planning a radical event like a conference may be so committed to vegan diets that planning meetings for the gathering get bogged down in the details of providing vegan food, at the expense of other concerns. It may also mean that the actual event is alienating to meat-eaters when they feel that their own dietary choices have been judged unacceptable.[12] But there is such a thing as strategic attention to lifestyle, in contrast with astrategic preoccupation with lifestyle. If one of the goals of an event is to inform about and promote veganism and to connect it to other struggles against exploitation, paying a good bit of attention to the menu—and how it is framed for attendees—would be a worthwhile endeavor. And it's not always the case that lifestyle draws attention away that would otherwise be devoted to "serious" issues. It is fair to say that there are some anarchists who get caught up in interpersonal drama over issues of lifestyle, and it is reasonable to think that such drama takes up time and energy that might be better spent elsewhere. However, it's speculative to assume that were lifestyle practices not an issue for anarchists, they would spend all their newly found free time engaged in "serious" struggle. The idea that lifestyle is a distraction from "authentic" politics presumes that both cannot coexist and even be productively coordinated within an overall movement strategy. The question is in what instances are puristic lifestyle commitments getting in the way of other goals, and what are the relative merits of those goals in comparison with that which is accomplished by the lifestyle practices.

A strategic integration of lifestyle politics within radical activist projects requires an analysis that is able to distinguish between and accurately connect micropolitical and macropolitical tactics and outcomes. This means that activists must recognize that efficacy at transforming one's own life or even one's local situation does not necessarily imply efficacy at changing larger structures and processes, since there are different interventions that must be made at these different scales. So, for example, choosing to seek consent before pursuing sexual contact with another individual can be an efficacious way of enacting an anarchist sexual politics in that particular situation. It does not, however, alter the larger culture in which, in very regular and patterned ways, women's consent is frequently not sought by men who interact with them sexually. When this kind of analysis is missing, disagreements about the effectiveness of lifestyle activism arise, since people have not really staked the terms of the debate—they have not established what they are arguing that lifestyle politics is effective *for* (perhaps because they have not even quite thought about it for themselves). Take for example these two views, one from an interviewee (and which began the introduction to this book), and another coming from an anarchist blogger:

> . . . it gets abstract sometimes, because it's like, where do I attack it, where do I attack patriarchy, where do I attack capitalism? And that's why I think lifestylism is so important, cuz I think that you do attack it by being vegan, or by not buying from Walmart, or not being subjected by the beauty standards. Like, by building those alternative communities and alternative infrastructure, we're not paying attention to them, so we're not demanding anything from them. (Raychel, interviewee)

> Well, wake up people, we live in the triumphantly (and some would say late) capitalistic world of the 21st century, and, I'm sorry, but a couple of anarchist co-ops and squats, food not bombs projects and urban vegetable farms spread thinly around the world are not going to rot away the leviathan from within – regardless of what the cyberpunks say about the networking capacities of the internet. A more apt metaphor would be sprinkling water on a bonfire – if you think that the small centers of resistence [sic] we have are going cool this raging capitalist exploitation, you're underestimating the heat of the fire. ("Anarchism and Decadence" 2008)

For Raychel, political success is at least somewhat defined by being able to live without being personally dependent on the most objectionable institutions of consumer society. The blogger has something else in mind when thinking about the purpose of radical activism, asserting, probably correctly, that lifestyle tactics will be unsuccessful at actually destroying the objectionable institutions of consumer society, let alone consumer society itself. Each has something to say about the effects of lifestyle-based activism; their "disagreement" stems from implicit differences in the way they define the goals of resistant lifestyle practices.

Fantasies of individual resistance as systemic subversion are often both induced and foreclosed by the logic of neoliberalism. Neoliberal discourses of individual autonomy promote the idea that we are each endowed with the agency to choose the best way of life and that the means to realize our choices are readily available if only we will commit to them. Yet, this sense of autonomy may obfuscate the fact that in many cases our "choices" are constrained by conservative economic, political, and cultural networks of power. To be fair, the case of anarchist lifestyles has shown that activists are not really restricted to a homogeneous set of lifestyle choices, nor are their choices fully containable by the commodity market. In many instances, anarchists' practices and beliefs *are* qualitatively different from those of most participants in the hegemonic order. Their activism *is* distinguishable from the kind of commodity activism that involves merely choosing the lesser of many evils from among the options on offer in the marketplace. Yet, the individualist logic of neoliberalism is often implicit in anarchists' efforts to free their minds and bodies from the grips of repressive forces by choosing a different way. Though anarchists may not exemplify the "possessive or competitive individualism" of the thoroughly integrated capitalist subject (Marcuse 2001), lifestyle practices are still fundamentally individual responses to power, and thus are not adequately equipped to, by themselves, radically rearrange power relations. They don't, for instance, win power that was not already available within the capitalist system. They are what Scott (1985) calls, "weapons of the weak"—attempts by disenfranchised subjects to do what they can, where they can. Such tactics may lay the groundwork for further collective struggle by solidifying and sustaining radical identities and critiques and building community among those who share a vision for social change (Kelley 1996). But the turn to lifestyle may also signify the constricted scope of resistance enabled by (and ultimately potentially recuperable by) the present system.

A purely individualist anarchist politics would refer to an individual's attempt to produce the conditions of anarchy for oneself through one's own lifestyle choices. This would be consistent with lifestyle anarchism in the most pejorative sense. But, as I said above, most people who self-identify as anarchists assume a relationship between the individual and the collective. They wish not only to liberate themselves, but also to generate broader change through collective activities. Raychel, quoted above, may not only see herself as retreating to an alternative community free of misogyny and economic exploitation—her words insinuate that she actually sees herself as *attacking* patriarchy and capitalism through this retreat. The trouble here is then not selfish or malignant intent on the part of lifestyle activists. It may rather be a misapprehension or simple inattention to the actual mechanisms by which individual change might empirically result in collective change. In other words, lifestyle politics may seem to rest on a kind of untested *faith* in the potential of individual action to change the world in a larger sense. It may assume, without much basis, that drawing support away from troubling institutions ("not demanding anything from them" as Raychel put it), one individual at a time, will weaken those institutions once enough individuals have been recruited to the cause and choices have an aggregate effect.[13]

Mechanisms of prefiguration

Lifestyle politics leaves itself open to criticism when individual resistance is conflated with systemic subversion, or when the connection between the two is left in a black box that simply assumes one can "be the change you wish to see in the world" and the world will change as a consequence of that "being." For one thing, the individual's very capacity to "be the change"—to personally enact what one values—is shaped by macropolitical structures. The phenomenon of manarchism (discussed in Chapter 4) is proof of this—acknowledging that patriarchy is a problematic system that they do not want to reproduce hasn't stopped countless anarchist men from unconsciously "cashing in" on their male privilege within activist communities. Even when these men mean well, it is no easy thing to undo a lifetime of ideological conditioning toward oppressive performances of masculinity. Much as the ideology of neoliberalism does, the ideology of lifestyle politics may overstate the power that individuals actually have to actively resist many of the social forces that, in fact, heavily shape everyday experience. In recognition of this, Jeremy, an interviewee, called it a "flawed idea that one can individualize capitalism or 'drop out' of it." The fact that completely dropping out of capitalism is, in reality, an impossibility, further attests to this incommensurability between individual refusal and systemic power. Capitalism is so well integrated into every aspect of life that there is no getting away from it completely, no matter how much the individual might intend to liberate oneself from its hold. Beyond the material conditions of capitalism, the ideological conditions are always already present in our subjectivities. One doesn't lose their influence simply because one realizes that one might like to. Radical social change, under the conditions of which radical ideological change would be possible, would be a necessary precondition for all people, not just those who have the wherewithal to choose lifestyle anarchism, to realize the experience of liberation. This is a catch-22 that is hard to reason one's way out of.[14]

Even assuming that some individuals are effective at resisting the reproduction of the objectionable aspects of the dominant society in their own lives, it is questionable how alternative ways of life—even if they are demonstrably better than the dominant ones—are to become widely practicable to the point where they replace the old ways on a broad scale. The process of *how* the new world might fully emerge in the shell of the old is unclear. The immediate personal benefits of prefigurative lifestyle practices may be clear to those who undertake them, but the connection

)etween these prefigurations and actual broad cultural shifts is hazy, even "magical" at times (Epstein 1991: 157). One of the justifications offered for individuals making lifestyle choices in line with their political ideals is that "if enough people did this, then the system would have a real battle on its hands" (in the words of a commenter on an anarchist email list). Yes, "if enough people did this . . ." it would make a difference, but the operative word there is "if." Rossinow (1998: 292–3) points out that prefiguration, as a tactic, seems to rest on an assumption of a "marketplace of ideas" in which people observe and adopt new ways of doing things based purely on their intrinsic merits. But without a carefully considered mechanism for disrupting hegemonic ideologies, the embrace of alternative lifestyles, even if meant to be a prefiguration for a new society, may be indistinguishable from the individualist retreat that is so characteristic of the neoliberal status quo. By merely hoping that withdrawal and leading by example will effect a cultural shift, lifestylists may, at best, form a subcultural enclave that is no threat to hegemony whatsoever. Activists' subcultural practices may even be successfully co-opted as the next in a never-ending series of consumer lifestyles that drive capitalist consumer culture.

Alberto Melucci (1985: 812) suggests that the kind of prefigurative forms developed by social movements constitute "new media," meaning that they communicate about the current political system by giving a name to the "silence, violence, irrationality which is always hidden in dominant codes." He continues, "through what they do, or rather through how they do it, movements announce to society that something 'else' is possible." One of the questions people who study "new media" often ask when encountering a particular medium is, "what is the reach of this medium?" or, to put it another way, "how many people does this medium speak to, who are these people, and how effectively does it speak to them?" (Baym 2010). If we are to follow Melucci and consider anarchists' lifestyle practices as a medium for the communication of political critique—if, in other words, we are to consider lifestyle as propaganda by deed, as discussed in Chapter 1—we will want to know the *reach* of this medium under given conditions. This question is an empirical and historical one that ought to be answerable with situational evidence, rather than assumed to have a universal answer. One then wants to know under what conditions lifestyle prefiguration has ever been an effective form of political propaganda. With this knowledge, specific conditions in the present could be assessed for their amenability to such a tactic.

The conditions under consideration must include the context in which communication between radical activists and other political subjects takes place. As I argued in Chapter 3, alternative lifestyles may not be particularly aesthetically attractive to non-participants in the subculture, nor may outsiders be able to make sense of the political appeal of the practices either. The choice by some to adopt alternative lifestyle habits has no intrinsically persuasive function—just because a deed is done by an individual doesn't make it effective propaganda. Alternative consumer aesthetics may be just as likely to alienate potential anarchists as to recruit them. As has been pointed out before, for every person who likes punk music, there are many more who find its harsh aesthetic distasteful (Cornell 2011b: 181). Mainstream consumption patterns are powerfully sustained by deeply ingrained taste preferences (Bourdieu 1984), thus the majority of people are unlikely to be attracted to alternative lifestyles purely on the basis of their aesthetic appeal. Lifestyle alternatives are probably, in fact, *more* likely to alienate than inspire, precisely because of their implicit critique of the status quo; mainstream observers may defensively interpret subcultural lifestyle choices as a negative judgment of their own habits (Holt 2000).

If part of the logic of lifestyle politics is that it sets an example for others to follow (i.e. it prefigures an alternate way of life), there is a problem when the example is one that people don't find compelling for reasons of taste. Take for instance the Really Really Free Market as a demonstration of the viability of an alternative to commercial exchange (as described in Chapter 2). The idea of picking through a pile of someone else's discarded items on a blanket in a public park is just not appealing to many people. One could deconstruct the ideological forces that *make* the idea unappealing (e.g. consumers have been trained by capitalism to want sterile, brightly lit retail spaces full of brand new objects), but the mere presence of alternatives does not necessarily effectively combat those forces. And even if people are made aware of the political motivations behind alternative consumption practices, they may simply not *want* to consume like anarchists. This speaks to one of the nagging problems of prefigurative politics—if the conditions prefigured by radical alternatives are not desirable to observers, their propagandistic function is null. As I suggested in Chapter 3, discursive common ground and ideological symmetry must be already present, or actively forged, in order for cultural challenges to be legible and attractive to those not already involved with the movement. Careful analysis of the conditions under which some actions do succeed at winning over new supporters would be a step toward validating the implicit hopes behind prefiguration as a strategic approach.

One also wants to know to what extent prefigurative practices are defused or deformed when taken out of the context of activist communities and given (often sold) to the mainstream as lifestyle alternatives. Without the ideological underpinnings of anarchist political theory, practices such as dumpster diving, body modification, and polyamorous relationships would lose nearly all their value *as* political interventions. And not merely because people might start doing the "right" things for the "wrong" reasons. Polyamory, for example, when not undertaken with a perseverant commitment to its feminist and anti-capitalist interventions, may drift toward the sexual dynamics of mainstream patriarchal culture, as discussed in Chapter 5. The material effects of the practice thus become quite different from what was initially prefigured by the activists who saw the practice as a radical political tactic and good in itself. This validates Bookchin's (1995: 3) fear that "the revolutionary and social goals of anarchism are suffering far-reaching erosion to a point where the word *anarchy* will become part of the chic bourgeois vocabulary of the coming century—naughty, rebellious, insouciant, but deliciously safe." This doesn't only have to refer to lifestyle practices being co-opted by the market directly. It may also simply be about "radical" lifestyle practices becoming integrated into mainstream culture or into other subcultures that lack the political analysis that anarchists were hoping to express and embody through their practices.

The degradation in meaning caused by commodification and decontextualization are what make the contemporary incarnation of lifestyle politics a characteristically postmodern problem. While the tensions between the personal and the political have been present throughout radical movements for some time, prefiguration becomes particularly shaky under conditions in which cultural practices are easily and often circulated in forms that are divorced from their original justifications and strategic orientations. It's not hard to see how the propagandistic function of prefigurative lifestyles would be even further muddled than what is already inherent within the limited capacity for representations to fully convey what their producers intend (Hall 1997). Practices, beliefs, and their representations will circulate freely among people who don't necessarily share discursive frameworks and ideological commitments, who may, in fact, hold opposite commitments. There is therefore no ensuring that the practices of lifestyle anarchism will hold the same significance across all these contexts, let alone bring about the same material effects.

Subcultures and movements

Jeremy Gilbert (2008) argues that, in fact, the most meaningful social contribution that radical movements can make is to find acceptance for their ideas and practices among people who would not necessarily identify with the movements themselves. From this point of view, the ideal outcome of co-optation and re-presentation would be that ethical lifestyle practices get collectivized and established to the extent that they become adoptable by people and movements who think of themselves as more mainstream. However, this "ideal" may not be fully commensurate with the function of lifestyle for radical activists. As I discussed in Chapter 2, lifestyle is a carrier of social meaning, in addition to being a source of personal fulfillment and potential activist change. From this angle, the diffusion or mainstreaming of anarchist subcultural practices is a big problem, as they can no longer function in the same way if they no longer mark their practitioner as a member of a specific subculture or as holding a specific set of political beliefs. We can see here the inherent tension within lifestyle politics—the material and symbolic dimensions of it may, in fact, be working at cross-purposes. A strategy that embraces diffusion of anarchist lifestyle practices may require that activists reconcile themselves to becoming less recognizable as anarchists. The question is whether this is a cultural sacrifice that also interferes with the political work of activist groups. Do they depend on their cultural identities to be effective in achieving their goals, or are their desired outcomes independent from their ability to maintain themselves as a culturally distinct movement?

The tension just described brings up again the fact that contemporary anarchism combines elements of alternative subculture and political movement, and is, in fact, profoundly characterized by this dualism. As a subculture, diffusion and mainstreaming are a kind of cultural death. As a movement, growing in numbers and winning over new, diverse people to the cause are crucial. Subcultures struggle to preserve the space to be different; movements aim to make all spaces in society different from what they currently are. The different kinds of "work" done by political lifestyle practices highlight that the contemporary anarchist formation has features of both subculture and movement. Indeed, the case of contemporary anarchism shows that subcultures and movements are not dichotomous social formations at all—the self-identified anarchists who engage in lifestyle politics do so neither purely for stylistic reasons nor purely for practical reasons. Admitting that there are stylistic or "merely cultural" motivations and effects of lifestyle politics does not have to mean that anarchists are unserious or adolescent or not "real" activists. Recognizing that politics are personal does not make them any less political.

The tensions cannot be resolved, then, by taking sides. Activists cannot choose *not* to be a cultural formation while they are also being a political movement. They cannot choose *not* to engage with power at an individual level while they are also attempting to engage with it collectively. They cannot choose for their actions to *not* have symbolic import while they also have material effects. It's not that there is an unbridgeable chasm between lifestyle and politics; rather, their intertwinedness is only solidified by contemporary conditions. The "chasm" exists only in the minds of those who have not come to terms with the reality that social movements are always cultural formations as well. The way to resolve Bookchin's issue is not—as he seemed to advocate—to cast off the unserious subcultural arm of "the movement". This is an untenable solution in any case, since as I have shown, many of the "serious" movement activists are engaged in lifestyle activism to some extent at least. And as multiple interviewees observed, lifestyle activities may be a precursor to further involvement in other forms of activism. What these tensions invoke is, again, the strategic necessity to acknowledge and embrace the multiple "functions" of lifestyle within the anarchist community and to commit to nuanced, situational critique that accepts the presence of lifestyle as a site of engagement while aiming to maximize its most promising potentials.

What *can* radical activists do about lifestylism under conditions of postmodernity and neoliberalism then? As I have demonstrated in the chapters of this book, an ethical critique of lifestyle politics would balance a recognition of the positive potential of lifestyle politics under certain conditions, with a sensitivity to the specific conditions that may make them less practicable and less productive on other occasions. This means approaching political lifestyle practices as tactics rather than an overall strategy or goal, as something to be deployed when appropriate and downplayed when the situation is less amenable. It means recognizing that lifestyle practices are undertaken with multiple and varying motivations, some of which are perhaps more appropriate to certain conditions than others. As a site of political engagement, a lifestyle is not a fixed program, it is a collection of practices and is thus open to contestation and infinite tinkering and situational adaptation. In this way, lifestyles are quintessential sites of postmodern political activism. They attempt to represent, or give a face and name to a diffuse collection of political subjects. And they provide a kind of disciplinary guide for living like an "actual anarchist" amid conditions that encourage hierarchy, not anarchy, as the hegemonic norm. Yet, such strengths also give rise to special challenges and pitfalls that are not easily overcome. What the issues of individualism, privilege, taste boundaries, etc., speak to is not perhaps a weakness by anarchists in their attempts to navigate those pitfalls of lifestyle politics, but rather the intrinsicality of such pitfalls to any activist strategy that includes lifestyle-based tactics. The same conditions that give lifestyle its political potential are also those which limit it.

Does this mean that lifestyle politics is thoroughly unbridgeable to any strategy with any hope of success at transforming a deeply flawed social order? I don't have an answer to that at this point. It's clear that under neoliberalism, lifestyle politics will continue to exist in some form as a component of activist strategy. And as long as there are anarchists who live within non-anarchic conditions, the labels they adopt and the personal aesthetic choices they make will continue to be significant as sites for enacting and representing their political identities and visions. Lifestyle practices will do other cultural work than inciting revolution, and this work will be valuable, perhaps even necessary, to the survival of radical activist movements. At the same time, lifestyle practices will continue to bring up fundamental problems and tensions. And anarchist activists will continue to critique and debate them, in the interest of creating the other world they hope is possible.

Working through the tensions posed by present conditions forces movements to respond to the problematic features of the present in which they find themselves—which is precisely what movements exist to do.

Movements are premised on there being an identifiable difference between what is and what could be (Butler 1997b). To constitute oneself as a radical, in particular, is to question the received order or truth, to throw into question the very rules by which one has been accustomed to living and seeing the world (Butler 2004b). Radicals, anarchists, are subjects who cannot quite exist within the regime of truth in which they find themselves—present conditions will, by definition, be impossible to live with for radicals, and yet they live and must form their radical identity amid them. The potential of an anarchist movement, or any movement at all, lies in its ability to productively negotiate the obstacles thrown up by the conditions it exists to protest.

This is perhaps then a promising thing about the ongoing struggle to determine whether and how much lifestyle-based forms of resistance are politically effective as activism, the struggle I've focused on in this chapter. Though, as I've argued, there are no easy answers to whether any tactic is finally "effective" or not, perhaps what matters more is the critical stance activists are willing to take toward their own methods. For Foucault, debate and questioning of authoritative truth is an ethical practice, a good in itself. While the project of self-scrutiny has been mobilized for the aims of institutional power, such as the state (as in Foucault's [2009] account of governmentality), it may be that internal criticism could also tend toward discovering a way to be governed "otherwise" (Butler 2004b), a different set of ends that might ask or require us to conduct ourselves differently. As Foucault (1997c) argues, there is no originary or outside moral code by which a set of laws might be authorized or declared invalid. We cannot thus make any final judgment on lifestyle politics as a style of being in the world as a resistant subject. Rather, we can only endlessly critique in the interest of never letting the existing authority get away with going unquestioned. This in itself is an entirely anarchistic project, and it is fitting that contemporary anarchists would be engaged in such a thing. Yet, the critical consciousness and even preoccupation with debating the merits or drawbacks of lifestylism as a mode of political engagement is, I think, indicative or typical of the tensions all would-be activists—particularly radicals—struggle with under contemporary conditions.

7

Conclusion: Learning from lifestyle anarchists

The issues faced by anarchist activists are not unique to this particular group. They are experienced by all sorts of resistant subjects within contemporary society, and even have historical antecedents that predate the current social order. Certainly, theorists of the mid twentieth-century counterculture perceived some of the same issues, as when Herbert Marcuse (1972) noted in his book *Counterrevoluttion and Revolt* that the modes of political engagement he observed among disaffected American youth in the 1960s "raise[d] the problem of the relation between personal and political rebellion, private liberation and social revolution" (48). In the present day, other radical projects, such as queer liberation, struggle to navigate tensions between the pursuit of individual pleasure and the project of social transformation, which would bring liberatory conditions to more than just the most privileged of non-normative sexual subjects. All contemporary movements are operating in conditions where activism is fluidly defined, and where the objects one chooses to buy or not buy, the way one chooses to present oneself in public, the words one uses to refer to oneself, even the partners and practices of one's sexual life, are understood as meaningful political acts.

Such conditions should give pause to any who would dismiss the issue of activists' lifestyles as "merely cultural" or marginal to the realities of contemporary politics. This designation—"merely cultural"—has long been used to marginalize the concerns of certain actors within political movements, by both opponents and allies to these movements. Many of the liberationist streams arising out of, and in response to, the New Left, were belittled on just such a basis (Duggan 2003). Because their analyses included thoughtful critiques of the everyday, personal freedoms which were constricted by systems such as capitalism, patriarchy, and the white supremacist state, and because these constrictions were seen as only applying to the personal freedoms of some (as opposed to the supposedly universal constrictions imposed on those who happened to be white, straight, and male), their projects have been understood and portrayed as "factionalizing, identitarian, and particularistic" (Butler 1997b). Like the "cultural focus of left politics" described by Butler, activism mounted at the level of lifestyle is subject to accusations that it "substitutes a self-centered and trivial form of politics that focuses on transient events, practices, and objects rather than offering a more robust, serious and comprehensive vision of the systematic interrelatedness of social and economic conditions" (34). But what one person calls "self-centered and trivial" *is* often an important element of "social and economic conditions" for someone else, and the presumption that one can make such a judgment for someone else is simply evidence of one's own ideological, social, and economic biases.

It's clearly false that movements on the Left such as feminism, anti-racism, and gay liberation have lacked "robust, serious and comprehensive vision[s] of the systematic interrelatedness of social and economic conditions," though it may be true that some individuals, organizations, and texts from these movements have failed to effectively *articulate* their "focuses on transient events, practices, and objects" *to* those robust visions. A failure of articulation is probably what accounts for lifestylism's susceptibility to similar critiques within the anarchist milieu (Slack 1996). When activists are not able to more than superficially link their lifestyle concerns to those of the broader anarchist project, when they are not able to connect the microscopic difference their actions make to the macroscopic changes that would be necessary for a real power shift in society, when they overstate the power of lifestyle to bring on the revolution—this is when lifestyle politics comes to seem like a retreat, a distraction, a delusion.

As this book has illustrated, lifestyle is inflected by politics all the way down, so to say that concerns with lifestyle are not political or are less political than other concerns is to misunderstand how politics and power work. Lifestyle is implicated in politics whether one is an anarchist or just a mainstream political subject. The measurable macrostructural impact of one's lifestyle choices may be small to the point of insignificance in the eyes of some, but as sites of meaning making, identity constitution, and social negotiation, politicized lifestyle practices are nothing if not *significant,* in the sense that they *signify.* But, it is true that subversive lifestyle practices like the ones examined in this book are inadequate to achieve all that activists might hope they could. However, the contradictions between the hopes of lifestyle activists and their actual achievements should be evidence of the contradictions endemic to life within postmodernity and neoliberalism at large, more so than an indication of failings in their analysis or project. Instead of assuming that those who attempt lifestyle-based interventions are dupes or tools of the system, perhaps one can productively read their mode of engagement as an implicit (possibly even unconscious) critique of what is foreclosed by neoliberalism *and* by traditional forms of activist politics, which are themselves hobbled under neoliberal conditions as well. As was demonstrated with the Occupy mobilizations of 2011, radical movements that attempt to seize physical and discursive public space for the airing of their critiques are both directly repressed by state force and minimized by unfriendly commercial media portrayals. Even mainstream, "non-resistant" subjects find themselves in positions where the things they might hope to achieve in life are ideologically portrayed as achievable while simultaneously foreclosed in reality by forces that serve the interests of political and economic elites. So, it should be no surprise that radical activists are especially disempowered to achieve their aims inside the ideological and material structures of neoliberalism. The problem, of course, is that there is not much in the way of an *outside* to those structures.

Positioning lifestyle activism within the cultural conditions of neoliberalism also helps in understanding why some functions of resistant lifestyles are achieved while others are not. It may be that the aims most effectively realized are those that are most compatible with neoliberalism. This isn't to say that every aspect of lifestyle politics is recuperated for neoliberal ends. Yet, as movements have no choice but to operate within given cultural conditions, some of the techniques they adopt will respond to or make use of those conditions. Critics of lifestylism have a point when they identify some of the trends in radical activism as being formally similar to the trends of neoliberal individualism and consumerism, but to assume that we can stop there in our understanding of lifestyle practices is to assume that identification or orientation toward radical political projects is meaningless in itself. If the people who wish to subvert neoliberalism are just as complicit in it as those who uncritically buy into the system, then is there a point to resistance at all? If the only difference between anarchist lifestylists and neoliberalist individualists is what they call themselves or how they think of themselves in relation to the dominant ideology, is this a difference that makes a difference?

This is a question that must be answered through empirical observation. If people who orient themselves toward the radical restructuring of hierarchical power relationships do not actually do anything that enacts or measurably works toward that end, then perhaps the difference does not matter much. If, for instance, a manarchist perpetuates the same conditions for women within the activist scene that women can expect to experience within the mainstream, patriarchal society, then perhaps there is no value to his identification with anarchism. But I argue that orientation to or identification with radicalism does matter, because at least it provides a starting point in the form of an ideological framework that is receptive to reflexive critique and adjustment. Anarchist scenes may reproduce problematic forms of sexism, but at least they are spaces where a critique along those lines can be mounted and not dismissed out of hand as unnecessary, since in theory at least, everyone there has committed to recognizing and rejecting patriarchal power (even if they are still struggling to figure out how to really do it). I argue then that there is a difference between "neoliberal radicals" and "neoliberal neoliberals," though it may lie mostly in the *ideological space* they make for critique of current systems. This is a necessary condition for projects of material social change, if not sufficient to effectively accomplish them.

Perhaps one of the most surprising sociological observations to come out of this book is the amount of discursive work that activists are involved in to make their everyday activities count as meaningful expressions of political resistance. To me, this is indicative of an absence of conditions that make the full realization of utopian alternatives possible. For radicals, daily life is a never-ending stream of ethical compromises, and at times it is only through signification that the personal experience of resistance is plausible. At some level, anarchists are aware of all the ways in which they are forced to betray their own ideals, and so they are doing the best they can to hold onto those ideals in the face of hugely daunting systems that push their bodies and minds in the direction of hegemonic power. Through the work of signification, lifestyle practices may actually be experienced as real alternatives, even if the ultimate material differences between these practices and those of the mainstream are small, and even if their adoption by radicals fails to generalize them as alternatives accessible beyond a subcultural milieu.

As much as anything then, lifestyle politics may be about the *representation* of utopian difference, the representation of a desire for a different world, in the absence of that world. Even while lifestyle practices do not make a new world in the shell of the old, they do *represent* that project as a goal. And this representation, while its limits must be acknowledged, should not be underestimated as a necessary element of political projects. The lifestyles of radical anarchists may be less important for how they prefigure a different world than for the fact that they make visible the existence of subjects who desire a different world. Though true authenticity as a pure anarchist might be impossible to achieve within present conditions, lifestyle is a way of gesturing toward a desire for different conditions, the kind that would make different kinds of subjectivities truly possible. While critics may dismiss lifestyle activism as a "self-delusion" with the central purpose of presenting a virtuous identity (Schutz 2009b), this is not sufficient grounds for the dismissal of lifestyle activism. Rather, it just points up a set of ethical concerns that will have to be addressed in specific times and places, such as whether potential allies are being excluded or relations of domination are being reproduced.

This case of anarchist lifestyle activism can also tell us something about the nature of radical identity and orientation within postmodernity. As I showed in Chapter 4, "anarchist" is a contested sign: there is no universal consensus about what that label must refer to, and everyone is aware that their identification as an anarchist is open to doubt. They may even doubt their own authenticity as anarchists, seeing the term as something to which they can aspire but never completely measure up. Furthermore, no one can ever fully exemplify anarchy—contemporary society is so thoroughly shaped by conditions of economic exploitation, political hierarchy, and ideologies of oppression that no one is quite at liberty to step outside any of these systems. In the absence of conditions under which it would be possible to achieve a truly anarchistic existence, anarchism remains always an orientation rather than an achievable state of fixed identity. This lesson applies just as well to any radical project, since by definition, a radical project seeks a reality that is radically outside the boundaries of the currently real.

A more theoretical implication of this book, and one that I hope will be clear to those who recognize aspects of anarchist culture in their own social groups, is that, radical or not, all personal identity projects are bound to fail in one way or another. This is something postmodern theorists have been saying for quite a while.[1] As Linda Martín Alcoff (2000: 77) puts it, "Identities are not and can never be accurate representations of the real self, and thus interpellation always in a strict sense *fails* in its representational claim even while it succeeds in inciting and disciplining one's practice." This book has shown some of the particular reasons and conditions under which one specific identity is so problematic. But it's not a problem unique to anarchists (though as I've just argued, there may be particular features of the contemporary political economic system that make anarchism particularly problematic as an identity). We are each in some ways failing to truly "be" all the things we say we are, or think we are, or are recognized as in certain times and places, because any identity is always an ideal that, when pushed up against all the conditions and interlocking forces each of us is subject to, will never be fully realized. The anxieties and tensions around anarchist identity and the manifestations of these anxieties in commitments to lifestyle practices, in conjunction with postmodern theories of identity, suggest that perhaps many or most of the social identities that define us are anxiety provoking in their ultimate unachieveability and that this is itself a major engine of the contemporary preoccupation with lifestyle, both within the anarchist context and far beyond it. As the individual figures in this book show, the stakes are particularly high when the identity one is defined by is one informed by a utopian political vision—the unachieveability of the anarchist ideal is not just a personal frustration but actually an addition of insult to the injury of neoliberal capitalism.

To identify with radicalism is to recognize the great power and pervasiveness of systems that are deeply flawed; if you're a radical it's because you seek radical change and have a radical analysis that sees the fundamental defects at the root of the present system. A radical orientation will thus necessarily introduce contradictions, inconsistencies, and "hypocrisies" between the way one lives day to day—because one lives within the defective system—and the way one wishes it were possible to live. A radical identity that relies on personal authenticity for its verification is thus always bound to "fail," but only if such inconsistencies are read and treated as failures, which they often are, within the "call out" culture of contemporary activist communities. The question then, is what do we do with our failures and the failures we observe in those around us? What is the appropriate response to contradiction? This is an axiological question that each community must answer for itself.

One possible response would be to embrace the risk of failure to achieve an "authentic" radical reality in the hope that something better might be achieved without any such guarantee being offered. This doesn't mean romanticizing failure or embracing failure as a way of life. Rather, it means making a commitment to test and reassess the extent to which one's actions have achieved something better, and even to be willing to redefine what "better" means. One would proceed with a "strategic orientation" rather than a "singular ideology" or "singular imagined goal" (Gilbert 2008: 228). Localized, specific critique also allows for the possibility that lifestyle politics does valuable cultural work for activists, despite its final effects not being determinable in advance.[2] This might look suspiciously like the flexible, nimble labor and assessment induced by neoliberalism itself, but it could also be a way of most effectively using some of the techniques of neoliberalism against itself. Lynn Comella (2012: 43) argues that "elements of neoliberalism, including the care of the self and the role of the marketplace in promoting technologies of empowerment, can be rearticulated and marshaled toward socially progressive ends." Likewise, the will and capacity to be reflexive and adaptive toward the way tactics work within given nodes in a broad, connected network might be used to coordinate activist projects.

In trying to answer the question of what is at stake for those who debate the value of lifestyle politics, I've come to the conclusion that many things are at stake, and the stakes are not always necessarily compatible or commensurable with each other. Radical activists who attempt to put their political values into their lifestyle practices are responding to a variety of conditions: a postmodern world that casts into doubt the stability of any identity category, let alone one defined through philosophical commitments which are subject to constant, collective, and cross-contextual debate and revision; a neoliberal political climate in which personal action and responsibility are touted as the privileged form of civic participation; a commodity culture that fosters the construction of alternative ways of life while simultaneously attempting to recuperate them for profit motives; and profoundly unjust social relations that make themselves felt at the most personal levels and thus incite resistance there as well. A tactical move that responds effectively to one of these conditions may look markedly less adaptive when considered from the perspective of another condition. Lifestyle politics is thus a complex phenomenon and no easy judgments can or should be offered.

In the afterword to his study of everyday politics among working-class African Americans, Robin Kelley (1996) urges social movement critics to look at the limits and effects of any political action, in order to assess its ultimate value to a larger project. I have presented all the above issues and debates in the interest of critically interrogating the ways in which lifestyle politics constitutes a set of tactics that can be integrated into the political strategy of radical movements. The phenomenon of lifestyle politics in anarchist movements bears out Kelley's observation that "certain forms of resistance create their own limits" (231). And, as he goes on to say, they are "limits that can be understood only in specific historical and spatial context" (231). This book does not offer a final answer on whether lifestyle is effective as politics. Indeed, it argues that such a question cannot be answered at all in a final way. Rather, we must ask, in every instance, what is lifestyle politics effective for. Only by attending to the situational factors that affect the outcome of any particular instance of lifestyle politics can we assess its usefulness and its place in radical activist strategy. Movements and their participants will have to answer for themselves whether the effects of their lifestyle-based tactics are consistent with their philosophical ideals and pursuant to their material goals.

If what one means by activism is practices which effect material changes in systems of power, then clearly lifestyle politics are "mere" "weapons of the weak," unsuited to the necessary task of restructuring social conditions. Lifestylism may even be read as a "false consciousness" response to the weakness of the individual engendered by the capitalist system. But neoliberalism does not only *disempower* individuals. In fact, part of its logic is to empower them, to spur them to make life decisions, to take responsibility for themselves, to stitch their daily experience into aesthetically and politically coherent—if multifaceted—narratives. By turning to lifestyle politics from this angle, we see that its practitioners are, in some respects, strong—not weak—given their demonstrated capacity to make choices far outside the dominant norms. And yet, overarching systems shape even these choices, so that resistant lifestyle practices may be differently appealing and achievable by different kinds of subjects–men, women, straight, queer, white, non-white, citizen, immigrant— each will have particular forces acting on the choices they make. Because the whole phenomenon of lifestyle politics looks so different depending on the angle from which one approaches it, the only final argument this book can make is that understanding and assessing the value of politicized lifestyle practices for radical activism must be seen as a project of "limitless critique" that constantly displaces its own assumptions, out of a recognition that they are always shaped by authority whose own legitimacy must be open to question (Foucault 1997c). The politics of lifestyle must neither be romanticized nor dismissed out of hand by radical activists and those who study political activism; rather, it must be constantly held in hand, to be wielded at appropriate moments, and with a humble commitment to learn when and where those moments are.

NOTES

Chapter 1

1 All interviewee names used in this book are pseudonyms.

2 Somewhat ironically, given his early championship of lifestyle politics, the most famous critic of "lifestyle anarchism" is Murray Bookchin, who published a polemical essay on the topic in the 1990s. In this essay, titled *Social Anarchism or Lifestyle Anarchism: An Unbridgeable Chasm* (1995), he seemed to reveal his disillusionment with the use of lifestyle as a political tactic. I discuss some of the reasons for this apparent shift in Bookchin's position in Chapter 6.

3 There are inherent limitations introduced by my status as a relative outsider to the movement I study in this book. My knowledge, like all knowledge, is "situated" within my own subjectivity and experience and is therefore partial (Haraway 1988). My own political identities, namely feminist and queer, inevitably colored the questions I asked and the way I interpreted my observations during the research process.

4 For further definitions of the term lifestyle, see Featherstone (1987) and Binkley (2007b).

5 There is an extensive and growing literature on "ethical consumption" but see especially Barnett et al. (2005), Connolly and Prothero (2008), Harrison et al. (2005), Littler (2009), Micheletti (2003), and Mukherjee and Banet-Weiser (2012).

6 See, for instance, Adam's (1995) history of the gay and lesbian movements of the twentieth century; Braunstein and Doyle's (2002) collection of histories of the 1960s counterculture; Cornell's (2011a, 2011b) histories of anarchist organizing in the twentieth century; Denning's (1997) history of the "Cultural Front" during the Cold War; Kaplan and Shapiro's (1998) collection of personal accounts of the children of Communist Party activists of the 1930s; Klatch's (1999) sociological history of New Left and conservative activists of the 1960s and 1970s; Lipsitz's (1994) history of mid twentieth-century labor movements; McKinley's (1982) history of early twentieth-century anarchists' occupational choices; Ogbar's (2004) history of the Black Power movement; Roszak's (1969) account of the youth counterculture of the 1960s; Rossinow's (1998) study of New Leftists and the 1960s counterculture; Veysey's (1973) study of reform movements in the pre-Civil War era; and the many accounts of radical lesbian feminism of the 1960s and 1970s (Echols 1989; Freeman 1975; Stein 1997; Taylor and Whittier 1995; Whittier 1995; Millett 2000; Phelan 1989).

7   For social movement research that discusses the cultural vibrancy of radical activism in the face of official repression, see Polletta (2002), Taylor and Whittier (1992), and Whittier (1995).

8   The sense in which I use the terms "tactics" and "strategy" here is rooted in the work of de Certeau (1984) and Foucault (1990a). I have also found useful Gilbert's (2008) discussion of "strategic orientation." The sense in which I use the term "articulation" is usefully explained by Slack (1996).

9   For examples of these critiques, see Bevington and Dixon (2005), Cornell (2011b), Eschle (2004), and Martínez (2000).

10 "Lifestyle change or revolution?" thread in the Infoshop Forums (www. forums.infoshop.org/viewtopic.php?f=29&t=6340&p=22961).

11 The concept of "strategic ethnography" comes from Marcus and Fischer (1999: 132). Even within the delimited scope of my research on one particular aspect of anarchist movements, I had to be further selective about the dimensions of anarchist lifestyle politics I chose to address in this book due to inevitable limitations on time and space. There are some specific lifestyle practices that I do not cover, such as child-rearing practices or occupational choices. I also do not closely trace changes in lifestyle practices over the lifecycle of individual anarchists, or the relationship between age and commitment to lifestyle politics. Such topics should be explored in future research.

12 See *Security Culture: A Handbook for Activists*, a pamphlet available online at www.security.resist.ca/personal/securebooklet.pdf.

13 Several works trace the anarchist philosophical and practical tradition through the history of US countercultural movements. See especially Cornell (2011a), Davis (2010), Farrell (1997), Rossinow (1998), and Veysey (1973).

14 This approach is inspired by Juris's (2008a) study of anarchist activist networks, in which he took the generalized practice of networking as his object of analysis, instead of focusing on the structure of any one specific group or location. My approach is also reminiscent of Berlant and Freeman's (1993) work on Queer Nation, also a decentralized, radical movement. They describe their scholarship as "falsely bringing into narrative logic and collective intentionality what has been a deliberately unsystematized politics" (200).

15 Ross Haenfler (2006: 195) suggests that collective identity is especially important to diffuse social movements because there is "no formal structure to ensure continuity, consistency, action, and commitment." He goes on to say that "collective identity is a *support structure*; people call on collective identity (that is, look to the identity for guidance) in a variety of situations where they might otherwise rely on the guidance of an organization and/or a leader" (196).

16 The informal hierarchies of power that emerge within radical political movements have been described by Jo Freeman in her much circulated essay, "The Tyranny of Structurelessness" (2002). Gordon (2008) also describes how such dynamics can be found within contemporary anarchist movements. I extend this discussion by examining the specific role of taste and lifestyle in these power dynamics.

17 For further discussion of "politics of articulation" see Reed (2005) and Hall (1996b).

18 "Movement culture" is a term introduced by Goodwyn (1978) and is further elaborated by Denning (1997) and Reed (2005).

19 See Olson (2009) for more on infoshops and their importance to anarchist social formations.

20 The term "zine" is short for magazine, and refers specifically to a hand-assembled, do-it-yourself style publication. See Duncombe (2008) for an in-depth study of zines and zine cultures.

21 In addition to using these texts to develop what anthropologist Lanita Jacobs-Huey (2002: 794) calls "communicative competence" in the relational norms of anarchist cultures (which aided me in my fieldwork), I also treated contemporary anarchist publications as sources of information about anarchists' lifestyle practices. Paul Atkinson and Amanda Coffey (2004) refer to the method of utilizing texts like this as sources of data as the analysis of "documentary realities." They caution against using such texts as sources of evidence about material realities. Although no representation can unproblematically capture reality, I did, to some extent, take it on faith that the lifestyle practices commonly described by anarchist texts are actually undertaken in the real world. In many cases, textual accounts were corroborated by interviewees and my own observations.

22 The alterglobalization movement, also known as the antiglobalization movement or alternative globalization movement, is the umbrella name given to the global justice movements against neoliberalism that flourished worldwide in the 1990s. It is widely recognized as being anarchistic in its tactics, aims, and organizing structures (Graeber 2002).

23 This phrase, "building a new world in the shell of the old," is generally attributed to the International Workers of the World, an anarchist labor organization founded in 1905. See the organization's website, www.iww.org.

24 See Sheehan (2003) for further discussion of media representations of anarchists.

Chapter 2

1 The concept of mutual aid as an anarchist ethos comes from nineteenth-century Russian scientist and anarchist, Peter Kropotkin (2009). While Kropotkin's account of mutual aid derived from his observations of animal behavior, and thus attributed the practice to natural rather than ethical impulses, mutual aid has since been taken up by anarchist organizers as an ethically mandated expression of solidarity with fellow activists.

2 Food Not Bombs is a decentralized network of autonomous collectives who, usually on a weekly basis, acquire free food (often obtaining it from the dumpsters of restaurants and grocery stores), cook it in mass quantities, and serve it to homeless communities. They may also provide prepared food to other activists at protest and cultural events. Food Not Bombs groups exist all over the United States; most major cities and many smaller towns have active Food Not Bombs groups. In Los Angeles, for example, there are multiple groups—on two occasions, I participated in food preparation with

the Downtown LA "chapter," which happened to meet near my apartment. In addition to its official aim of providing food to hungry people on the streets and at political events, Food Not Bombs is a social hub and frequently serves as an entry point for people who are beginning to get involved with anarchist activism. As the founders of Food Not Bombs observe in their handbook, "The Food Not Bombs table is often a landmark for activists and street folks looking to connect with the movement in a new city" (Butler and McHenry 2000: 26).

3 Other studies of ethical consumption have noted the overlap of multiple motivations by consumers. See Connolly and Prothero (2008) and Sassatelli and Davolio (2010).

4 Some anarchists might take exception to this logic, arguing that to vote, either in an electoral or an economic sense, is to legitimate a situation in which one must choose the least of many evils. As a writer of the *Why Freegan?* zine put it, "I don't vote because no matter who I vote for, the government always wins and when you 'vote with your dollars,' consumerism always wins, capitalism always wins" (koala!, n.d.: 4). The only ideologically supportable course, according to this argument, is to abstain from the system altogether (i.e. to not vote at all and to not spend money on consumption at all.) Whether one adequately extracts oneself from capitalism by not spending money or from the state by not voting is open to debate.

5 There is an extensive literature on the consumer strike as a mode of anti-consumption. See, for example, Smith (1990) and Micheletti (2003).

6 As Leiss et al. (2005: 200) explain, "The product has become a totem, a representation of a clan or group that we recognize by its activities and its members' shared enjoyment of the product. The response to consumption seems to be less concerned with the nature of satisfaction than with its social meaning—the way it integrates the individual into a consumption tribe. Meaning here focuses on questions such as: Who is the person I become in the process of consumption? Who are the other consumers like me? What does the product mean in terms of the type of person I am and how I relate to others?"

7 While Binkley (2007a) positions the individualist anti-consumer against the collectivist anti-consumer, arguing for a distinction between those who are pursuing projects of self-realization and those who approach consumption as a means for realizing the shared objectives of a social movement, this dichotomy doesn't really hold up among anarchist anti-consumers. Binkley's work is important in recognizing that consumption practices are not always already self-interested; I want to extend Binkley's analysis a step further by exploring the strategic implications of the multitude of motivations and outcomes of anti-consumption lifestyles.

Chapter 3

1 There is extensive literature from a variety of disciplines on the associations between subcultures and body modification. See, for example, Bell and Valentine (1995), DeMello (2000), and Vale and Juno (1989). Much of the theoretical work of these studies is applicable to anarchists as well.

2 My approach here is strongly influenced by the models of cultural studies provided by Richard Johnson (1986), Paul du Gay et al. (1997), and Stuart Hall (1997, 2006). It should be made clear here that I am using "production" and "consumption" in the sense of sending and receiving communicative messages. We might alternatively think of producers and consumers as performers and audience. Production and consumption in this sense do not imply commodity fabrication and exchange.

3 In the southwestern United States at least, the bandana also carries connotations of solidarity with Latin American political causes, such as the indigenous, revolutionary Zapatista movement based in Mexico. Zapatista-made bandanas, among other garments, are sometimes sold at anarchist events to raise funds for that movement.

4 Although my account here should look familiar to those knowledgeable of Butlerian theories of performativity, an identity like anarchist is different from an identity like woman, with which Butler and other post-structuralist feminist theorists have been concerned. Specifically, I am rather less concerned with the unconscious and its relation to subjectivity since this is less instructive for understanding the kind of activist identity and performances on which this book focuses. In a way, anarchist identity is much easier to understand in terms of performativity than gender identity is, since the notion that "one is not born an anarchist activist" is a rather uncontroversial one, while the idea that one is not born a woman (pace Beauvior) is harder for many people to wrap their heads around.

5 The similarity between sexual and political identities—namely, that they are both "invisible"—is also noted by Gross (2001) and McKenna and Bargh (1998).

6 See Kobena Mercer (1987) for an excellent discussion of the "sense of solidarity" cultivated by African-American radicals through stylistic performance in the post-Black Power era. Many parallels can be drawn between the subjects of Mercer's work and the anarchist activists described here.

7 *Agents provocateurs* are police or other state officials who infiltrate organizations and protest actions disguised as activists and then incite violent confrontation, effectively justifying overt police repression of activist efforts.

8 This phenomenon has been much discussed by historians of the US lesbian feminist movement of the 1970s. Women in this movement experienced enormous pressure to adopt a very limited style of self-presentation, and women whose tastes diverged from the subcultural norm had their political commitments to feminism called into question. As a result, many women reported being driven away from feminist activist communities. See Echols (1989), Stein (1997), Faderman (1992), Taylor and Whittier (1992), Whittier (1995), and Phelan (1989).

9 This is a perennial question for scholars of spectacular subculture style. See, for example, Bell and Valentine (1995: 152) who lament, "the ways in which body modifications articulate a politics of dissent other than through well-worn notions of the refusal to conform remain unclear."

10 The blog post and its comments can be accessed at www.thelede.blogs. nytimes.com/2009/04/02/protesters-fail-to-bring-down-global-capitalism-with-costumes-puppets.

11 Radical black activists of the 1960s, for example, saw their stylistic innovations—such as the afro hairstyle and the raised fist gesture—appropriated by marketing campaigns targeted at mainstream black audiences (often by white-owned companies) (Van Deburg 1992; Mercer 1987). Feminist politics as well have been enlisted in the marketing of commercial products; often these are products that tap into retrograde constructions of femininity, such as cleaning supplies and personal hygiene products (Goldman et al. 1991).

12 I am referring here to a line of products sold by the Unilever Corporation, under the Axe brand name.

13 This is a not-so-subtle reference to the hard rock band Rage Against the Machine, whose songs are known for their radical political content, but who achieved commercial success after releasing an album on the Sony record label in the early 1990s.

Chapter 4

1 This problem is discussed informally in many places. For some more formal observations and critiques, see Cornell (2011b), Olson (2009), and Thompson (2010).

2 See Chapter 1, fn. 7 for histories that detail such "pictures of the proper or normative activist subject" with respect to lifestyle practices.

3 I understood that people may be hesitant to identify as anarchists (Graeber 2002; Juris 2009). Therefore, when I recruited people to participate in my study, I was always careful to stipulate only that they have an affinity to anarchism, whether or not they felt comfortable claiming the identity outright.

4 My use of the word sincere here comes from John L. Jackson's (2005) discussion of "sincerity" versus "authenticity" with respect to racial identity. For Jackson, sincerity refers to the strength of one's subjective investment in a particular identification, regardless of how convincingly one performs according to the social expectations for that identity in a given context.

5 This resistant subject is not located *outside* the state or the market's networks of power, but rather the subject has multiple networks of power converging on it, one of which is that of the radical movement. Recognizing this intersection of power helps to explain why attempting to achieve a puristic movement subjectivity and a pure activist lifestyle is a futile pursuit: one will never be able to fully align with *just one* disciplinary discourse since one is pulled in different directions by different discourses. I will return to this idea again in future chapters.

6 For Foucault, the authority or institution in question is often one of domination, such as the state. He uses the term "anatamo-politics" to refer to the exercise of power upon the individual human body; this exercise of power is distinct from punishment, rather it generally takes the form of *self*-discipline

toward some positive state of "optimization" and "usefulness" (Foucault 1990a: 139).

7 In the context of "ethical consumption," Jo Littler (2009: 14) describes such purism as being characterized by "sanctimonious righteousness." Drawing on the work of Wendy Brown (2005), Littler asserts that self-righteous moralism ends up shutting down productive debate over ethical goods, rather than bringing people together for political projects. Littler also points out that, "the celebration of a kind of 'purity' of activism can give it a mythic force which, while potent and generative, can also exclude a wide range of people without particular forms of social and cultural capital from identifying with it" (44).

Chapter 5

1 See also an essay by Goldman's contemporary Voltarine De Cleyre titled "They Who Marry Do Ill" (2004) and Greenway's (2009) discussion of late nineteenth-century British anarchists' views on marriage.

2 For a typology of various polyamorous relationship structures involving more than two people, see the alt.polyamory FAQ at www.faqs.org/faqs/polyamory/faq/.

3 For a discussion of the specific valence of the term "queer" within sexual activist movements, see Warner (1993). For an introduction to the intellectual movement known as queer theory, and its roots in the homosexual activist tradition, see Jagose (1996).

4 "Homonormativity" is a term used by radical queers to critique homosexual identities and relationships that conform to heterosexual ideas of normalcy; for example, gender dichotomous, monogamous, and legally sanctioned. See Sycamore (2008) and Warner (1999).

5 See, for example, the websites for Radical Homosexual Agenda (www. radicalhomosexualagenda.org), and Black and Pink (www.blackandpink.org), and posts and forum discussions of queer anarchism on more general anarchist sites like Infoshop (www.infoshop.org), Anarkismo (www.anarkismo.net), and Anarchist News (www.anarchistnews.org).

6 Ze and hir are non-gendered, singular, third-person subject and object pronouns. They have been put into use by queer/trans activists as a remedy for the lack of non-gendered, singular, third-person pronouns in the English language.

7 I use straight as a synonym for heteronormative, not for heterosexual. To some extent, this means that straight also describes homonormative identities, though any form of homosexuality is relatively "less" hegemonic or straight by virtue of its not being the heterosexual norm. When I say straight, I don't mean to specify heterosexuality or homosexuality, just relative conformity to heteronormativity.

8 I'm not sure how to interpret Minty's slippage from sexual identity (which was how I framed my question) to "gender identity." Although gender and sexuality are clearly related, I am unsure whether to interpret Minty's statement about

"loving womyn" as more about her identification *as* a woman or about her erotic attraction *to* women. Unfortunately, after I received this response (in an email follow-up to our in-person interview), Minty got too busy with work to continue exchanging emails, and so I was unable to clarify her answer.

9   The way the author uses the term bisexual in this particular essay is closer to the way I have defined queer here. The use of bisexual is unfortunately confusing; it is clear that the author does not mean to indicate that each and every anarchist is sexually attracted to both men and women, which is what bisexuality is generally taken to signify.

10 This is not a new dynamic within political movements that have supported the subversion of mainstream sexual mores. In Emma Goldman's autobiography she describes an encounter with a supporter of free love who attempts to seduce her, and recounts her subsequent frustration when she discovers that he is merely a married man looking to engage in "clandestine affairs" (Goldman 1977: 197). Scholars of the hippie counterculture of the late 1960s and early 1970s have documented the ways in which critiques of sexual moralism were used within the subculture to facilitate men's unrestricted access to women's bodies. Picking up on this issue, Beth Bailey (2002) argues that while images of liberated sexuality were initially used by the counterculture to symbolize a rejection of mainstream repression and conformity, such images stopped being so revolutionary once they began to mirror misogynist fantasies and commonplace marketing techniques. Bailey observes that ultimately, "what were formerly markers of opposition now signaled revolutionary intent less than they demonstrated belonging in a vast and powerful peer culture" (322). Kreutzer (2004) makes an explicit link between this history and contemporary political subcultures: "The recent rise of polyamory as the preferred lifestyle in the radical leftist/anarchist circles parallels the 'sexual revolution' of the late 1960s. In both instances, the supposed sexual freedom for women has not been done for our benefit, but for the benefit of men." It would probably be overly cynical to assume that male proponents of sexual liberation have long been engaged in a coordinated campaign to reassert patriarchal social dynamics within radical movements. However, it seems reasonable to think that, by movements failing to adequately understand and address the ways that resistant practices may reproduce hegemonic privileges, on the whole these practices may benefit individual men more frequently than they benefit individual women. The consequence is that systemic hierarchies are reinforced rather than subverted.

11 This phenomenon is discussed at length in a widely reproduced essay titled "The Tyranny of Structurelessness," by women's liberation activist Jo Freeman (2002). The essay appears in a collection of anarcha-feminist writings alongside a rejoinder titled "The Tyranny of Tyranny," by Cathy Levine (2002).

12 The document, authored by the Pittsburgh G-20 Resistance Project Sexual Assault Group, is titled "Consent Guidelines for G-20 Resistance Spaces and Housing" and can be found at www.resistg20.org/policies.

13 BDSM is an umbrella acronym that designates sexual encounters involving dynamics of bondage, discipline, domination, submission, sadism, slave/master relations, and masochism. The erotic appeal of these encounters is founded

upon the participants' role-playing with uneven power dynamics. Practitioners of BDSM understand consensuality to be crucial—the willing consent of all parties involved ensures that the fantasy of coercion remains physically and emotionally safe for the participants. Certainly, not all sex between anarchists is based on the fantasmatic eroticization of power differentials, but it is telling that this discussion posited the condition of consent as the common link between anarchism and BDSM.

14 The method of "calling people out" is not limited to the sphere of sexual violence. It is used as a technique of discipline around all sorts of practices, as discussed in other chapters of this book.

15 A remarkably similar sentiment is expressed in CrimethInc.'s *Days of War, Nights of Love* (2000: 40): "Every time one of us remembers not to accept at face value the authority of the powers that be, each time one of us is able to escape the system of domination for a moment (whether it is by getting away with something forbidden by a teacher or boss, relating to a member of a different social stratum as an equal, etc.), that is a victory for the individual and a blow against hierarchy."

16 Butler's body of work on performativity and subversion is another venue in which personal acts of transgression are attributed with the power to disrupt systems of domination. Butler's theoretical explication of "gender insubordination" (1997a) has been taken up by those who see personal refusals to conform to hegemonic norms as a means of detracting from the hegemony of those norms. In Gramscian terms, by refusing to consent to being governed by gender norms, insubordinate subjects weaken the overall force of these norms. In this vein, it might be thought that anarchist sexual practices make trouble for the hegemonic sexual order. Again though, it is unclear to many readers of Butler in what precise capacity "speech and gesture" are able to intervene in the material realities generated by power differentials (Nussbaum 1999). It can be argued, along Nussbaum's lines, that to merely identify as one thing versus another is a superficial gesture that does little to undercut the material privileges that will still accrue to the disidentifier as a result of their actual participation in heterosexual sexual arrangements, and by the same token, be denied to the oppressed due to their non-participation.

17 This is similar to the logic behind the construction, within gay liberation discourses, of "coming out" as a political act. Publicly acknowledging—or outing—one's non-normative sexual identity has been a central tactic of queer activism. It is thought that "declaring one's deviant, transgressive erotic autobiography is a political act brimming with the potential to subvert repression and to facilitate the exploration of sexual practices and beings" (Wilson 1999: 109). Within queer activist projects, there are other reasons for outing: to promote tolerance by showing that already beloved figures may be non-straight, or to expose hypocritical public figures (Gross 1993). These motivations do not figure as prominently in the anarcha-queer project. In the case of queer identification of the kind performed by anarchists, what is happening is less the airing of an erotic autobiography and more the refusal to allow a straight biography to go assumed or unquestioned, even if, empirically, the events of one's sexual life could more or less fit within a straight narrative.

Chapter 6

1 "Lifestyle change or revolution?" thread in the Infoshop Forums www.forums. infoshop.org/viewtopic.php?f=29&t=6340&p=22961.

2 "Debunking Nonsense in the Anarchist Movement" www.infoshop.org/page/ MovementDebunker.

3 www.infoshop.org/wiki/Lifestyle_anarchism.

4 Cornell's (2011a) discussion of anarchist culture in the pre-WWI period shows that activists were debating these ideas even then. Cornell describes, for example, how anarchist activist Harry Kelly mounted a critique of bohemianism among anarchists, a critique which "presciently warned against the tendency, which grew later in the century, for purported anarchists to simply live their own lives in as free a fashion as their social status allowed for (as 'bohemians' or 'drop-outs') without investing themselves in the organized struggle to create lasting structural transformations that would increase security and liberty for the least privileged" (91). In the interwar period, the journal *Vanguard* wanted to separate its anarchist-communism/anarcho-syndicalism from anarchist-individualism, so it avoided any issues that "smacked of individualism"—"anything 'bohemian,' such as consideration of modern art, or the promotion of progressive gender roles, was out" (290).

5 The co-optation of radical critique by capitalist apparatuses such as advertising is discussed by Frank (1997), Klein (1999), and Binkley (2007a).

6 "Debunking Nonsense in the Anarchist Movement" www.infoshop.org/page/ movementdebunker.html.

7 Interestingly, Pritha went on to say, "However, I do not want to want to deny those types of anarchists their struggle- I just don't agree with it and will continue to be critical of it." This speaks to the ethical obligations anarchists feel both to respect others' autonomy and to hold each other accountable for the political effects of their actions. These two ethical principles can, themselves, spawn contradictory feelings and responses among activists who are interested in developing anarchist strategy—another factor that makes the internal debate over lifestylism a tricky one.

8 Milstein (2010: 42) explains this dilemma with specific regard to anarchists: "the gap between what anarchists imagine to be fully ethical and the series of bad choices we all make under the present conditions illustrates that hierarchical social relationships will forever preclude our ability to be free. Anarchism's emphasis on the whole of life underscores that the current social order already frames the world for everyone down to the tiniest interactions; 'choice' itself is already hobbled."

9 See Plant (1992) for a historical discussion of the concept of recuperation as developed by the theorists of the Situationist International in the mid twentieth century. Plant explains that, for the Situationists, recuperation involves dissenting voices not only being co-opted and weakened by the forces of "the spectacle," but also, through their co-optation, enhancing the power of the commodity system itself (75).

10 Harvey (2007: 200) notes this limitation as a common one for grassroots movements against neoliberalism: "They draw strength from being embedded in the nitty-gritty of daily life and struggle, but in doing so they often find it hard to extract themselves from the local and the particular to understand the macro-politics of what neoliberal accumulation by dispossession and its relation to the restoration of class power was and is all about." Harvey observes that movements of the US Left, from 1968 on, have largely "failed to recognize or confront, let alone transcend, the inherent tension between the quest for individual freedoms and social justice" (43).

11 This dichotomy of ideal types of consumers is used by Binkley (2008).

12 See Cornell (2011b: 181) and Leondar-Wright (n.d.) for more examples in this vein.

13 Even assuming the possibility of individual resistance by significant numbers of people, it may not be the case that there are enough activists out there to have a quantitatively significant impact on the whole capitalist system, or even on one industry or corporation within that system. In this vein, writer Derrick Jensen (a controversial figure among anarchists who take differing stances on lifestyle politics) argues that even if ethical consumption practices were to be adopted by masses of individuals, their material impact might still be relatively small. In an essay titled "Forget Shorter Showers: Why Personal Change Does Not Equal Political Change," Jensen (2009) points out that the environmental damage caused by individuals is minuscule when compared with that of government and corporate institutions. Thus, exhortations for individuals to minimize their detrimental effect on the planet through changes in personal consumption have the dual negative consequence of displacing responsibility, and perhaps inconvenience, onto those who are least equipped to cope with it, and allowing the worst offenders to go on conducting (unethical) business as usual.

14 Indeed, this echoes one of Bookchin's most convincing criticisms of lifestyle anarchism in *Social Anarchism or Lifestyle Anarchism* (1995).

Chapter 7

1 See, for example, Alcoff (1988, 2005), Butler (1990, 2004a), and Hall (1996b).

2 My thinking here is indebted to Wendy Brown's (2005) discussion of Michel Foucault's (1997c) concept of "local criticism."

REFERENCES

Adam, Barry D. (1995). *The Rise of a Gay and Lesbian Movement*. Rev. ed. New York: Twayne Publishers.

AK Press. n.d. "About Us." *AK Press*. www.akpress.org/about.html. Accessed 23 November 2012.

Alcoff, Linda Martín. (1988). "Cultural Feminism vs. Poststructuralism: The Identity Crisis in Feminist Theory." *Signs: Journal of Women in Culture and Society* 13(3): 405–36.

—. (2000). "Who's Afraid of Identity Politics?" In *Reclaiming Identity: Realist Theory and the Predicament of Postmodernism*, edited by Paula Moya and Michael Hames-Garcia, 312–44. Berkeley, CA: University of California Press.

—. (2005). *Visible Identities: Race, Gender, and the Self*. New York: Oxford University Press.

Althusser, Louis. (2006). "Ideology and Ideological State Apparatuses (Notes Toward an Investigation)." In *Media and Cultural Studies: Keywords*, edited by Meenakshi Gigi Durham and Douglas M. Kellner, 79–88. Malden, MA: Blackwell.

Amster, Randall, Abraham DeLeon, Luis A. Fernandez, Anthony J. Nocella, II, and Deric Shannon, (eds) (2009). *Contemporary Anarchist Studies: An Introductory Anthology of Anarchy in the Academy*. London: Routledge.

"Anarchism and Decadence." (2008). *Anarchy Is for Everyone* (blog) 19 February. www.anarchyisforeveryone.blogspot.com/2008/02/anarchism-and-decadence-5.html.

Anarchist Federation. (2009). "Queer: An Anarchist Deconstruction." *Anarchist Federation* (blog) 19 May. www.afed.org.uk/blog/community/76-queer-an-anarchist-deconstruction.html.

Anderson, Benedict. (1991). *Imagined Communities: Reflections on the Origin and Spread of Nationalism*. Rev. ed. New York: Verso.

Anonymous Queers. (1999). "Queers Read This: I Hate Straights." In *The Columbia Reader onLesbians and Gay Men in Media, Society, and Politics*, edited by Larry Gross and James D. Woods, 588–94. New York: Columbia University Press.

Appiah, Kwame Anthony. (1996). "Race, Culture, Identity: Misunderstood Connections." In *Color Conscious: The Political Morality of Race*, edited by Kwame Anthony Appiah and Amy Gutmann, 30–105. Princeton, NJ: Princeton University Press.

Ardent Press. (2008). *Complicated Relationships: Conversations on Polyamory and Anarchy*. San Francisco, CA: Ardent Press.

Atkinson, Paul, and Amanda Coffey. (2004). "Analysing Documentary Realities." In *Qualitative Research: Theory, Method and Practice*, edited by David Silverman, 56–75. 2nd ed. London: Sage.

Austin, J. L. (1975). *How to Do Things with Words*. Cambridge, MA: Harvard University Press.

Bailey, Beth. (2002). "Sex as a Weapon: Underground Comix and the Paradox of Liberation." In *Imagine Nation: The American Counterculture of the 1960s and '70s*, edited by Peter Braunstein and Michael William Doyle, 305–24. New York: Routledge.

BAMF! Productionz. (2009). *Bash Back!: An Unofficial Zine*. www.zinelibrary. info/bash-back-fan-zine.

Banet-Weiser, Sarah, and Roopali Mukherjee. (2012). "Introduction: Commodity Activism in Neoliberal Times." In *Commodity Activism*, edited by Mukherjee and Banet-Weiser, 1–22. New York: New York University Press.

Barnett, Clive, Paul Cloke, Nick Clarke, and Alice Malpass. (2005). "Consuming Ethics: Articulating the Subjects and Spaces of Ethical Consumption." *Antipode* 37(1): 23–45.

Bartky, Sandra Lee, (ed.) (1990). "Foucault, Femininity, and the Modernization of Patriarchal Power." In *Femininity and Domination: Studies in the Phenomenology of Oppression*, 63–82. New York: Routledge.

Bauman, Zygmunt. (2001). "Consuming Life." *Journal of Consumer Culture* 1(1): 9–29.

Baym, Nancy K. (2010). *Personal Connections in the Digital Age*. Cambridge: Polity.

Bell, David, and Gill Valentine. (1995). "The Sexed Self: Strategies of Performance, Sites of Resistance." In *Mapping the Subject: Geographies of Cultural Transformation*, edited by Steve Pile and Nigel Thrift, 143–57. London: Routledge.

Bennett, Andy, and Keith Kahn-Harris. (2004). Introduction to *After Subculture: Critical Studies in Contemporary Youth Culture*, edited by Andy Bennett and Keith Kahn-Harris, 1–18. New York: Palgrave Macmillan.

Berlant, Lauren, and Elizabeth Freeman. (1993). "Queer Nationality." In *Fear of a Queer Planet: Queer Politics and Social Theory*, edited by Michael Warner, 193–229. Minneapolis, MN: University of Minnesota Press.

Berlant, Lauren, and Michael Warner. (1998). "Sex in Public." *Critical Inquiry* 24(2): 547–66.

Beuchler, Steven M. (1995). "New Social Movement Theories." *The Sociological Quarterly* 36(3): 441–64.

Bevington, Douglas, and Chris Dixon. (2005). "Movement-relevant Theory: Rethinking Social Movement Scholarship and Activism." *Social Movement Studies: Journal of Social, Cultural and Political Protest* 4(3): 185–208.

Binkley, Sam. (2007a). *Getting Loose: Lifestyle Consumption in the 1970s*. Durham, NC: Duke University Press.

—. (2007b). "Governmentality and Lifestyle Studies." *Sociology Compass* 1(1): 111–26.

—. (2008). "Liquid Consumption: Anti-consumerism and the Fetishized De-fetishization of Commodities." *Cultural Studies* 22(5): 599–623.

Bookchin, Murray. (1979). "Post-scarcity Anarchism." In *Contemporary Anarchism*, edited by Terry M. Perlin, 257–72. New Brunswick, NJ: Transaction. First published in 1971.

—. (1995). *Social Anarchism or Lifestyle Anarchism: An Unbridgeable Chasm*. San Francisco, CA: AK Press.

Bourdieu, Pierre. (1984). *Distinction: A Social Critique of the Judgment of Taste*, translated by Richard Nice. Cambridge, MA: Harvard University Press.

—. (1987). "What Makes a Social Class? On the Theoretical and Practical Existence of Groups." *Berkeley Journal of Sociology: A Critical Review* 32: 1–17.

—. (1989). "Social Space and Symbolic Power." *Sociological Theory* 7(1): 14–25.

Braunstein, Peter, and Michael William Doyle, (eds) (2002). *Imagine Nation: The American Counterculture of the 1960s and '70s*. New York: Routledge.

Breines, Wini. (1982). *Community and Organization in the New Left: 1962–1968*. New York: Praeger Publishers.

Brown, Gavin. (2007). "Mutinous Eruptions: Autonomous Spaces of Radical Queer Activism." *Environment and Planning A* 39(11): 2685–98.

Brown, Wendy. (2005). *Edgework: Critical Essays on Knowledge and Politics*. Princeton, NJ: Princeton University Press.

Butler, C. T. Lawrence, and Keith McHenry. (2000). *Food Not Bombs*. Rev. ed. Tucson, AZ: See Sharp Press.

Butler, Judith. (1990). *Gender Trouble: Feminism and the Subversion of Identity*. New York: Routledge.

—. (1993). *Bodies that Matter: On the Discursive Limits of "Sex"*. New York: Routledge.

—. (1997a). "Imitation and Gender Insubordination." In *The Second Wave: A Reader in Feminist Theory*, edited by Linda Nicholson, 300–15. New York: Routledge.

—. (1997b). "Merely Cultural." *Social Text* 52/53: 265–77.

—. (2004a). *Undoing Gender*. New York: Routledge.

—. (2004b). "What is Critique? An Essay on Foucault's Virtue." In *The Judith Butler Reader*, edited by Sara Salih with the assistance of Judith Butler, 302–22. Malden, MA: Blackwell.

—. (2005). *Giving an Account of Oneself*. New York: Fordham University Press.

Canclini, Nestor García. (2001). *Consumers and Citizens: Globalization and Multicultural Conflicts*. Translated by George Yúdice. Minneapolis, MN: University of Minnesota Press.

Carrington, Ben, and Brian Wilson. (2004). "Dance Nations: Rethinking Youth Subculture Theory." In *After Subculture*, edited by Andy Bennett and Keith Kahn-Harris, 65–78. New York: Palgrave MacMillan.

Castells, Manuel. (1996). *The Rise of the Network Society*. Vol. 1 of *The Information Age: Economy, Society, and Culture*. Oxford: Blackwell.

—. (2003). *The Power of Identity*. 2nd ed. Vol. 2 of *The Information Age: Economy, Society, and Culture*. Malden, MA: Blackwell.

Cavarero, Adriana. (2000). *Relating Narratives: Storytelling and Selfhood*. New York: Routledge.

Chaney, David C. (1996). *Lifestyles*. London: Routledge.

—. (2001). "From Ways of Life to Lifestyle: Rethinking Culture as Ideology and Sensibility." In *Culture in the Communication Age*, edited by James Lull, 75–88. London: Routledge.

Clark, Danae. (1991). "Commodity Lesbianism." *Camera Obscura* 9 (1–2, 25–26): 181–201.

Clarke, John. (2005). "Style." In *Resistance Through Rituals: Youth Subcultures in Post-war Britain*, edited by Stuart Hall and Tony Jefferson, 175–91. London: Routledge.

Clarke, John, Stuart Hall, Tony Jefferson, and Brian Roberts. (2005). "Subcultures, Cultures and Class." In *Resistance Through Rituals: Youth Subcultures in Post-war Britain*, edited by Stuart Hall and Tony Jefferson, 9–74. London: Routledge.

Cohen, Lizabeth. (2003). *A Consumer's Republic: The Politics of Mass Consumption in Postwar America*. New York: Vintage Books.

Collins, Patricia Hill. (1986). "Learning from the Outsider Within: The Sociological Significance of Black Feminist Thought." *Social Problems* 33(6): S14–S32.

Comella, Lynn. (2012). "Changing the World One Orgasm at a Time: Sex Positive Retail Activism." In *Commodity Activism,* edited by Mukherjee and Banet-Weiser, 240–53. New York: New York University Press.

Connolly, John, and Andrea Prothero. (2008). "Green Consumption: Life-Politics, Risk and Contradictions." *Journal of Consumer Culture* 8(1): 117–45.

Cornell, Andrew. (2011a). "'For a World Without Oppressors': U.S. Anarchism from the Palmer Raids to the Sixties." PhD diss., New York University.

—. (2011b). *Oppose and Propose! Lessons from Movement for a New Society*. Oakland, CA: AK Press and the Institute for Anarchist Studies.

Cosgrove, Stuart. (1984). "The Zoot Suit and Style Warfare." *History Workshop* 18: 77–91.

CrimethInc. Ex-Workers' Collective. (2000). *Days of War, Nights of Love: Crimethink for Beginners*. Canada: CrimethInc. Free Press.

—. (2005a). *Recipes for Disaster: An Anarchist Cookbook*. Olympia, WA: CrimethInc. Free Press.

—. (2005b). We are all survivors, we are all perpetrators. *Rolling Thunder: An AnarchistJournal of Dangerous Living* 1(Summer): 37–41.

—. n.d. *Fighting for our lives: An anarchist primer*. www.crimethinc.com/tools/downloads/zines.html. Accessed 23 November 2012.

Curran, Giorel. (2007). *21st Century Dissent: Anarchism, Anti-globalization and Environmentalism*. New York: Palgrave Macmillan.

Davis, Laurence. (2010). Social Anarchism or Lifestyle Anarchism: An Unhelpful Dichotomy. *Anarchist Studies* 18(1): 62–82.

de Certeau, Michel. (1984). *The Practice of Everyday Life*. Translated by Steven F. Rendall. Berkeley, CA: University of California Press.

de Cleyre, Voltairine. (2004). "They Who Marry Do Ill." In *The Voltairine de Cleyre Reader*, edited by A. J. Brigati, 11–20. San Francisco, CA: AK Press.

DeMello, Margo. (2000). *Bodies of Inscription: A Cultural History of the Modern Tattoo Community*. Durham, NC: Duke University Press.

Denning, Michael. (1997). *The Cultural Front: The Laboring of American Culture in the Twentieth Century*. London: Verso.

Dollimore, Jonathan. (1991). *Sexual Dissidence: Augustine to Wilde, Freud to Foucault*. Oxford: Clarendon Press.

Douglas, Mary, and Baron Isherwood. (1979). *World of Goods: Towards an Anthropology of Consumption*. New York: Basic Books.

du Gay, Paul, Stuart Hall, Linda Janes, Hugh MacKay, and Keith Negus. (1997). *Doing Cultural Studies: The Story of the Sony Walkman*. Milton Keynes: The Open University/Sage.

Duggan, Lisa. (2003). *The Twilight of Equality?: Neoliberalism, Cultural Politics, and the Attack on Democracy*. Boston, MA: Beacon Press.

Duncombe, Stephen, (ed.) (2002). *The Cultural Resistance Reader*. London: Verso.

—. (2008). *Notes from Underground: Zines and the Politics of Alternative Culture*. 2nd ed. Bloomington, IN: Microcosm.

Echols, Alice. (1989). *Daring to Be Bad: Radical Feminism in America, 1967–1975*. Minneapolis, MN: University of Minnesota Press.

Epstein, Barbara. (1991). *Political Protest and Cultural Revolution: Nonviolent Direct Action in the 1970s and 1980s*. Berkeley, CA: University of California Press.

Eschle, Catherine. (2004). "Constructing 'the Anti-globalisation Movement'." *International Journal of Peace Studies* 9(1): 61–84.

Evans, Sara. (1979). *Personal Politics: The Roots of Women's Liberation in the Civil Rights Movement and the New Left*. New York: Alfred A. Knopf.

Faderman, Lillian. (1992). "The Return of Butch and Femme: A Phenomenon in Lesbian Sexuality of the 1980s and 1990s." *Journal of the History of Sexuality* 2(4): 578–96.

Farrell, James J. (1997). *The Spirit of the Sixties: Making Postwar Radicalism*. New York: Routledge.

Featherstone, Mike. (1987). "Lifestyle and Consumer Culture." *Theory, Culture & Society* 4(1): 55–70.

—. (1991). *Consumer Culture and Postmodernism*. London: Sage.

Feigenbaum, Anna, Fabian Frenzel, and Patrick McCurdy. Forthcoming. *Protest Camps: Experiments in Alternative Worlds*. London: Zed.

Feixa, Carles, Ines Pereira, and Jeffrey S. Juris. (2009). "Global citizenship and the 'New, New' Social Movements: Iberian Connections." *Young: Nordic Journal of Youth Research* 17(4): 421–42.

Foucault, Michel. (1984a). "On the Genealogy of Ethics: An Overview of a Work in Progress." In *The Foucault Reader*, edited by Paul Rabinow, 340–72. New York: Pantheon.

—. (1984b). "Politics and Ethics: An Interview." In *The Foucault Reader*, edited by Paul Rabinow, 373–80. New York: Pantheon.

—. (1988a). *The History of Sexuality*. Vol. 3, *The Care of the Self*. Translated by Robert Hurley. New York: Vintage.

—. (1988b). "Technologies of the Self." In *Technologies of the Self: A Seminar with Michel Foucault*, edited by Luther H. Martin, Huck Gutman, and Patrick H. Hutton, 16–49. Amherst, MA: University of Massachusetts Press.

—. (1990a). *The History of Sexuality*. Vol. 1, *An Introduction*. Translated by Robert Hurley. New York: Vintage.

—. (1990b). *The History of Sexuality*. Vol. 2, *The Use of Pleasure*. Translated by Robert Hurley. New York: Vintage.

—. (1995). *Discipline and Punish: The Birth of the Prison*. Translated by Alan Sheridan. New York: Vintage.

—. (1997a). "The Birth of Biopolitics." In *Essential Works of Foucault*, edited by Paul Rabinow, 73–9. Vol. 1, *Ethics: Subjectivity and Truth*. New York: The New Press.

—. (1997b). "The Ethics of the Concern for Self as a Practice of Freedom." In *Essential Works of Foucault*, edited by Paul Rabinow, 281–302. Vol. 1, *Ethics: Subjectivity and Truth*. New York: The New Press.

—. (1997c). "What is Critique?" In *The Politics of Truth*, edited by Sylvere Lotringer and translated by Lysa Hochroth and Catherine Porter, 41–82. Los Angeles: Semiotext(e).

—. 2001. "So Is It Important to Think?" In *Power: Essential Works of Foucault, 1954–1984*, edited by James D. Faubion, 454–8. New York: The New Press.

—. (2009). *Security, Territory, Population: Lectures at the Collège de France 1977–1978*. Edited by Michel Senellart. Translated by Graham Burchell. New York: Picador.

Frank, Thomas. (1997). *The Conquest of Cool: Business Culture, Counterculture, and the Rise of Hip Consumerism*. Chicago, IL: University of Chicago Press.

Frank, Thomas, and Matt Weiland, (eds) (1997). *Commodify your Dissent*. New York: Norton.

Freeman, Jo. (1975). *The Politics of Women's Liberation: A Case Study of an Emerging Social Movement and Its Relation to the Policy Process*. New York: Longman.

—. (2002). "The Tyranny of Structurelessness." In *Quiet Rumors: An Anarcha-Feminist Reader*, edited by Dark Star Collective, 54–61. San Francisco, CA: AK Press.

Fuss, Diana. (1989). *Essentially Speaking: Feminism, Nature and Difference*. New York: Routledge.

Garber, Marjorie. (1992). *Vested Interests: Cross-Dressing and Cultural Anxiety*. New York: Routledge.

Gauthier, Isabelle, and Lisa Vinebaum. (1999). *Hot Pants: Do It Yourself Gynecology*. Montreal: Blood Sisters.

Geertz, Clifford. (1993). *The Interpretation of Cultures*. London: Fontana Press.

Gelder, Ken. (2007). *Subcultures: Cultural Histories and Social Practice*. London: Routledge.

Gemie, Sharif. (1994). "Counter-community: An Aspect of Anarchist Political Culture." *Journal of Contemporary History* 29(2): 349–67.

Giddens, Anthony. (1991). *Modernity and Self-identity*. Stanford, CA: Stanford University Press.

Gilbert, Jeremy. (2008). *Anticapitalism and Culture: Radical Theory and Popular Politics*. Oxford: Berg.

Goffman, Erving. (1959). *The Presentation of Self In Everyday Life*. New York: Anchor Books.

Goldman, Emma. (1969). "Marriage and Love." In *Anarchism and Other Essays*, 227–40. New York: Dover.

—. (1977). *Living My Life*, edited by Richard Drinnon and Anna Maria Drinnon. Abr. ed. New York: New American Library.

Goldman, Robert, Deborah Heath, and Sharon L. Smith. (1991). "Commodity Feminism." *Critical Studies in Mass Communication* 8(3): 333–51.

Goodwyn, Lawrence. (1978). *The Populist Moment: A Short History of the Agrarian Revolt in America*. New York: Oxford University Press.

Gordon, Uri. (2005). "Anarchism and Political Theory: Contemporary Problems." *The Anarchist Library*. www.ephemer.al.cl.cam.ac.uk/~gd216/uri/. Accessed 23 November 2012.

—. (2008). *Anarchy Alive! Anti-authoritarian Politics from Practice to Theory*. London: Pluto Press.

Graeber, David. (2002). "The New Anarchists." *New Left Review* 13(1): 61–73.

Gramsci, Antonio. (1971). *Selections from the Prison Notebooks*. Edited and translated by Quintin Hoare and Geoffrey Nowell Smith. New York: International Publishers.

Greenway, Judy. (2009). "Speaking Desire: Anarchism and Free Love as Utopian Performance in Fin de Siecle Britain." In *Anarchism and Utopianism*, edited by Laurence Davis and Ruth Kinna, 153–70. Manchester: Manchester University Press.

Gross, Larry P. (1993). *Contested Closets: The Politics and Ethics of Outing*. Minneapolis, MN: University of Minnesota Press.

—. (2001). *Up from Invisibility: Lesbians, Gay Men, and the Media in America*. New York: Columbia University Press.

Haenfler, Ross. (2006). *Straight Edge: Clean-living Youth, Hardcore Punk, and Social Change*. New Brunswick, NJ: Rutgers University Press.

Haenfler, Ross, Brett Johnson, and Ellis Jones. (2012). "Lifestyle Movements: Exploring the Intersection of Lifestyle and Social Movements." *Social Movement Studies: Journal of Social, Cultural and Political Protest* 11(1): 1–20.

Hall, Stuart. (1977). "Culture, the Media and the Ideological Effect." In *Mass Communication and Society*, edited by James Curran, Michael Gurevitch, and Janet Woollacott, 315–48. London: Edward Arnold.

—. (1993). "Minimal Selves." In *Studying Culture*, edited by Ann Gray and Jim McGuigan, 28–34. London: Edward Arnold.

—. (1996a). "The Problem of Ideology: Marxism Without Guarantees." In *Stuart Hall: Critical Dialogues in Cultural Studies*, edited by David Morley and Kuan Hsing-Chen, 25–46. London: Routledge.

—. (1996b). "Who Needs 'Identity'?" In *Questions of Cultural Identity*, edited by Stuart Hall and Paul du Gay, 1–17. London: Sage.

—, (ed.) (1997). *Representation: Cultural Representations and Signifying Practices*. Milton Keynes: The Open University/Sage.

—. (2006). "Encoding/Decoding." In *Media and Cultural Studies*, edited by Meenakshi Gigi Durham and Douglas M. Kellner, 163–73. Malden, MA: Blackwell.

Hall, Stuart, and Tony Jefferson, (eds) (2005). *Resistance Through Rituals: Youth Subcultures in Post-War Britain*. London: Routledge.

Haraway, Donna. (1988). "Situated Knowledges: The Science Question in Feminism and the Privilege of Partial Perspective." *Feminist Studies* 14(3): 575–99.

Harrison, Rob, Terry Newholm, and Deirdre Shaw, (eds) (2005). *The Ethical Consumer*. London: Sage.

Harvey, David. (2007). *A Brief History of Neoliberalism*. Oxford: Oxford University Press.

Heath, Joseph, and Andrew Potter. (2004). *Nation of Rebels: Why Counterculture Became Consumer Culture*. New York: HarperCollins.

Hebdige, Dick. (1981). *Subculture: The Meaning of Style*. New York: Routledge.
—. (1997). "Posing . . . Threats, Striking . . . Poses: Youth, Surveillance and
    Display." In *The Subcultures Reader*, edited by Ken Gelder and Sarah Thornton,
    393–405. London: Routledge.
Heckert, Jamie. (2004). "Sexuality/Identity/Politics." In *Changing Anarchism:
    Anarchist Theory and Practice in a Global Age*, edited by Jonathan Purkis and
    James Bowen, 101–16. Manchester: Manchester University Press.
Hennessey, Rosemary. (1994–1995). "Queer Visibility in Commodity Culture."
    Cultural Critique 29(Winter): 31–76.
Holt, Douglas B. (2000). "Does Cultural Capital Structure American
    Consumption?" In *TheConsumer Society Reader*, edited by Juliet B. Schor and
    Douglas B. Holt, 212–52. New York: The New Press.
Imani, John A. (2011). "Who Are RAC-LA, and What Are They Doing in
    MacArthur Park?" *Revolutionary Autonomous Communities-LA*, (blog) 2
    December. www.revolutionaryautonomouscommunities.blogspot.com/2011/12/
    who-are-rac-la-and-what-are-they-doing.html.
Jackson, John L., Jr. (2005). *Real Black: Adventures in Racial Sincerity*. Chicago,
    IL: University of Chicago Press.
Jacobs-Huey, Lanita. (2002). "The Natives are Gazing and Talking Back:
    Reviewing the Problematics of Positionality, Voice, and Accountability
    Among 'Native' Anthropologists." *American Anthropologist* 104(3):
    791–804.
Jagose, Annamarie. (1996). *Queer Theory: An Introduction*. New York: New York
    University Press.
Jakobsen, Janet R. (1998). "Queer Is? Queer Does? Normativity and the Problem
    of Resistance." *GLQ* 4(4): 511–36.
Jensen, Derrick. (2009). "Forget Shorter Showers: Why Personal Change Does Not
    Equal Political Change." *OrionMagazine*. July/August. www.orionmagazine.org/
    index.php/articles/article/4801/. Accessed 23 November 2012.
Jeppesen, Sandra. (2003). "Do Make Think: Anarchy and Culture." In
    Culture + the State: Alternative Interventions, edited by James Gifford and
    Gabrielle Zezulka-Mailloux, 64–75. Edmonton, Canada: CRC Humanities
    Studio.
Johnson, Richard. (1986). "What Is Cultural Studies Anyway?" *Social Text*
    16(Winter): 38–80.
Juris, Jeffrey S. (2004). "Networked Social Movements: Global Movements for
    Global Justice." In *The Network Society: A Cross-cultural Perspective*, edited by
    Manuel Castells, 341–62. Cheltenham: Edward Elgar.
—. (2008a). *Networking Futures: The Movements Against Corporate
    Globalization*. Durham, NC: Duke University Press.
—. (2008b). "Performing Politics: Image, Embodiment, and Affective Solidarity
    During Anti-corporate Globalization Protests." *Ethnography* 9(1): 61–97.
—. (2009). "Anarchism, or the Cultural Logic of Networking." In *Contemporary
    Anarchist Studies: An Introductory Anthology of Anarchy in the Academy*,
    edited by Randall Amster, Abraham DeLeon, Luis A. Fernandex, Anthony J.
    Nocella II, and Deric Shannon, 213–23. Abingdon: Routledge.
Kanouse, Sarah. (2006). "Cooing over the Golden Phallus." *Journal of Aesthetics
    and Protest* 4. www.journalofaestheticsandprotest.org/4/kanouse.html.

Kaplan, Judy, and Linn Shapiro, (eds) (1998). *Red Diapers: Growing Up in the Communist Left*. Champaign, IL: University of Illinois Press.

Kauffman, Leslie A. (1990). "Anti-Politics of Identity." *Socialist Review* 20(1): 67–80.

Kelley, Robin D. G. (1996). *Race Rebels: Culture, Politics, and the Black Working Class*. New York: The Free Press.

Kissack, Terence. (2008). *Free Comrades: Anarchism and Homosexuality in the United States, 1895–1917*. Oakland, CA: AK Press.

Klatch, Rebecca E. (1999). *A Generation Divided: The New Left, the New Right, and the 1960s*. Berkeley, CA: University of California Press.

Klein, Naomi. (1999). *No Logo*. New York: Picador.

koala! n.d. *Why Freegan? An Attack on Consumption: In Defense of Donuts*. Sarasota, FL. www.zinelibrary.info/files/whyfreegan.pdf. Accessed 23 November 2012.

Kozinets, Robert V., and Jay M. Handelman. (2004). "Adversaries of Consumption: Consumer Movements, Activism, and Ideology." *Journal of Consumer Research* 31(3): 691–704.

Kreutzer, Kimberley. (2004). "Polyamory on the Left: Liberatory or Predatory?" *off our backs* 34(5/6): 40–1.

Kropotkin, Peter. (2009). *Mutual Aid: A Factor of Evolution*. London: Freedom Press.

Laing, Dave. (1997). "Listening to Punk." In *The Subcultures Reader*, edited by Ken Gelder and Sarah Thornton, 406–19. London: Routledge.

Larrain, Jorge. (1996). "Stuart Hall and the Marxist Concept of Ideology." In *Stuart Hall: Critical Dialogues in Cultural Studies*, edited by David Morley and Kuan Hsing-Chen, 47–70. London: Routledge.

Leiss, William, Stephen Kline, Sut Jhally, and Jacqueline Botterill. (2005). *Social Communication in Advertising: Consumption in the Mediated Marketplace*. 3rd ed. New York: Routledge.

Leondar-Wright, Betsy. n.d. "It's Not 'Them'—It's Us!" *Class Matters*. www.classmatters.org/2006_07/its-not-them.php. Accessed 27 November 2012.

Levine, Cathy. (2002). "The Tyranny of Tyranny." In *Quiet Rumors: An Anarcha-Feminist Reader*, edited by Dark Star Collective, 54–61. San Francisco, CA: AK Press.

Linthicum, Kate. (2010). "Bookfair Draws an Array of Anarchists." *Los Angeles Times*, January 25. www.articles.latimes.com/2010/jan/25/local/la-me-anarchists25-2010jan25. Accessed 27 November 2012.

Lipsitz, George. (1994). *Rainbow at Midnight: Labor and Culture in the 1940s*. Champaign, IL: University of Illinois Press.

Littler, Jo. (2009). *Radical Consumption: Shopping for Change in Contemporary Culture*. Berkshire: Open University Press.

Maeckelbergh, Marianne. (2011). "Doing is Believing: Prefiguration as Strategic Practice in the Alterglobalization Movement." *Social Movement Studies* 10(01): 1–20.

Marcus, George E., and Michael M. J. Fischer. (1999). *Anthropology as Cultural Critique: An Experimental Moment in the Human Sciences*. Chicago, IL: University of Chicago Press.

Marcuse, Herbert. (1972). *Counterrevolution and Revolt*. Boston, MA: Beacon Press.

—. (2001). "Cultural Revolution." In *Towards a Critical Theory of Society: Collected Papers of Herbert Marcuse*, Vol. 2, edited by Douglas Kellner, 122–62. London: Routledge.

—. (2002). *One-Dimensional Man: Studies in the Ideology of Advanced Society*. London: Routledge.

Martínez, Elizabeth Betita. (2000). "Where Was the Color in Seattle? Looking for Reasons Why the Great Battle Was So White." *Colorlines* 3(1): 11. www. colorlines.com/archives/2000/03/where_was_the_color_in_seattlelooking_for_ reasons_why_the_great_battle_was_so_white.html.

Marx, Karl. (1978). "Capital, Volume One." In *The Marx-Engels Reader*, edited by Robert C. Tucker, 294–438. New York: Norton.

McGee, Micki. (2005). *Self-help, Inc.: Makeover Culture in American Life*. London: Oxford University Press.

McKenna, Katelyn Y. A., and John A. Bargh. (1998). "Coming out in the Age of the Internet: Identity 'Demarginalization' through Virtual Group Participation." *Journal of Personality and Social Psychology* 75(3): 681–94.

McKinley, Blaine. (1982). "'The Quagmires of Necessity': American Anarchists and Dilemmas of Vocation." *American Quarterly* 34(5): 503–23.

McRobbie, Angela. (1991). *Feminism and Youth Culture: From "Jackie" to "Just Seventeen."* Boston, MA: Unwin Hyman.

Melucci, Alberto. (1985). "The Symbolic Challenge of Contemporary Movements." *Social Research* 52(4): 789–816.

Mercer, Kobena. (1987). "Black Hair/Style Politics." *New Formations* 3(Winter): 33–56.

Micheletti, Michelle. (2003). *Political Virtue and Shopping: Individuals, Consumerism and Collective Action*. New York: Palgrave MacMillan.

Millett, Kate. (2000). *Sexual Politics*. Champaign, IL: University of Illinois Press. First published 1969.

Milstein, Cindy. (2010). *Anarchism and Its Aspirations*. Oakland, CA: AK Press.

Mohanty, Chandra Talpade. (2003). *Feminism Without Borders: Decolonizing Theory, Practicing Solidarity*. Durham, NC: Duke University Press.

Molyneux, John. (2011). *Anarchism: A Marxist Criticism*. London: Bookmarks Publications.

Moore, Mignon R. (2006). "Lipstick or Timberlands? Meanings of Gender Presentation in Black Lesbian Communities." *Signs: Journal of Women in Culture and Society* 32(1): 113–39.

Morley, David. (1983). "Cultural Transformations: The Politics of Resistance." In *Language, Image, Media*, edited by Howard Davis and Paul Walton, 104–17. New York: Palgrave MacMillan.

Morrish, Elizabeth. (2002). "The Case of the Indefinite Pronoun. Discourse and the Concealment of Lesbian Identity in Class." In *Gender Identity and Discourse Analysis*, edited by Lia Litosseliti and Jane Sunderland, 177–92. Amsterdam: John Benjamins.

Mukherjee, Roopali, and Sarah Banet-Weiser, (eds) (2012). *Commodity Activism: Cultural Resistance in Neoliberal Times*. New York: New York University Press.

Muñiz, Albert M., Jr., and Thomas C. O'Guinn. (2001). "Brand Community." *Journal of Consumer Research* 27(4): 412–32.

Musuta, Selina, and Darby Hickey. (2008). "No Justice and No Peace: A Critique of Current Social Change Politics." *Illvox*, 8 May. www.illvox.org/2008/05/no-justice-and-no-peace-a-critique-of-current-social-change-politics/.

Newholm, Terry. (2005). "Case Studying Ethical Consumers' Projects and Strategies." In *The Ethical Consumer*, edited by Rob Harrison, Terry Newholm, and Deirdre Shaw, 107–24. London: Sage.

Nomous, Otto. (2007). "Race, Anarchy and Punk Rock: The Impact of Cultural Boundaries Within the Anarchist Movement." *Illvox*, 22 June. www.illvox.org/2007/06/race-anarchy-and-punk-rock-the-impact-of-cultural-boundaries-within-the-anarchist-movement/.

Nussbaum, Martha. (1999). "The Professor of Parody." *The New Republic*, 22 February.

Ogbar, Jeffrey O. G. (2004). *Black Power: Radical Politics and African American Identity*. Baltimore, MD: Johns Hopkins University Press.

O'Hara, Craig. (1999). *The Philosophy of Punk: More Than Noise*. London: AK Press.

Olson, Joel. (2009). "The Problem with Infoshops and Insurrection: US Anarchism, Movement Building, and the Racial Order." In *Contemporary Anarchist Studies: An Introductory Anthology of Anarchy in the Academy*, edited by Randall Amster, Abraham DeLeon, Luis A. Fernandex, Anthony J. Nocella II, and Deric Shannon, 35–45. Abingdon: Routledge.

Ouellette, Laurie. (2004). "'Take Responsibility for Yourself': Judge Judy and the Neoliberal Citizen." In *Reality TV: Remaking Television Culture*, edited by Susan Murray and Laurie Ouellette, 231–50. New York: New York University Press.

Phelan, Peggy. (1993). *Unmarked: The Politics of Performance*. London: Routledge.

Phelan, Shane. (1989). *Identity Politics: Lesbian Feminists and the Limits of Community*. Philadelphia, PA: Temple University Press.

Plant, Sadie. (1992). *The Most Radical Gesture: The Situationist International in a Postmodern Age*. New York: Routledge.

Polletta, Francesca. (2002). *Freedom Is an Endless Meeting: Democracy in American Social Movements*. Chicago, IL: University of Chicago Press.

Polletta, Francesca, and James M. Jasper. (2001). "Collective Identity and Social Movements." *Annual Review of Sociology* 27: 283–305.

Purkis, Jonathan, and James Bowen, (eds) (2004). *Changing Anarchism: Anarchist Theory and Practice in a Global Age*. Manchester: Manchester University Press.

Reed, Thomas Vernon. (2005). *The Art of Protest: Culture and Activism from the Civil Rights Movement to the Streets of Seattle*. Minneapolis, MN: University of Minnesota Press.

Rich, Adrienne. (1980). "Compulsory Heterosexuality and Lesbian Existence." *Signs* 5(4): 631–60.

Robson, Ruthann. (1996). "Living our Lives." In *Reinventing Anarchy, Again*, edited by Howard J. Erlich, 323–6. San Francisco, CA: AK Press.

Rose, Nikolas. (1996). "Governing 'Advanced' Liberal Democracies." In *Foucault and Political Reason: Liberalism, Neo-Liberalism, and Rationalities of Government*, edited by Andrew Barry, Thomas Osborne, and Nikolas Rose, 37–64. Chicago, IL: The University of Chicago Press.

—. (1999). *Governing the Soul: The Shaping of the Private Self.* 2nd ed. London: Free Association Books.

Rossinow, Doug. (1998). *The Politics of Authenticity: Liberalism, Christianity, and the New Left in America.* New York: Columbia University Press.

Roszak, Theodore. (1969). *The Making of a Counter Culture: Reflections on the Technocratic Society and its Youthful Opposition.* Garden City, NY: Doubleday.

Rubin, Gayle. (1984). "Thinking Sex: Notes for a Radical Theory of the Politics of Sexuality." In *Pleasure and Danger,* edited by Carol S. Vance, 267–319. New York: Routledge and Kegan Paul.

—. (1997). "The Traffic in Women: Notes on the 'Political Economy' of Sex." In *The Second Wave: A Reader in Feminist Theory,* edited by Linda Nicholson, 27–62. New York: Routledge.

Rupp, Leila J., and Verta Taylor. (1987). *Survival in the Doldrums: The American Woman'sRights Movement, 1945 to the 1960s.* New York: Oxford University Press.

Ryan, Christopher, and Cacilda Jethá. (2010). *Sex at Dawn: The Prehistoric Origins of Modern Sexuality.* NewYork: HarperCollins.

Sassatelli, Roberta and Davolio, Federica. (2010). "Consumption, Pleasure and Politics: Slow Food and the Politico-Aesthetic Problematization of Food." *Journal of Consumer Culture* 10(2): 202–32.

Sawer, Marian. (2007). "Wearing Your Politics on Your Sleeve: The Role of Political Colours in Social Movements." *Social Movement Studies: Journal of Social, Cultural and Political Protest* 6(1): 39–56.

Schlichter, Annette. (2004). "Queer at Last? Straight Intellectuals and the Desire for Transgression." *GLQ* 10(4): 543–64.

Schutz, Aaron. (2009a). "The Distortions of Lifestyle Politics." *OpenLeft,* 24 July. www.openleft.com/diary/14295/part-ii-the-distortions-of-lifestyle-politics-core-dilemmas-of-community-organizing. Accessed 27 November 2012.

—. (2009b). "Self-delusion and the Lie of Lifestyle Activism." *OpenLeft,* 26 April. www.openleft.com/diary/13032/selfdelusion-and-the-lie-of-lifestyle-politics-core-dilemmas-of-community-organizing.

Scott, James C. (1985). *Weapons of the Weak: Everyday Forms of Peasant Resistance.* New Haven, CT: Yale University Press.

Scott, Joan W. (1992). "Experience." In *Feminists Theorize the Political,* edited by Judith Butler and Joan W. Scott, 22–40. New York: Routledge.

Security Culture: A Handbook for Activists. n.d. www.security.resist.ca/personal/securebooklet.pdf. Accessed 29 November 2012.

Sedgwick, Eve Kosofsky. (1990). *Epistemology of the Closet.* Berkeley, CA: University of California Press.

Seidman, Steven. (1993). "Identity and Politics in a 'Postmodern' Gay Culture." In *Fear of a Queer Planet,* edited by Michael Warner, 105–42. Minneapolis, MN: University of Minnesota Press.

Sender, Katherine. (2006). "Queens for a Day: Queer Eye for the Straight Guy and the Neoliberal Project." *Critical Studies in Media Communication* 23(2): 131–51.

Sheehan, Seán M. (2003). *Anarchism.* London: Reaktion Books.

Shoplifting: The Art and the Science. n.d. www.zinedistro.org/zines/54/shoplifting/by/an-unknown-author. Accessed 29 November 2012.

Slack, Jennifer Daryl. (1996). "The Theory and Method of Articulation in Cultural Studies." In *Stuart Hall: Critical Dialogues in Cultural Studies*, edited by David Morley and Kuan-Hsing Chen, 112–27. London: Routledge.

Smith, N. Craig. (1990). *Morality and the Market: Consumer Pressure for Corporate Accountability*. London: Routledge.

Soper, Kate. (2007). "Re-thinking the 'Good Life': The Citizenship Dimension of Consumer Disaffection with Consumerism." *Journal of Consumer Culture* 7(2): 205–29.

—. (2008). "Alternative Hedonism, Cultural Theory and the Role of Aesthetic Revisioning." *Cultural Studies* 22(5): 567–87.

Spivak, Gayatri Chakravorty. (1987). *In Other Worlds: Essays in Cultural Politics*. London: Taylor & Francis.

—. (1997). Interview with Ellen Rooney. "'In a Word': Interview." In *The Second Wave: A Reader in Feminist Theory*, edited by Linda Nicholson, 356–78. New York: Routledge.

Stein, Arlene. (1997). *Sex and Sensibility: Stories of a Lesbian Generation*. Berkeley, CA: University of California Press.

—. (1999). "Becoming Lesbian: Identity Work and the Performance of Sexuality." In *The Columbia Reader on Lesbians and Gay Men in Media, Society, and Politics*, edited by Larry Gross and James D. Woods, 81–92. New York: Columbia University Press.

—. (2006). *Shameless: Sexual Dissidence in American Culture*. New York: New York University Press.

Stepp, Brooke. (2008). "NW APOC Reportback." *Illvox*, 18 October. www.illvox. org/2008/10/nw-apoc-reportback/.

Sycamore, Mattilda Bernstein. (2008). "Gay Shame: From Queer Autonomous Space to Direct Action Extravaganza." In *That's Revolting: Queer Strategies for Resisting Assimilation*, edited by Mattilda Bernstein Sycamore, 268–95. 2nd ed. New York: Soft Skull Press.

Taylor, Verta, and Nancy E. Whittier. (1992). "Collective Identity in Social Movement Communities: Lesbian Feminist Mobilization." In *Frontiers in Social Movement Theory*, edited by Aldon D. Morris and Carol McClurg Mueller, 104–30. New Haven, CT: Yale University Press.

—. (1995). "Analytical Approaches to Social Movement Culture: The Culture of the Women's Movement." In *Social Movements and Culture*, edited by Hank Johnson and Bert Klandermans, 163–87. Minneapolis, MN: University of Minnesota Press.

Thompson, A. K. (2010). Black Bloc White Riot: Anti-Globalization and the Genealogy of Dissent. Oakland, CA: AK Press.

Thompson, Stacy. (2004). *Punk Productions: Unfinished Business*. Albany, NY: State University of New York Press.

Thornton, Sarah. (1996). *Club Cultures: Music, Media and Subcultural Capital*. Hanover, CT: Wesleyan University Press.

Tinnell, Adam. (2008). "Intro to Radical Mens Fashion." *The Boulevardier*, 19 November. www.boulevardier4eva.wordpress.com/2008/11/19/intro-to-radical-mens-fashion/#more-16. Accessed 27 November 2012.

—. (2009). "Court Fashion and Ariel Attack! Part 1." *The Boulevardier*, 9 September. www.boulevardier4eva.wordpress.com/2009/09/09/court-fashion-and-ariel-attack-part-1/. Accessed 27 November 2012.

Vale, Valerie, and Andrea Juno. (1989). *Modern Primitives: An Investigation of Contemporary Adornment and Ritual*. San Francisco, CA: Re/Search Publication.

Van Deburg, William L. (1992). *New Day in Babylon: The Black Power Movement and American Culture, 1965–1975*. Chicago, IL: University of Chicago Press.

Veblen, Thorstein. (1994). *The Theory of the Leisure Class*. New York: Dover.

Veysey, Lawrence. (1973). *The Communal Experience: Anarchist and Mystical Counter-cultures in America*. New York: Harper & Row.

W. (2006). "Rethinking Crimethinc." *anarkismo.net* (blog) 4 September.

Warner, Michael, (ed.) (1993). *Fear of a Queer Planet*. Minneapolis, MN: University of Minnesota Press.

Warner, Michael. (1999). *The Trouble with Normal: Sex, Politics, and the Ethics of Queer Life*. Cambridge, MA: Harvard University Press.

Weber, Max. (1978). *Economy and Society*. Vol. 1. Berkeley, CA: University of California Press.

Wehling, Jason. (1995). "Anarchism and the History of the Black Flag." *Spunk Library*. 14 July. www.spunk.org/library/intro/sp001492/blackflg.html. Accessed 27 November, 2012.

Weston, Kath. (1997). *Families We Choose: Lesbians, Gays, Kinship*. New York: Columbia University Press.

Whittier, Nancy. (1995). *Feminist Generations: The Persistence of the Radical Women's Movement*. Philadelphia, PA: Temple University Press.

—. (1997). "Political Generations, Micro-cohorts, and the Transformation of Social Movements." *American Sociological Review* 62: 760–78.

Williams, Leonard. (2007). "Anarchism Revived." *New Political Science* 29(3): 297–312.

Wilson, Ara. (1999). "Just Add Water: Searching for the Bisexual Politic." In *The Columbia Reader on Lesbians and Gay Men in Media, Society, and Politics*, edited by Larry Gross and James D. Woods, 108–12. New York: Columbia University Press.

Woodcock, George. (1979). "Anarchism Revisited." In *Contemporary Anarchism*, edited by Terry M. Perlin, 23–36. New Brunswick, NJ: Transaction.

Yoshino, Kenji. (2007). *Covering: The Hidden Assault on our Civil Rights*. New York: Random House Trade Paperbacks.

INDEX